STAYING
ALIVE WHILE
LIVING THE LIFE

STAYING ALIVE WHILE LIVING THE LIFE

Adversity, Strength, and Resilience in the Lives of Homeless Youth

SUE-ANN MACDONALD
& BENJAMIN ROEBUCK

FERNWOOD PUBLISHING
HALIFAX & WINNIPEG

Editing: Erin Seatter
Cover design: John van der Woude
Printed and bound in Canada

Published by Fernwood Publishing
32 Oceanvista Lane, Black Point, Nova Scotia, B0J 1B0
and 748 Broadway Avenue, Winnipeg, Manitoba, R3G 0X3
www.fernwoodpublishing.ca

Fernwood Publishing Company Limited gratefully acknowledges the financial support of the Government of Canada, the Canada Council for the Arts, the Manitoba Department of Culture, Heritage and Tourism under the Manitoba Publishers Marketing Assistance Program and the Province of Manitoba, through the Book Publishing Tax Credit, for our publishing program. We are pleased to work in partnership with the Province of Nova Scotia to develop and promote our creative industries for the benefit of all Nova Scotians.

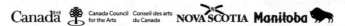

Library and Archives Canada Cataloguing in Publication

MacDonald, Sue-Ann, 1972-, author
Staying alive while living the life: adversity, strength, and resilience in the lives of homeless youth / Sue-Ann MacDonald, Benjamin Roebuck.

Issued in print and electronic formats.
ISBN 978-1-55266-932-7 (softcover).—ISBN 978-1-55266-933-4 (EPUB).—ISBN 978-1-55266-934-1 (Kindle)

1. Homeless youth. 2. Homeless youth—Social life and customs.
3. Homeless youth—Social conditions. 4. Homelessness. I. Roebuck, Benjamin, 1982–, author II. Title.

HV4493.M33 2018   362.7'75692   C2018-903945-0
C2018-904545-0

CONTENTS

*This research is dedicated to the young people of
Ottawa sleeping on sidewalks and park benches;
in elevators, stairwells, and parking garages; under
bridges and along riverbanks; on the couches of friends
and strangers; in shelters and transitional housing;
and camped out in the forests of the Greenbelt. Your
stories have moved us, challenged us, and inspired our
hearts. You are so strong. Do not allow your hope for
a better tomorrow to slip away. Grasp it tightly!
This book would have never come to fruition without
the trust the youth offered us. These experiences, the
sharing of intimate parts of their daily lives, have been
humbling, inspiring, and all too often angering and
saddening. We wish you all the best in the pursuit of your
dreams, and we remain inspired by your perseverance
and creativity in the face of so much injustice.*

ACKNOWLEDGEMENTS

SUE-ANN

This project would not have been possible without the support and blind trust of homeless youth organizations and the numerous service providers that I worked with for many years, who encouraged me in my doctoral research and embraced the complexity of the researcher-practitioner dynamic. I deeply admire your passion for your work and efforts to serve and help others, as well as your constant drive to innovate and renew practice.

Coupled with this unwavering support, the judicious counsel of my thesis supervisor, Céline Bellot, over so many years cannot be overlooked. Her deep passion for combatting social injustice in innovative ways offers a constant source of inspiration. Similarly, I am grateful for Kate Bezanson's wisdom, editorial talents, and, most importantly, her friendship and mentoring.

Lastly, this project took up more than a decade of my life, including having four children. To my wonderfully supportive partner, Alain, and to our children, Guillaume, Isabelle, Henri, and Hugo, as well as to my family and parents who have inspired me by their passion for their work, I want to thank you for your patience and support.

BENJAMIN

Thank you to my research supervisor and friend, Ross Hastings. I miss you. Under your keen editorial vision (and affinity for Howard Becker's writing style), I have learned to abandon the notion that there is "one right way" to approach the organization of ideas, and I have become passionate about writing — and rewriting. Thank you for your patience, encouragement, willingness to let me explore ideas, and thirty-seven pages of hand-drawn charts that I collected from our meetings together. I owe my completion of this project to the motivation I find in striving to hear you say, "I think we're in good shape."

Thank you to my community partners, who welcomed my presence and made it easy to do this research. I admire your continual energy and the strength-based, solution-focused approach you embody in your work.

Thank you to Kathryn Campbell, Tim Aubry, Christine Gervais, Christine Bruckert, and Jeff Karabanow for your mentoring and feedback on earlier versions of this work.

I would like to thank the Social Sciences and Humanities Research Council of Canada for supporting this research in part through a doctoral fellowship.

Thank you to my parents for having the courage to start raising a family in the back end of an open custody facility for young offenders and for teaching me about the power of second chances.

To my beautiful wife, Maryann, and to Isaac, Mavis, and Tian, thank you for all that you have given. I love you all dearly.

1. INTRODUCTION

It's Monday morning. Kristin opens her eyes and scans the parking lot to ensure no cars have arrived. She spent another night under the bleachers at her school — it's safer than her old spot downtown. She stretches and opens the backpack she used as a pillow to look for her toothbrush and water bottle. She knows it'll be hard to get a job and afford a place to live if she can't graduate from high school. She'll go to classes and get in trouble for not having her homework done, and she'll use her time in the computer lab to search for housing and get in trouble for being off task. Even so, today Kristin will try her best.

Every day, young people like Kristin live without shelter and protection and do their best to achieve their goals. People tend to believe that youth are cared for and have their needs met, but there is a darker reality in every city and most rural communities across Canada that remains hidden. *Staying Alive While Living the Life* exposes the complex and high-stakes reality of street life from the perspectives of youth who are homeless. Moving past the simplistic label of "at-risk youth," we introduce you to young people with hopes and dreams, with skills and strengths, navigating their environment and negotiating with those around them to live their best lives without access to many of the resources and relationships that can be taken for granted. Experiencing homelessness requires youth to make heavy decisions that most people will never face, such as choosing between hunger and theft or trying to rationalize sexual exploitation in exchange for shelter or protection. Youth are making these decisions during crucial developmental transitions to adulthood and while discovering who they are.

3

Too often the experiences of homeless youth are oversimplified, leaving little room for understanding the complexity of how they make decisions. Despite adverse conditions, social exclusion, and oppression, many youth who experience homelessness demonstrate tremendous resilience, both in eventually securing more stable housing and in achieving a subjective feeling of well-being (Bender, Yang, Ferguson, and Thompson 2015; Kidd 2008). How do they do it? How do they maintain hope for the future? How do they manage their well-being on the streets? What role do families, peers, and service providers play in their process of resilience? And what do these youth think about their own lives?

This book comes from our own practice, community engagement, and academic research. Sue-Ann has supported homeless and street-involved youth for over a decade as a social worker, while Benjamin comes from the youth justice sector and volunteered at an urban youth drop-in centre as part of this research. You will be immersed in the lives of fascinating and resilient youth and invited to confront the complex dilemmas they face and gain a deeper understanding of their points of view. We show a collision of structural obstacles with youth who are presented as active agents responding to their circumstances and making choices influenced by the constraints imposed on them. Our aim is to amplify the voices of the youth themselves, revealing how they understand their place in the world and on the streets.

Writing about youth homelessness often focuses on the external constraints imposed on youth and portrays them as passive recipients of negative circumstances, as if their lives were happening to them. While we acknowledge the adversity, marginalization, and social exclusion experienced by young people, we are interested in exploring how they think about their circumstances and the kind of approaches they use to solve problems. This line of questioning brings human agency into the centre of the analysis and allows us to explore the internal and external resources that young people draw on when making decisions about their lives. Describing human agency, Elder, Kirkpatrick Johnson, and Crosnoe (2003: 11) wrote:

> Individuals construct their own life course through the choices and actions they take within the opportunities and constraints of history and social circumstance.... Children, adolescents, and adults are not passively acted upon by social influence and structural constraints.

Instead, they make choices and compromises based on the alternatives that they perceive before them.

While the relationship between human agency and social structures is a classic debate within the social sciences (see Archer 1982; Giddens 1984; Vaughan 2001), we hope that our research contributes to a balanced exploration of how young people demonstrate agency on the streets. Conceptually, this process of young people navigating and negotiating their social circumstances is framed within the concept of resilience, which at its core implies *adapting positively* despite significant adversity (Masten and Powell 2003; Ungar 2004a, 2004b, 2005, 2008).

Our aim is to provide a comprehensive portrait of homeless youth experiences and to combat unnuanced images of youth that oscillate between victimhood and deviance. Homeless youth face many barriers, including structural constraints (poverty; lack of affordable and stable housing; rigid education, social services, and health systems; and precarious labour markets; MacDonald 2013) and symbolic obstacles (stigma, social representations, and identity constructs). This analysis illuminates these challenges and showcases the resilient ways in which youth seek to cope with and overcome obstacles, while still experiencing life.

YOUTH HOMELESSNESS IN CANADA

The Canadian Observatory on Homelessness (COH) has developed a common definition of homelessness to help with research, measurement, policy, and intervention. It has been endorsed by academics and service providers across Canada.

> Homelessness describes the situation of an individual, family or community without stable, safe, permanent, appropriate housing, or the immediate prospect, means and ability of acquiring it. It is the result of systemic or societal barriers, a lack of affordable and appropriate housing, the individual/household's financial, mental, cognitive, behavioural or physical challenges, and/or racism and discrimination. Most people do not choose to be homeless, and the experience is generally negative, unpleasant, unhealthy, unsafe, stressful and distressing. (Gaetz et al. 2017: 1)

This definition balances different types of housing instability with the social experiences that contribute to homelessness and are reinforced by it. The COH has also developed a housing typology that delineates four categories of homelessness:

> 1) Unsheltered, or absolutely homeless and living on the streets or in places not intended for human habitation; 2) Emergency Sheltered, including those staying in overnight shelters for people who are homeless, as well as shelters for those impacted by family violence; 3) Provisionally Accommodated, referring to those whose accommodation is temporary or lacks security of tenure, and finally, 4) At Risk of Homelessness, referring to people who are not homeless, but whose current economic and/or housing situation is precarious or does not meet public health and safety standards. It should be noted that for many people homelessness is not a static state but rather a fluid experience, where one's shelter circumstances and options may shift and change quite dramatically and with frequency. (Gaetz et al. 2017)

However, homelessness is not only about extreme poverty and not having a roof over one's head but also about the failure of society to provide adequate supports to facilitate social inclusion and well-being and to safeguard citizens' rights. As the COH tweeted in May 2018, "Homelessness is more than a social problem; it is a human rights violation."[1]

The COH has also developed a definition of youth homelessness that endorses a human rights approach: "the situation and experience of young people between the ages of 13 and 24 who are living independently of parents and/or caregivers, but do not have the means or ability to acquire a stable, safe or consistent residence" (Gaetz et al. 2017). The COH explains that youth homelessness is a complex social issue involving the denial of basic human rights — all young people have the right to safety and security, adequate housing, food, education, and justice.[2] They further differentiate youth homelessness from adult homelessness because of the developmental process and the challenges presented by the lack of a safe and nurturing environment in the transition to adulthood.

We include all forms of youth homelessness in this book. At one end of the spectrum are youth whose lives are completely entrenched in street life, and at the other end are the less socially disenfranchised who live in transitional housing, rarely socialize downtown, and go to school or have part-time jobs. We spoke with youth in emergency shelters, whether youth-specific or adult, youth who sleep "rough" (e.g., outside, in parks, in cemeteries, on the street, in alleys and parking garages), youth who sleep or stay in places not specifically designed for human habitation (e.g., apartment or businesses entrances), youth who squat (i.e., stay in an unoccupied or abandoned space or building that they do not own, rent, or otherwise have permission to use), and youth who couch-surf (i.e., stay temporarily at a friend's, family member's, or acquaintance's place). We agree with researchers who have found that "the majority of homeless youth are not visible on the street, but are couch-surfing or living in overcrowded conditions, unsuitable housing, or housing that they cannot afford" (Kraus, Eberle, and Serge 2001: 3), so we made every attempt to include this hidden nature of youth homelessness in our studies. It should be noted too that the fluid nature of youth homelessness is rather integral to the experience — that is, we did not necessarily have to go looking for it, because it was present and innate to most of our interactions with youth.

There are roughly a quarter of a million absolutely homeless people in Canada, and youth make up an estimated 20 percent of that population (Gaetz 2014). While recognizing that gender remains a rather fluid category, research shows that these youth are predominantly male (57.6 percent), with females comprising an estimated 36.4 percent of the population, resulting in a two-to-one ratio of males to females (Gaetz 2014).

In a first pan-Canadian study on youth homelessness that canvassed 1,103 respondents from forty-seven communities across Canada (*Without a Home: The National Youth Homelessness Survey* by Gaetz, O'Grady, Kidd, and Schwan 2016), 40 percent of participants reported that they had their first experience of homelessness before age sixteen. These youth tended to experience greater hardship during their childhood years prior to becoming homeless but also greater adversity once they hit the streets. According to Gaetz et al. (2016: 7), youth who leave home at an early age are more likely to experience multiple episodes of homelessness, be involved with child protection services, experience bullying and learning difficulties, be victims of crime once homeless, have greater mental health and addiction symptoms, experience poorer quality of life, attempt suicide, and become chronically homeless.

Gaetz et al. (2016: 6) claim that almost 30 percent of youth were identified as members of racialized communities, and in some regions of Canada over 30 percent identified as Indigenous. There is also evidence to suggest that a high proportion of the population self-identifies as LGBTQ2S (lesbian, gay, bisexual, transgender, queer, questioning, and two-spirit), with estimates ranging from 20 to 45 percent. Conflict around sexual orientation and gender identity has often been cited as a reason that youth leave or are expelled from home (Abramovich 2013; Abramovich and Shelton 2017; Gaetz and O'Grady 2002; Gaetz, O'Grady, and Vaillancourt 1999; Karabanow 2008). Coolhart and Brown (2017: 230) note that LGBTQ2S youth are at higher risk of homelessness (two to thirteen times) than their heterosexual cisgender counterparts.

The Homeless Youth Landscape

Young people who are homeless enter the streets for a variety of reasons, including poverty, family conflict or breakdown, aging out of child welfare programs, release from correctional facilities without adequate discharge planning, and a lack of access to affordable housing (Hagan and McCarthy 2005; Kidd 2008; Roebuck 2008). Our book recognizes that there are many different understandings about how people become homeless. Simply put, two streams of thought have dominated thinking around the causes of homelessness. The liberal paradigm has focused on individual causes, while structuralists argue that homelessness is a function of the way society organizes and distributes its resources. The focus on individual responsibility has been criticized for diverting attention away from the contribution of macro-level variables such as the lack of affordable and stable housing, poverty, cuts in social welfare programs, and the lack of employment opportunities at a wage above the poverty level for individuals with limited education or work skills. Like others before us, we believe that much homelessness research and discourse has existed outside of a broader analysis of burgeoning social inequality embedded in unequal social relations (Farrugia and Gerrard 2016). According to Karabanow (2004), the last two decades have witnessed a greater understanding of the structural elements that place youth at risk. In sum, without diminishing the heterogeneity of the homeless youth population, it is fair to state that this group is unevenly and markedly characterized by having common experiences of childhood victimization (abuse, neglect, abandonment), being more vulnerable to victimization once on the streets (e.g., sexual assault, physical and psychological violence, addictions), and being greatly affected by structural transformations (e.g., precarious and changing labour and housing markets, disinvestment of the state, unstable family structures), which culminate in consequences for their ability to carve out a future.

In an effort to understand what makes some youth more susceptible to homelessness or street involvement, there has been a desire to uncover "pre-existing risk factors" as a way to develop programs and policies that will stop kids from becoming homeless. A preponderance of research has examined the etiological reasons for youth homelessness, with a significant emphasis on theories about "running away" from families because of sexual and/or physical abuse, neglect, abandonment, and family dysfunction (Karabanow 2004: 2). A number of the intermediate factors that contribute to home-lessness may actually be caused by trauma associated with childhood abuse. Severe childhood abuse is linked to developmental delays, poor school adjustment, disruptive classroom behaviour, school-age pregnancy, truancy and running away, delinquency and sex work, early use of illicit drugs and alcohol, and suicide attempts (Kidd 2004; Novac, Hermer, Paradis, and Kellen 2006). These social problems can interfere with the development of healthy relationships, and lead to social isolation and low levels of social support, revictimization, and self-medication. All of these, in turn, are linked to homelessness (Novac, Hermer, Paradis, and Kellen 2006). Some have argued that childhood events leading to youth homelessness are so problematic that they can result in chronic forms of adult homelessness (Baker Collins 2013).

Most research on homeless youth suggests that they have experienced childhoods rife with abuse, neglect, and abandonment that set them on a negative developmental course, pushing and pulling them to the streets (Baron 2003; Cauce et al. 2000; Gaetz 2004, 2014; Gaetz and O'Grady 2002; Karabanow 2004; Karabanow et al. 2005; Kidd 2013; Mounier and Andujo 2003). According to Heerde and Hemphill (2018), "these youth have often experienced trauma, that is, 'threats to life or bodily integrity, or a close personal encounter with violence and death' (Herman 1992: 33), and maltreatment in their family of origin" (1). Research shows that poor parent-child relationships and parenting practices (see DiPaolo 1999; Stefanidis, Pennbridge, MacKenzie, and Pottharst 1992; Whitbeck, Hoyt, and Yoder 1999), along with family breakdown, instability, and recompo-sition (Bearsley-Smith, Bond, Littlefield, and Thomas 2008; Laird 2007), place youth at increased risk for homelessness, further victimization, mental health problems (Brown, Begun, Bender, Ferguson, and Thompson 2015; Kidd 2013; Narendorf et al., 2017), and engagement in deviant activities (Baron, Forde, and Kennedy 2007; Reid 2011). Youth report exposure to violent behaviour on the streets as victims and as perpetrators (Heerde and Hemphill, 2017), resulting in a cumulative form of trauma (Hamilton, Poza, and Washington, 2011). These historical push-pull factors intertwine and create a certain forecasting of future behaviours. In the literature, homeless youth are characterized as incredibly vulnerable to further victimization or deviance (either as perpetrators or victims of violence and exploitation, poor health, or drug use), magnifying their fragile status as an "at-risk" group.

Gender, Sexuality, and Victimization

Pregnancy is an important issue among young women who are homeless. They become pregnant at exceptionally high rates, and such pregnancies often pose serious emotional, social, and physical health concerns. According to Begun (2017: ii), "many homeless youth intentionally seek to become pregnant or involved in pregnancy, as pregnancy and parenthood are viewed as conduits toward accessing social services and meaningful social connections to others that this group often lacks." She argues that most pregnancy prevention efforts focus on individual efforts (attitudes and behaviours) and neglect the contextual and structural realities that shape young homeless women's experiences of pregnancy, "such as desired pregnancy and pregnancy ambivalence, the influence of youths' social networks and perceived social norms regarding pregnancy, youths' desire for social connection, and their dire needs for tangible resources, each of which may influence youths' reproductive and sexual health behaviors" (Begun 2017: ii). Further, these young women are more likely to have experienced sexual assault, creating conflicted emotions about their pregnancies.

In general, young women who are homeless are more likely to be sexually abused, raped, and physically assaulted than homeless men or the general population (D'Ercole and Struening 1990; Jasinski, Wesely, Wright, and Mustaine 2010; Novac, Brown, and Bourbonnais 1996). Sexual assaults against homeless women are reported as being more violent and are often perpetrated by strangers in public places (Stermac and Paradis 2001). Among a sample of people who were homeless in Ottawa, 16 percent of female young people reported that they had experienced a miscarriage resulting from a physical assault (Aubry, Klodawsky, Hay, and Birnie 2003). Gaetz, O'Grady, and Buccieri (2010) also found that victimization is not evenly distributed, and young women were more likely to experience victimization than males on the street, with minority and queer female youth experiencing the highest rates of victimization. Age was also a significant predictor of victimization, with those who left home at an earlier age being more likely to experience victimization on the streets.

Youth who identify as LGBTQ2S frequently leave home because of conflict over their sexual identity or the fear that they will not be accepted if they come out to their parents (Cochran, Stewart, Ginzler, and Cauce 2002; Gattis 2009). They report higher rates of abuse in their family home and of victimization on the street than other young people who are homeless (Abramovich and Shelton 2017; Cochran et al. 2002; Fournier et al. 2009; Gattis 2009).

At-Risk and Risky Homeless Youth

Many youth arrive on the streets from the child welfare system (Aubry, Klodawsky Nemiroff, Birnie, and Bonetta 2007; Karabanow 2004; Karabanow et al. 2005; Kraus, Eberle, and Serge 2001) or are released from detention centres and have nowhere else to go (Gaetz and O'Grady 2002; Public Health Agency of Canada 2006), revealing a systemic and structural dimension to the problem of youth homelessness. Some researchers have gone one step further in arguing that youth exiting the foster care system through emancipation are at an increased risk for homelessness (Bender et al. 2015). In Ontario, young people have the right to leave "home" at age sixteen, and many choose to do so. However, significant gaps that contribute to youth homelessness have been identified in Ontario's child welfare and protection services, especially for sixteen- and seventeen-year-olds (Kraus, Eberle, and Serge 2001). Structural constraints abound for this population; inadequate social assistance and supportive housing systems and the changing labour market make it difficult for this age group to gain access to scarce resources and to eke out a living in socially legitimate ways (Bender et al. 2015; Bessant 2001; Farrell, Aubry, Klodawsky, and Pettey 2000). What's more, due to their lack of a private sphere, their daily activities are frequently carried out in public and are thus under the microscope of health, social, and judicial actors. For example, while it is common for young people to experiment with drugs and alcohol, youth with access to private housing are less likely to be observed by police than young people in an alley downtown.

A Montreal study found that 22,685 tickets had been distributed to people who were homeless for violations of municipal bylaws from 1994 to 2004. In 72 percent of cases, convicted individuals were sent to jail for their inability to pay the fine (Bellot, Raffestin, Royer, and Noël 2005). An article in local newspaper *Le Devoir* (April 16, 2007) revealed that people who were homeless in Montreal owed over $3.3 million in unpaid fines to the city. The largest proportion of tickets (20 percent) were given for sleeping or being spread out on a bench or on the ground in a public space (Bellot, Chesnay, and Royer 2007). Further investigation by the Quebec Human Rights Commission (Avila, Campbell, and Eid 2009) found that young people who were homeless were frequently ticketed for jay walking, and people who were homeless were often subjected to the discriminatory practice of social profiling. This phenomenon is not unique to Quebec. Criminalizing poverty via the social profiling of homeless people takes place across the country (Chesnay, Bellot, and Sylvestre 2013; O'Grady, Gaetz, and Buccieri 2011). It reinforces images of homeless youth as different, deficient, or deviant and in need of surveillance and punishment.

In much of the key literature on youth homelessness, the streets are charac-terized as intensely dangerous spaces in which these young people congregate. As Hagan and McCarthy (1997: 3) state in their watershed study of youth homelessness, entitled *Mean Streets: Youth Crime and Homelessness*, "the street is a downward spiral of deviance, danger, and despair." Others have remarked that the objective dangers of street life are well documented: rates of violence and victimization on the streets are greater than those experienced by the Canadian public (Gaetz 2004; 2009) and victimization is likely to increase based on length of time spent without a home (Boivin, Roy, Haley, and Galbaud du Fort 2005). While on the street, youth also are known to engage in activities that increase their chances of becoming victims of violence, such as sex work or using and selling drugs (Heerde and Hemphill 2015; Hoyt, Ryan, and Cauce 1999). Many researchers have noted a rise in criminal involvement among youth who do not have access to legitimate means of self-support, without which a significant number are drawn into illegal activities as a method of survival on the streets (Baron 2003; Baron, Forde, and Kennedy 2007; Hagan and McCarthy 1997). Experience with deviant behaviours increases the likelihood of victimization (Gaetz 2004, 2009; Krause, Eberle, and Serge 2001; McCarthy and Hagan 1992; Whitbeck, Hoyt, and Ackley 1997) and the likelihood of further involvement with deviance and crime

(Hagan and McCarthy 1997; McCarthy and Hagan 2005). Homelessness disrupts important social bonds and impairs personal networking that could be instrumental to getting off the street, and many individuals become trapped in an environment where they will be further victimized (D'Ercole and Struening 1990). Victimization on the street is psychologically distressing and can lead to depression and low self-esteem, which in turn contributes to apathy and feelings of futility, making it more difficult to escape further abuse (D'Ercole and Struening 1990; Simmons, Whitbeck, and Bales 1989). Young people experiencing homelessness have much higher levels of mortality through violence and disease than the general population; rates are estimated to be eight to eleven times higher than for similarly aged youth who are not homeless (Roy, Haley, Leclerc, Sochanski, Boudreau, and Boivin 2004). Young people on the streets who feel "trapped, hopeless, worthless and alone" are also at a higher risk of suicide and suicide attempts (Kidd 2004: 47). The majority of youth experiencing homelessness in Canada face severe mental health challenges, including depression, anxiety, post-traumatic stress disorder, psychosis, substance use disorders, and attention-deficit/hyperactivity disorder (Kidd, Slesnick, Frederick, Karabanow, and Gaetz 2018). According to a proposal submitted to the different levels of government, *Mental Health Care for Homeless Youth* (Schwan, Kidd, Gaetz, O'Grady, and Redman 2017: 3), 85.4 percent of homeless youth are experiencing a mental health crisis, 42 percent report at least one suicide attempt, and 35.2 percent report at least one drug overdose requiring hospitalization. More specifically, Indigenous, LGBTQ2S, and female homeless youth are affected disproportionately, as they are at the highest risk of experiencing a mental health crisis, along with youth who become homeless before the age of sixteen.

> These mental health struggles are the culmination of challenges faced by these youth in their homes, schools, and communities before becoming homeless, combined with exposure to violence and stigmatization once on the streets. The gravity of this situation is highlighted by the fact that suicide and drug overdose are the leading causes of death for Canadian homeless youth. (Schwan et al. 2017: 3)

Faced with so many challenges, it can be hard to understand how youth who are homeless survive and live their lives on the street. The personal and structural challenges they experience cut across the sectors of mental health, criminal justice, health care, social services, employment, family systems, education, and housing, making solutions to youth homelessness complex. There is so much to learn about how youth navigate these different systems, and about how solutions to youth homelessness require "policy fusion," breaking down the siloed mandates of different branches of government and social services to create structural change (Nichols 2014).

Because of these challenges, discussions about youth homelessness tend to focus on the risk factors that lead to homelessness or exist when young people are on the streets. A consequence is that homeless youth themselves may be perceived as "at-risk," as "risk-takers," or as "risky." Similarly, ideas about "the streets" are associated with fear, danger, victimization, and deviance. Such a culture of fear in relation to risk affects how homeless youth are understood and depicted (Kelly 2000, 2001). It magnifies perceptions of their vulnerability and fragility due to their young age and their marginalized social status and minimizes their capacity. This focus on risk tends to homogenize homeless youth experiences, notably from researchers' social standpoints, situating their experiences within a context of victimization and delinquency and perpetuating "at-risk" and "risky" discourses. We redress this imbalance by listening to the voices of youth to learn from their unique vantage points and decision-making processes within a strength-based framework. We believe that there are untold stories that can shed light on the strengths and resilience of these youth. It is important to highlight the adaptability and creativity of homeless youth in the face of so many obstacles — dimensions of their experience that are rarely portrayed.

RESILIENCE: A CONCEPTUAL FRAMEWORK

Young people who are not homeless may also experience marginalization, but for young people who are homeless, marginalization is reinforced and compounded by the multiple forms of adversity that are part of life on the streets (e.g., lack of shelter, food, and safety; experiences of violence, discrimination, and stigma). While this marginalization has the potential to be very damaging, many young people are able to recover. Resilience research attempts to examine how this recovery takes place, with a goal of identifying the types of interventions that can stimulate recovery. Understanding how resilience occurs for young people who are homeless will assist communities to respond in a more effective manner.

Resilience research focuses on children who develop well in the context of significant adversity. Many academics conducting research on resilience share the belief that their findings may inform preventative interventions and social policies to improve the lives of vulnerable children and families (Cicchetti 2003; Fraser 1997; Greene 2002; Ungar 2005; Walsh 1998). While the general concept of resilience comprises overcoming adversity, there are numerous perspectives and debates on how resilience functions. The term "resilience" has achieved a degree of popularity in everyday speech and may be considered a buzzword within contemporary social science research, but it is frequently used out of its proper context and remains quite ambiguous (Tisseron 2009; Tremblay 2005). Throughout its evolution, resilience has referred to a characteristic attributed to an individual, an outcome, and most recently a process (Ahern 2006). Resiliency and resilience can be defined in the following ways:

- Resiliency refers to an *attribute* or the capacity of people to adapt positively to adversity.
- Resilience refers to either the *demonstration of positive outcomes* despite experiences of adversity or the *process of adapting positively* to adversity. Both of these perspectives imply a degree of subjectivity in determining what may be defined as a positive adaptation. The value-laden use of the word "positive" is discussed further below.

Furthermore, resilience is generally seen in two different ways:

- as an *objective* phenomenon that can be studied and measured quantitatively and
- as a *subjective* social construction that changes based on the interpretations of people with different interests.

For our purposes, we define resilience as a *process* of adaptation in adversity. Overall, resilience is understood as the active process of young people adapting and achieving a personal sense of well-being despite adverse circumstances. This definition is consistent with that of a number of researchers who have chosen to operationalize resilience as "a dynamic developmental process reflecting evidence of positive adaptation despite significant life adversity" (Cicchetti 2003: xx; Egeland, Carlson, and Stroufe 1993; Luthar, Cicchetti, and Becker 2000; Masten 2001).

Critical Youth Studies

Riley and Masten (2005: 19) caution that the concept of resilience should not be used to cast blame on those who do not achieve positive outcomes, as this can lead to "blaming the victim." They explain that resilience must be understood within context as a complex process of developmental outcomes of individual children through interactions with families, schools, communities, and cultures. They explain that the concept of resilience deals with young people who experience significant risk and would not normally be expected to experience positive outcomes. Riley and Masten (2005) believe that resilience should never be used to shift blame on to those who have experienced adversity and have not been successful.

Even so, there are a growing number of critiques of the resilience discourse and its emphasis on the notion of risk (Foster and Spencer 2010; France 2007; Kelly 2000; Mallett, Rosenthal, Keys, and Averill 2010; Martineau 1999; O'Mahony 2009; te Riele 2006). Foster and Spencer (2011) borrow from Bourdieu's (1999) notion of symbolic violence to argue that the resilience discourse introduces an oppressive logic to the lives of young people, whereby they are seen through a risk framework and perceived as either "at-risk" or having narrowly averted risk and become "resilient." Furthermore, Mallett et al. (2010) express concern that the emphasis on risk factors and the designation of "at-risk" may individualize social problems and inequality, essentially stigmatizing the most marginalized and impoverished people in society as greater "risk-takers." Martineau (1999: 11–12) adds, "The resiliency discourse imposes prescribed norms of school success and social success upon underprivileged children.... The effect is that non-conforming individuals may be pathologized as non-resilient."

These critiques seem especially salient when applied to young people who are homeless; they may easily be considered "at-risk youth" since they are not living with their families (and for the most part these families are not considered stable, reliable, protective, or two-parent led), attending school, or accessing adequate shelter. Karabanow (2004) explains that young people who are homeless navigate through life on the streets, moving in and out of mainstream culture and community services, while often engaging in illegal and unconventional activities to meet their basic needs. However, he also argues, "Street youth are not 'social misfits' plagued by personal pathologies. For the majority, street life is the only viable alternative to extremely problematic (or nonexistent) family or child welfare settings" (Karabanow 2004: 91). Based on extensive longitudinal research with young people who are homeless, Mallett et al. (2010) believe that there is a need to challenge the stereotypes of young people who are homeless as leading chaotic, risky lives spiralling into drug use, mental health problems, and adult homelessness, finding that most young people who are homeless do transition off the streets.

One other related concern raised by critical youth scholars is the tendency to define young people who do not meet traditional developmental and economic milestones as "transitioning youth." Critical youth scholars argue that when adolescence is conceived as a linear journey from immaturity and dependence towards common desirable adult outcomes, any deviations from the projected path are conceived of as failures in transitioning to adulthood (Mallett et al. 2010). In this light, young people may be mistakenly considered "future adults" or "people-in-the-making" without recognizing the autonomy, capacity, and human agency of adolescents in their own right (Best 2007; Foster and Spencer 2011; Mallett et al. 2010). Barker (2005: 448) simply defines human agency as "the capacity of individuals to act independently and to make their own free choices." Best (2007) and Foster and Spencer (2011) describe how studies of adolescence have moved away from passive constructions of the human agency of young people and now focus on the capacities and decision-making of young people. Best (2007: 10–11) explains the impact of these "New Childhood Studies":

> New Childhood Studies provided a more complex portrait of young people as meaningfully engaged, independent social actors whose activities and practices influence a variety of social contexts and settings.... these emerging perspectives generated a cataclysmic shift in thinking about youth as they challenged the prevailing characterization of children as passive actors and instead emphasized children's autonomy and competence as actors in their own right.... For some time now, youth studies scholars have treated children and youth as reflexive social agents and producers of culture, active in the complex negotiations of social life and contributing in significant ways to the everyday construction of the social world.

Addressing the Gap

Critical youth studies today are generally informed by the perspective described by Best (2007) and seek to explore how young people understand their lives and how they make decisions. Furthermore, exploring the agency of youth is a growing theme in contemporary studies in contexts of youth adversity and marginalization, as this approach may be broadly applied to diverse contexts, such as young people experiencing family violence, child soldiers, and youth transitioning into adulthood (Best 2007; Bjarnason, Sigurdardottir, and Thorlindsson 1999; Denov 2010; Jones 2009; Larson 2006; Macmillan and Hagan 2004; Ungar 2004b). Exploring agency in these contexts allows researchers to gain a better understanding of how young people understand their social worlds and how they navigate through challenging environments while demonstrating capacity and resistance (Denov 2010; Jones 2009; Ungar 2004b). After a reading of the current research on resilience, we believe there is a great need to further explore the role of human agency in how young people adapt to adversity. Little attention is paid to how young people who are homeless think about their lives and how this understanding shapes their decision-making processes. Karabanow (2004: 68) validates this perspective:

> The vast majority of literature about street youth has focused on etiology and street culture with very little attention placed on the personal experiences of "being" a street youth. Few studies have attempted to account for the feelings, experiences, and sense of identity and meaning construction of street youth, as a way of extending our collective understanding of street culture and of how young people end up there.

It appears that there is a need to conduct research that fills this gap, raising awareness of how young people understand homelessness and how this understanding shapes how they navigate life on the streets. Given the heightened sensitization to the labelling of marginalized populations and passive constructions of young people, an alternative constructivist model of resilience has emerged to complement the conventional model of resilience and provide a more contextualized approach to understanding resilience among vulnerable populations affected by systemic inequality (see Ungar 2004a, 2004b, 2008).

The Constructivist Perspective of Resilience

An alternative to the objective perspective of resilience is a more subjective view that explores resilience through a social constructivist lens (Ungar 2004a, 2004b, 2005, 2008). This introduces the idea of subjectivity to the concepts of risk and protective factors, suggesting that people perceive risk and protective factors differently depending on their personal situation or social context. A constructionist model of resilience is framed around the personal narratives of people as they navigate through and negotiate with their social environments to obtain the resources they need to feel and define themselves as healthy (Ungar 2004b). It introduces the idea of resilience-seeking behaviours and the sense of a journey, as people deliberately make choices to access, or at times avoid, resources that may help them adapt to their adverse circumstances. This approach stresses the interaction of structure (social arrangements) and agency (individual responses and choices) and seeks to understand the experiences of young people as they interact, attribute meaning to, and respond to their circumstances. It draws on Anthony Giddens's (1976, 1979, 1983, 1984) theory of structuration, which examines the interaction and mutual reinforcement of human agency and social structures. He writes, "Social structures are both constituted by human agency, and yet at the same time are the very *medium* of this constitution" (Giddens 1976: 121; emphasis in the original).

Giddens's theory developed out of his concern that sociology had traditionally exaggerated the constraining nature of social structures on human decision-making.

> Structuration theory developed from the laudable viewpoint that human agents should not be seen as the puppets of social forces nor should they be seen as exercising unchecked autonomy. Structuration theory attempts to lend equal weight to the influences of both structure (and by implication culture) and agency. The means by which this is accomplished is to stop holding structure and agency apart, to no longer see them as discrete entities. To persist in this would be to repeat the dualisms which have bedevilled sociological analysis in the past (voluntarism and determinism; subjectivism and objectivism; macro and micro). (Vaughan 2001: 186)

Giddens (1976, 1979, 1983, 1984) sees humans as reflexive beings capable of monitoring their social environment and allowing their observations to influence their courses of action. This means that by reflecting on personal experiences, humans have the capacity, to some extent, to influence and even transform their social situations. Giddens (1976, 1979, 1983, 1984) sees social structures as the virtual rules and resources actors draw upon as they produce and reproduce themselves and society in their everyday actions. This view is important to understanding youth homelessness and resilience, as the decisions, choices, and economic realities of young people on the streets are constrained in very real ways by pre-existing structures. However, this does not mean that their choices are predetermined. This project seeks to explore how young people innovate or resist structures in ways that they perceive will meet their needs.

Navigation and Negotiation

A constructivist theory of resilience uses the interaction of agency and structure articulated in the theory of structuration to develop an understanding of how people navigate and negotiate through adversity (Ungar 2004a, 2004b, 2005, 2007, 2008). *Navigation* refers to a person's capacity to seek help, which Ungar (2005) argues is a function of both human agency and, at the same time, the availability of help to be sought, which he understands as structural. He writes, "The child seeking [to build] self-esteem or any other aspect of well-being requires access to experiences and relationships that build that self-esteem. One can only navigate to what is available and easily accessed" (225). So navigation refers to a young person's *capacity* and *choice* to access *available resources*.

Negotiation refers to the efforts of a young person interacting with resources to obtain personally relevant and meaningful services (Ungar 2005). Similar to navigation, it is a process comprising a youth's capacity to negotiate for personally meaningful resources and the adaptability of community services to participate in negotiation and provide structures that can meaningfully engage young people on their own terms. Ungar (2005: 441) argues that the assumption that community services will help produce positive outcomes may not align with the perceptions of adolescents, who may experience institutional care as intrusive or iatrogenic. Sometimes service providers produce barriers for young people, and the process of resilience emerges through a complex array of social and political relationships.

Rather than calculating the cumulative balance of risk and protective factors, Ungar (2008) proposes that youth experiences of resilience are framed around their ability to work through the many tensions that are central to their developmental trajectories. This may include access to material resources, development of healthy relationships, identity, a personal sense of power and control over personal outcomes, and the search for a fit within culture and community. Ungar (2008: 231) reasons that youth who experience resilience are "those that successfully navigate their way through these tensions, each in his or her own way, and according to the strengths and resources available to the youth personally, in his or her family, community and culture."

Pulling these pieces together, this project is conceptualized as a strength-based exploration of how young people overcome the adversity that they experience through homelessness. We provide a more nuanced understanding of the experiences of homeless young people and emphasize the role of human agency as youth respond reflexively to their circumstances. Although young people who are homeless experience significant adversity, they also possess many capacities. A constructivist model of resilience provides more theoretical space to recognize the successes and strengths of young people who are homeless, without this recognition being contingent on a prepackaged set of outcomes that might be considered normative for youth.

RESEARCHING YOUTH HOMELESSNESS

A significant amount of research has been conducted on the risk factors encountered by young people experiencing homelessness, but far less has been conducted on their strengths, assets, and resilience (e.g., Bender et al. 2007; Kidd and Davidson 2007). The emerging strength-based literature supports the idea that young people experiencing homelessness possess many strengths and resources and that these are important for young people navigating obstacles they encounter while homeless (Bender et al. 2007; Kidd and Davidson 2007; Ungar 2004b, 2005).

Bender et al. (2007) conducted focus groups with young people ages eighteen to twenty-four who were homeless and found that many young people develop a set of competencies, attitudes, and skills specific to life on the streets that help them to adapt to homelessness and that have the potential to be transferable to new contexts. Youth in Bender et al.'s study identified internal strengths such as street smarts, coping skills, motivation, attitudes, and spirituality as being important to their well-being, and highlighted the importance of peer networks and informal societal resources such as charity from strangers, restaurants, and churches as important external assets. In our research, we are interested in learning more about the strengths of young people navigating homelessness and exploring the role these strengths play in making decisions. Understanding these strengths is a prerequisite for enhancing the delivery of strength-based and solution-focused interventions. Saleebey (2013) explains that traditional intervention programs tend to share a deficit-based way of thinking that focuses on risk factors and problems such as poor attachment, substance use disorders, challenges in managing anger, learning disabilities, and anti-social peers. This type of thinking tends to overlook what is going well with young people and what resources they do have that might be used in planning solutions. Conversely, strength-based and solution-focused intervention approaches assess internal strengths and resources and build intervention strategies around them (Roebuck, Roebuck, and Roebuck 2011; Saleebey 2013). Internal strengths might include personal characteristics like being reflective, being willing to ask for help, being persistent, or resisting behaviours seen as oppressive, while external strengths might include having supportive friends or adults in a person's social network, having a family member who is willing to stay connected despite a strained relationship, or having access to community services. Identifying young people's strengths provides critical information and leverage to help them move towards their goals (Roebuck, Roebuck, and Roebuck 2011; Saleebey 2013).

Homeless youth can be difficult to study because they may not attend school and many are unlikely to seek help from emergency services such as shelters or drop-in centres (Gaetz 2004, 2009; Karabanow 2004; Kidd 2013), which happen to be the settings for most research (Hagan and McCarthy 1997; LaBoy 2018). Their extensive use of informal social networks (Tyler and Melander 2011) and "street families" to reduce victimization (Hagan and McCarthy 1997; McCarthy, Hagan, and Martin 2002) means that they remain a largely understudied group (Bradley 1997; Krause, Eberle, and Serge 2001; Marshall et al. 2008). There is a dearth of knowledge, and more particularly, longitudinal situated knowledge, about the subjective experiences of homeless youth (Aubry et al. 2007; Benoit, Jansson, and Anderson 2007; Kidd 2006; Tyler 2008). Research with young people experiencing homelessness tends to focus on psychological issues, such as self-esteem, mental illness, and measurements of individual developmental capacities, or on sociological aspects, such as structural risk factors for homelessness, social exclusion, and barriers to housing (see Baron 2003; Herman, Susser, Struening, and Link 1997; Karabanow 2004; Kidd 2004; Roy et al. 2004; Tanner and Wortley 2002). While both of these research agendas are important, we explore the intersection of agency and structure to learn more about how youth who are homeless attribute meaning to their circumstances and how they draw on internal and external resources to solve problems and navigate homelessness. We hope that our honest descriptions of the complexities of research in progress will be useful to others planning studies with transient and street-involved youth.

Sue-Ann's Research

In Sue-Ann's case, the use of ethnographic methods to build relationships with participants over a one- to four-year period was intended to capture the ontological complexity of the experiences of homeless youth. The use of participant observation and informal interviewing techniques offered an original point of departure, with the aim of producing knowledge that stemmed from participants' situated and evolving experiences, in recognition that these marginalized youth were social actors and experts of their own lives. This longitudinal approach captured the essence of experiences as they were unfolding, replacing traditional research methods in homelessness that have relied upon static snapshots taken at a single point in time.

As a social worker on a community outreach team serving homeless youth for almost a decade, Sue-Ann was well integrated within the community and thus able to recruit participants who would have been difficult to meet otherwise. Her aim was to "follow," with their permission, a minimum of fifteen youth (ages sixteen and seventeen), who were living on their own (legally emancipated) and experiencing homelessness. An important goal of her study was to also reach out to "shelter avoiders" — that is, youth who were "sleeping rough" (outside), squatting, or couch-surfing and chose not to a access emergency shelters. This population is more difficult to study precisely because they do not rely on emergency services such as shelters. There are many reasons why youth choose not to access shelters, including a lack of accommodation for their lifestyle or identity (e.g., shelters do not allow pets or couples, are cisgender-normative[3]), loss of autonomy and freedom, feeling threatened by others, and lack of appeal. It should also be noted that due to the fluid nature of youth homelessness, the participants' housing varied significantly throughout the study, transitioning between shelter life, couch-surfing, overcrowded apartments, and sleeping on the streets (particularly in the summer months). Research methods thus needed to match this fluidity, with the researcher available in the spur of the moment, meeting youth on the street, in coffee shops, in shelters and agencies, and staying in touch by phone and email — essentially being present, observing, and hanging out. The epistemological standpoint of this study meant that conceptualizations of risk sprung from the way in which youth understood risk in their everyday lives and how they described their experiences as they were unfolding.

This was a refreshing standpoint from Sue-Ann's traditional social work role. Fieldwork allowed for a broader, less circumscribed consideration of how youth creatively "got by" despite the very real omnipresence of oppressive structures. The starting point of interaction was directed by the youth themselves, based on what was important to them in that moment in time. Not directing the topic of the interview or observation allowed for a more natural flow of situated experience and loosened control over the research goals and relationship. Similarly, Acker et al. (1983 as cited in Shaw 2003: 19) attempted similar strategies in their research to "reduce the unequal power and acknowledge the subjectivity of the participants," including encouraging participants to "take the lead in deciding what to talk about." By deliberately searching out feedback from youth about their experiences and the themes and concepts that emerged (see Kirby and McKenna 1989 for more on using substantive feedback), youth assumed the role of raconteur, thus encouraging a repositioning and a power-sharing in the production of knowledge. While every effort was made to highlight youth voices, staying in contact over long periods of time (one to four years) was challenging at best. The use of substantive feedback could never and will never be enough to neutralize power dynamics, even if this were possible — just as all research is not value or judgment free — but it was an attempt to re-centre the production of knowledge and not transpose onto youth preconceived categories of experience.

Benjamin's Research

Benjamin's research methods combined multiple sources of data, including focus groups and in-depth interviews with young people experiencing homelessness and service providers. Benjamin also conducted feedback sessions with young people and service providers to report back on findings and discuss the relevance of conclusions. Benjamin conducted two focus groups (with some overlap in participants) and twenty-four interviews with young people. He also conducted three focus groups and four individual interviews with service providers. In total, Benjamin's study included thirty-five young people with experiences of homelessness and thirty service providers.

Both of the youth focus groups included youth who identified as transgender. These focus groups were held early in the research process to explore collective understandings of the strengths that young people rely on in difficult times and different indicators of resilience. The focus groups were intended to provide a broader response to the research questions than what could be obtained through individual narratives, and they also provided a snapshot into the group dynamics of peers who were homeless. The discussion in the focus groups helped Benjamin to better prepare for the individual interviews and helped to validate the themes that emerged from the interviews.

Benjamin also conducted one- to two-hour focus groups with three staff teams working in the youth homelessness sector, including the staff team from a youth shelter for young men, a youth shelter for young women, and a drop-in centre. These focus groups provided a checkpoint to explore themes he was hearing from young people and also provided an external perspective on the strengths and resilience seen in young people. After the three focus groups, Benjamin conducted four interviews with service providers to follow up in greater depth on the conversations of the three staff teams and again discuss emerging themes from the youth interviews.

Reflexivity (Locating the Researchers)

Ceglowski (2002) argues that social research is conducted on the stage of human interaction, where a researcher is influenced by the relationships formed with participants and the research setting. A researcher's personal perceptions, interactions, assumptions, and analytical approach all shape what the researcher is able to observe and understand about the phenomenon being studied. This makes it important for researchers to be aware of personal biases, not to eliminate them but to attempt to understand their influence on the research process.

For Sue-Ann, the impetus for her research was rooted in practice knowledge. Based on her years of social work practice with homeless youth before embarking on the project, one of the study's raisons d'être was clearly ethically motivated and directly related to the unjustness she perceived — notably, the gravity of structural constraints (difficulty accessing social assistance, housing, and labour markets) that push particularly younger youth into arenas of limited options (MacDonald 2013). The purposive sampling of sixteen- and seventeen-year-old youth was a deliberate choice to highlight a *risky* paradox of sorts. Not only is this group more marginalized because of structural and symbolic constraints that push them into more *risky* arenas of limited choices, since difficulties accessing job and housing markets frequently push them into illegal ways of surviving, but also they are considered to be more *at risk* due to their young age and marginalized social status. In a sense they are doubly disqualified: not only are they young, but they are homeless, thus bucking social norms and reducing the public's ability to view them as legitimate social actors. During our research in the province of Ontario, Canada, the simple act of sixteen- or seventeen-year-olds leaving "home" ultimately determined their legal autonomy.[4] There were no legislative provisions that allowed youth to become legally emancipated so that they could access adult resources, creating a significant equality rights issue. These youth were not required to submit to parental control, and yet they had not reached the age of majority and were consequently denied legislated adult benefits. Emancipated youth were in a kind of no-status limbo, where resources (e.g., housing, social assistance) were often paltry and difficult to access. Despite their designation as a more vulnerable group, the way the "system" was set up (e.g., social assistance, supportive and/or transitional housing, limited shelter options) often posed enormous challenges for them. Building relationships meant that Sue-Ann had to be present on a regular basis in the community where homeless youth congregated, in and outside agencies they frequented, proving that she could be trusted. It also meant making herself available on a moment's notice to discuss a topic of concern, go for a quick coffee, or "tag along" for a walk if invited. Being present and genuinely interested in what the youth had to share fostered closeness and trust, and lay the foundations for our relationships. Later on in the research, it also meant staying in contact through other methods (telephone, email) and sometimes involved seeing youth in new milieus — such as in their first apartments, after hitchhiking trips, or as first-time parents.

Unmapping the social work space that Sue-Ann had typically occupied with homeless youth meant doing away with the comforts and contours of clinical practice and being invited into their space. As the study unfolded, she became aware that her years of clinical experience documenting and evaluating histories of childhood and adolescent victimization, interpersonal and intrapersonal challenges, mental health and addiction problems, and so forth had supplied her with a particular victimization lens based on expert frameworks that she was not conscious of until she engaged with youth in a different way. Rather than essentializing their experiences into clinical categories, meanings, and actions, she needed their permission to observe and interact in their world in the role of observer-learner (which, in hindsight, was still invested with a certain amount of authority). Most importantly, it allowed her to connect with youth differently and to consider their experiences, and how decisions were shaped, in a different light, albeit taken up and interpreted through her power/knowledge framework. For instance, instead of framing youth experiences through a victim lens, she started to understand the other ways in which they framed their experiences.

Benjamin has been involved in training and advocacy for strength-based intervention with young people in Ontario and is aware that he has been strongly influenced by this strength-based perspective in his research. Through his long-term involvement with a youth-serving agency, he has co-authored a training manual on strength-based intervention with young people (see Roebuck, Roebuck, and Roebuck, 2011), and conducts training sessions with managers and service providers from youth justice, child welfare, and youth and adult mental health agencies on how to move away from deficit-based interventions and work effectively from a strength-based philosophy of care.

Conducting this research also opened his eyes to the social realities that young people were describing but that he had not previously seen. Ceglowski (2002) describes a similar experience about how conducting research with school-aged children living in poverty opened her eyes to the poverty in her own community. Best (2007: 3) also describes a similar experience in her research with young people: "I began to *see* and *sense* the world in a dramatically different way from how I had once *thought* of the world.... I came to see a conceptual rift between my everyday world and the youth worlds I studied." As Benjamin heard young people describe the places where they would sleep, the drug economy on the streets, and the types of criminal offences they would engage in, his view of the space around the drop-in changed dramatically. He became keenly aware of the drug pushers waiting outside the drop-in, he witnessed constant drug exchanges, and he noticed the types of spaces outside where youth might sleep. Benjamin's research was in the same neighbourhood where he had lived for eight years, and hearing young people's stories dramatically changed the way that he understood the social and physical environment.

Together, we recognize that a subjective, strength-based, resilience framework is inherently value laden, and although the same may be true of a risk-based framework, our projects allowed us to consider the experiences of homeless youth in a different way. For instance, while many youth experienced victimization on the streets or broke laws in their efforts to survive, they did not characterize their experiences as ones of victimization or deviance. Instead, many youth shared that their harmful experiences were character-shaping. They felt they were "warriors," "survivors," or "hustlers," describing themselves as resourceful and creative, actively practising resistance to those who tried to exert authority over them (e.g., police, other youth, helping professionals). We found that these young people were thoughtful about their lives, identities, stigma, and relationships with others. They inspired hope in the face of so many obstacles and demonstrated creative and adaptive responses to very difficult situations.

Given these extraordinary displays of resilience, we did not want our research involvement with youth to focus exclusively on what was going wrong in their lives, how their mental health was suffering, and how they experienced stigma, as we believed that having conversations exclusively about barriers had the potential to reinforce marginalization. It is our hope that by exploring their strengths, their abilities to solve problems, and the types of solutions they have found to problems in the past, our research approach invited them to share a more holistic rendering of their lives, their losses, and their wins.

A PERSONAL NOTE TO READERS

There is a danger of seeing the lives of young people who are homeless as so extraordinary and different that it becomes difficult to relate to their challenges and triumphs. As you read through our book, we invite you to imagine how you would react personally given the different circumstances described in these pages. We do not want to present a two-dimensional rendering of the lives of young people who are homeless, highlighting only the challenges that they experience, the multiple forms of exclusion and marginalization that surround them, and the benchmarks of adulthood that they have not yet achieved. This would limit our efforts and research engagement to a deficit perspective, and we do not believe that any of the young people who participated in this research would want to be described in that manner or would even recognize themselves in such language. The young people that we came to know navigated daily challenges, often with incredible courage, preserving their own dignity in a world where the decisions of adults have the power to wreak havoc in their young lives. In our projects, we were amazed to hear young people telling us what they have learned through homelessness, how they have grown, what strengths they have developed, and what they will take away from the experience. These discussions reshaped our understanding of youth homelessness, and we hope that you will have the same experience in the pages that follow.

Staying Alive While Living the Life is about the challenges and successes of young people navigating homelessness, working hard to survive while also living their lives as fully as they are able. The title emerged from our conversations with youth and reflects the paradoxes and tensions of street life. "Staying Alive" refers to their perseverance and resilience, the necessity to do whatever it takes to survive — including keeping hope. Annie, one of the youth in the study, said simply, "The challenge *is* to stay alive." The second part of this dialectic is "Living the Life," referred to by many youth in a glorified manner, as the taking up of the adventures and challenges of street life, including experimentation (e.g., sleeping outside, not being bound by shelter rules, bucking conformity, partying, trying different substances, testing out new relationships and group living), risk-taking, and mischief-making. This expression seemed to capture the moment in time, their journey through homelessness, as something symbolic of youthhood — as a time of taking risks. We hope that our writing does justice to the trust that the youth bestowed in us in allowing us to tell their stories.

2. BECOMING HOMELESS

Annie (age seventeen) stood outside the drop-in, waiting for it to open. She had been living on the streets for several months, after staying on and off in various shelters for about a year. She grew up in a small rural town outside of Ottawa, where she lived with her mother, whom she described as an alcoholic, and her stepfather, who works a lot at a "good government job." Annie described her relationship with her stepfather as tense and "fucked up," saying that she liked to provoke him and that he became violent, emotionally and physically. She said her mother escaped their constant fighting by drinking and turning the other way, trying to "save face" and maintain a good reputation in their small community. Her mother eventually told her it would be better for all of them if Annie left. Fed up with the constant tension and feeling abandoned by her mother and "disowned" by her family," she left last year for the city in search of what she called "freedom." After intermittent stays in a shelter, she began to feel suffocated by the rules and curfews and opted to "travel" by hitchhiking, squatting, or sleeping outdoors with friends. Over the year she travelled to Toronto several times, and she recently went there for an abortion, an experience she described as a "real wake-up call." She said this experience was pivotal in helping her to "change her life around," stop using drugs (methamphetamines), and try and get off the streets. "Being on the streets is just as violent as being at home," said Annie.

As Annie's story illustrates, her understanding of the risks, dangers, and vulnerabilities present in street life was inextricably linked to her sensibilities about risk in early life. Not only did violence and substance use characterize these early years, but so too did a sense of abandonment and general instability. For many participants, this translated into a higher tolerance for risk and unpredictability, leading to the impression that the streets were no more dangerous or unstable than what they had previously known. For Annie, her perception of risk was tied directly to what she had previously experienced. This may explain why Kipke and colleagues (Kipke, Simon, Montgomery, Unger, and Iversen 1997) found that participants displayed a cognitive dissonance between the significant amount of victimization they experienced and their fearlessness with respect to the risk of future victimization. Thus, even though the literature on homeless youth experiences suggests an increase of victimization once on the streets (Boivin et al. 2005; Gaetz 2004, 2009; Janus, Archambault, Brown, and Welsh 1995; Sleegers, Spijker, van Limbeck, and van Engeland 1998), Annie's prior experiences raised her threshold of risk tolerance. Karabanow and Kidd (2014: 18) explain:

> These are young people who have rarely experienced a stable, loving family unit — rarely did they feel loved, cared for, supported or experience a sense of belonging. As such, it is of little wonder why street life is consistently perceived by the vast majority of the street youth population as a safer and more stable environment than home.

Each young person that we spoke with had their own story of how they became homeless and how that experience had affected them. While each of their stories is unique, a number of themes recur and align with previous research on youth homelessness (Aubry et al. 2003; Karabanow 2004; Mallett et al. 2010; Novac, Hermer, Paradis, and Kellen 2006). Within these contexts, youth frequently portray themselves as survivors who need to take risks in order to survive daily challenges but also to experience what life on the streets — albeit constrained — can offer. This theme of survival and agency formed a common thread in youth narratives of how they perceived their circumstances and made choices when facing serious constraints and limited resources.

FAMILY CONFLICT

In our research, family conflict emerged as a primary pathway into homelessness, which is reflected in the dominant research in the field (Aubry et al. 2003; Karabanow 2004; Mallett et al. 2010; Novac, Paradis, Brown, and Morton, 2006). Many of the young people explained how multiple challenges within their family of origin led to an environment of instability that contributed to homelessness. In many cases, young people were kicked out or chose to leave home because of conflict with their parents, siblings, or grandparents. Some young people described their decision to leave home as a way to escape constant arguments with family members. Jay (age seventeen) acknowledged what a big decision it was for him to leave his home. He described how he weighed the pros and cons of staying in his family home versus his perceptions of what homelessness would be like:

> *I was about fourteen. Me and my mom had arguments daily. I eventually decided, "Fuck it.... I'm out of this house. I can't deal with this anymore. I'd rather be on the street." I ended up downtown right in front of McDonald's. [Laughs]. So ... I realized I'm homeless. The big decision was leaving my house or not.... Do I keep dealing with this, or do I leave and be me and not have someone over my shoulder all the time? I decided to leave. That was my big decision.*

Similarly, Marco (age twenty-one) was having challenges with his brother and felt the need to get some space away from the conflict. He described his choice very simply: "So, I had a little dispute with my brother, and I decided to leave home and see how it was in the shelters. I stayed there for eight months." Given the voluntary nature of our research, it is possible that there were other factors involved in the lives of the young people that they chose not to share, but in these two cases, the young people stated that they chose to leave home to gain some distance from family conflict. In the cases that follow, this environment of tension is a constant, but the young people provide further insight into what issues were contributing to their conflicts.

Family Instability, Substance Use, and Violence

Today many marriages and long-term romantic partnerships break up. The effects of divorce or separation on intimate partners and their children vary greatly. Several young people described how the difficult divorce of their parents left them torn between two worlds, as they were passed back and forth between parents. June (age eighteen) believed that the pressure she experienced from her parents to choose sides in their conflict contributed to her choices to "rebel" and to use drugs:

> *I was always happy when I was at home. I was always really spoiled. I actually came from a really rich family, and my parents got divorced 'cause my dad cheated on my mom. I guess I blame my mom a lot for it 'cause I was daddy's little girl, and I didn't see my dad at all ... like, ever. So I just started kind of rebelling and doing drugs.*

The combined tension of her parents' divorce and her mother's distress about June's drug use and truancy from school led to a situation where June was given an ultimatum to stop using drugs or to leave home. In the lead-up to the ultimatum, June was passed back and forth between her parents and was not able to find her fit:

> *But my mom kicked me out 'cause I started skipping class, and she was just fed up. She told me I was going to go live with my dad. So I went to go live with my dad. He kicked me out after a week, because I guess he couldn't handle it, and he just liked his single lifestyle. I went back to my mom, and she had enough of me. I said, "Whatever, I don't need you." And I left home.*

After she became homeless, June made a few attempts to come home, but these attempts would typically break down after about a week. She explained that her continued drug use created tension in her relationship with her mother:

> *At sixteen I started going really hard into drugs. I was really addicted to meth, and she found drugs in my purse 'cause she used to go through my stuff and read my diary. She didn't help me. She never said, "Oh, we'll go see a counsellor together." She'd just be like, "Get*

out of here." She never really offered help. So … I dropped out of
high school.

Young people reported that drug and alcohol use — by their parents or
themselves — was a common contributor to family instability. Many of
these young people lived in homes that were also characterized by violence
or other criminal activity. Vince (age twenty) explained how his home
environment led to his choice to leave:

I left home around the age of sixteen. My parents were really, really
heavy users. They were addicted to painkillers … OxyContin. My
mom left one Christmas and my dad was robbing so many banks.
He finally got caught, so I left for my friend's house.

Kathryn (age nineteen) had a similar family environment characterized
by instability, drugs, alcohol, and violence. This led her to reluctantly choose
to leave her mother's home at the age of fourteen:

I moved out of my mom's house willingly … kind of not willingly,
because I would've loved to stay with my mom. My parents are sepa-
rated, and my dad is remarried. My mom, on the other hand, she's
never going to change. We would move around.… I would have to
change schools every year, and that's not stable at all, you know? So
whenever I did have a home, it wasn't really a good place to be …
with drugs and drinking going on and … violence. It just doesn't
do any good for a kid growing up.

Kathryn's description of the tension between her willingness and unwill-
ingness to leave home highlights how her choices were constrained. Between
the limited options of remaining in an unstable environment with her family
or leaving for the street, she chose the instability of homelessness. This is a
heavy and difficult choice for a fourteen-year-old to make. Five years after
first becoming homeless, Kathryn continues to cycle through homelessness.
She described her decision with a lot of ambivalence:

If you don't have to, here's some advice, don't leave your parents. If
you have to … if you're mature enough to make that decision, then
you should be mature enough to keep on having to, because once
you make that decision, you're making that decision for the rest of

your life after that. You could either keep feeding into the bullshit, or you could do something with your life. I'm trying to, but it's kind of hard living in the streets.

In Adam's case (age eighteen), he stopped paying rent at home when he lost his job because of alcohol addiction. He was given time to find a new job and was then asked to leave home:

Ever since I was fourteen I've had a drinking problem. I am an alcoholic. I had a job. I was working every day, forty hours a week, making fifteen bucks an hour. I started drinking and eventually I started missing work. One day would turn into two days, then three days, then eventually I got fired. So I couldn't pay rent to my dad anymore. He let me live there for a few more months, and he told me I have so long to get a job. And I was just constantly drinking. I never went out and looked for a job at all. I ended up getting kicked out and going to live with my buddy ... who got evicted. And that's how I ended up on the street.

Adam highlights the tension that existed between his dad and stepmother in deciding to kick him out. Previous research indicates that children in blended families or with remarried parents may experience higher rates of homelessness than children from families where both parents have remained together, as a result of the conflict that arises from new expectations and roles within the family (Mallett and Rosenthal 2009). In his case, Adam believed that his father alone would not have asked him to leave, and that this decision was made by his stepmother:

My dad's wife is the one who kicked me out of the house, not my dad. My dad would never kick me out. The whole winter ... he had a shed in the backyard, and he put a blanket in there for me, and he's like, "You can sleep in the shed if you want." You know? But it's a shed with metal walls. It's still freezing, but ... that's where I slept most of the time. Eventually he had a futon mattress in there for me. He tried to help me. Either that or I slept on his porch.

Christine (age twenty-one) also experienced tension with her family because of her drug use. She did not feel her parents would understand her choice, so she tried to hide it from them. Christine described how her ongoing dishonesty with her parents about her drug use led them to ask her to leave home:

> *I was just lying a lot … making up stories as to where I was going and who I was hanging out with because … I didn't want to disappoint my mom. She inevitably found out through doing a bit of picking around and finding out different information. Her and my stepdad sat me down and I kept lying and lying, so they were like, "Okay, we know the truth and you just keep lying, so you're out." So I kinda got kicked out for the first time in my life, and my mom has never even threatened it before. The fact that I got kicked out is pretty hard. I just had to pack all my stuff, and they drove me to the bus stop and that was it.*

Christine's boyfriend, Ryan (age twenty-two), has a longer history of drug use and has participated in multiple treatment programs in Ottawa and in another region of Canada. During his attempts to clean up, his parents have allowed him to live with them periodically. He said, "I stayed with my parents for a little bit, but then I relapsed once or twice and got kicked out." When asked to share a little more about the conversation he had with his parents, he explained that he had gone for a job interview one day and met up with some people afterwards. He did not come home for three days. When he returned home, his parents were so angry that they told him he was no longer welcome to stay with them. Since he could not return home, he went to an adult shelter. Substance use is a central challenge for many young people who become homeless. Drugs are easily available, and many young people begin to use heavily to cope with the emotional stress of homelessness or to numb emotional pain. For young people on the margins of homelessness, who are still in and out of their family home, substance use can exacerbate pre-existing tensions and make a parent less willing to work through conflict.

Indeed, abandonment was a strong and recurring theme in participants' narratives. A sense of abandonment was also described by youth whose parents were heavily addicted; it gave youth the impression that their parents chose and prioritized their drug use over raising and taking care of them. For example, Chris (age seventeen), who did have some contact with his biological father, described him as a "good-for-nothing crackhead." Chris explained that he had attempted to reach out to him for help over the years but was tired of being disappointed. He had recently been to his father's apartment to see whether he could "crash on his couch." Upon visiting, he was horrified by the amount of drug paraphernalia present, such as crack and crack pipes, and observed that there were "too many crackheads crashing there already." He promptly decided to leave. His conclusion was that his father was too heavily addicted to be helpful to him at all: "My dad is too busy with keeping up his habit to be of any use to me."

Almost all of the youth described some level of abuse, neglect, abandonment, or extreme conflict in their residential settings prior to hitting the streets. About half left from their families of origin, while the other half left a foster home, group home, or detention centre. Three-quarters of the youth we met cited some level of physical, emotional, and/or sexual abuse or rejection that led to them being drawn or pushed to the streets. While the impact of abuse and rejection on identity construction is discussed further on, it is important to note here that almost all the youth cited extreme conflict as the impetus for leaving or being forced out by their parents or guardians. The types of conflict included abuse by parents, step-parents, and/or siblings; family instability and recomposition; and substance use (theirs or their parents). Young people often end up homeless as a way to escape violent physical and sexual victimization from their parents, siblings, or members of their extended families. Other young people may be perpetrators of family violence that is directed towards their parents or siblings. In these cases, parents may ask their child to leave or, after police and court involvement, the young person is no longer allowed to live at home. For example, Ezra (age eighteen) was asked to leave home after becoming enraged and punching holes in the walls, Dustin was asked to leave home after stealing to support his drug habit, Pete was kicked out after allegedly assaulting a younger sibling, and both Jake and Kristin were kicked out after physical altercations with their parents.

Almost half of the participants from Sue-Ann's research were from single-parent homes, particularly female-headed households, often living in poverty. These youth described being raised almost exclusively by their mothers, and when a new romantic partner entered the family scene, it introduced tension where youth felt unwanted. They described feeling betrayed and abandoned by their mothers, resulting in their perception that their mothers "chose" the partner over them, and glossing over perhaps the very real financial reasons their mothers might have needed or chosen to stay in such relationships. Participants emphasized the degree of conflict and violence between themselves and their mothers' partners. Some young men said that their mothers' short-term and shifting relationships with male partners contributed to their leaving home. They said they were physically assaulted by their mothers' partners, or they said they attacked in self-defence or in defence of their mothers. This tension and repetitive conflict pushed the youth to leave home.

Family Conflict over Sexual Orientation and Gender Identity

Society is organized around the dichotomy of male and female, but many people do not experience their gender along this binary. Further, some people experience a degree of fluidity in how they define their gender and sexual orientation. For young people who identify as gay, lesbian, bisexual, trans, queer, questioning, or two-spirit, it can be challenging to navigate a frequently hostile world and to cope with misunderstandings, especially in the family home. Previous research shows that youth who identify as LGBTQ2S are overrepresented among homeless youth (Abramovich and Shelton 2017; Fournier et al. 2009; Gaetz 2004; Gattis 2009; Kruks 2001). Roughly one-third of the youth we met identified as gay, queer, bisexual, transgender, queer, or questioning. In a focus group with service providers, Lynn confirmed that she saw a number of LGBTQ2S youth becoming home-less in Ottawa. She said, "If their parents have a really different value set that doesn't really include them in it, then they can end up on the streets."

Syrus (age twenty-one) is an example of this type of value conflict. He grew up in a traditional Muslim family and believed that his gender identity and sexual orientation conflicted with his family's traditional values. He called himself "male fluid" since he currently identified with the male gender but felt his gender was not fixed and may change with time and context. Syrus chose to run away from home at the age of eighteen as part of his decision to come out as queer:

> I ran away as I was coming out, a personal choice ... because I felt that my family was really Muslim and couldn't accept that or handle it. I left at 5 a.m. while everyone was sleeping. I packed up my stuff and left a note. I got guidance from a social worker who helped

me translate my letter into Arabic so that my family could really
understand it ... a coming out letter and a running away letter.

For Syrus, while his decision to leave home was not based on a particular conversation with his parents and he was not asked to leave, his perception of their likely reaction was based on his knowledge of their adherence to their faith, and it led him to make his choice. He engaged in a tremendous amount of planning and forethought in preparing a letter and seeking help from existing community services to have the letter translated into Arabic.

Thomas (age nineteen) grew up in Europe with his family. When he was twelve years old, his parents and his twin sister were killed in a car crash, and he moved in with his grandparents, whom he described as very traditional. His grandparents became aware of his sexual orientation when he was fourteen, and they kicked him out of their house. His grandma died just six months after asking him to leave, and his grandpa died shortly after her. Thomas had recently migrated to Canada to pursue an education, but he dropped out of school and became homeless. His hope was quickly depleted:

Everything that I was thinking about my future just went away. I
cried too much. I was desperate. I thought about killing myself, but
fortunately I saw the bright side. It has been hard for me. I don't
have any more family.

Family reactions to gender identity may also destabilize housing options for youth. Paul (age nineteen) was assigned female at birth but identified as a trans male. He had a very violent history in his family environment, and consequently spent time cycling through prison and periods of homelessness for more than five years. At the age of twelve, Paul was molested by his father, and he decided to run away because he felt his mother was not doing anything to protect him. Although Paul returned to his family home shortly after that incident, his parents told him to leave when he was fourteen and came out as transgender. Once again, Paul was later able to return home; however, after a serious incident of family violence, he was incarcerated and then left homeless. Several years later, Paul moved to Ottawa to live with his grandparents. They were as concerned about his gender identity as his parents were:

They found out I was "gay" ... in their terms. I told them I was

*transgender. They told me I was just gay, and they kicked me out
for it. Well ... they didn't really kick me out.... They threw out all
my guy clothes and everything, and they're like, "If you don't like
being straight, then you can get out of the house." And I was like,
"Fine, I'll leave."*

Young people who are discovering, learning about, and experimenting
with their sexual orientation and gender identity experience discrimination, harassment, and homophobia or transphobia in society. For many
adolescents these experiences occur not just in schoolyards and city streets
but also in the home, where family members may choose to terminate their
relationship with them as well as deny them access to safe housing and
other supports.

Youth mentioned that their perceived lifestyle "choices" (e.g., drug use,
school truancy, self-expression) could clash with their primary caretakers,
particularly when their search for more freedom was hampered by the imposi-
tion of more constraints (e.g., curfews and limits on phone calls, computer
use, and socialization with certain peers and partners considered bad influences). This tension exacerbated patterns of abuse, familial instability, and
conflict; escalated drug use by the youth; and, according to some youth,
was the final trigger for their departure to the streets, whether they were
ejected or left of their own accord. Examples of behaviours that magnified
tension between themselves and their parents, or their substitute caregivers, included quitting or being absent from school; using drugs, partying,
or spending an increasing amount of time on the streets; associating with
"deviant" peers; and taking on a "deviant" or "nonconformist" appearance
(gender-fluid, goth, punk, etc.). In general, the caregivers' censure of this
experimentation and activities that they considered deviant conflicted sharply
with young people's desire to have more freedom and ultimately pushed or
pulled young people to the streets.

Surprisingly, even though conflict was the decisive spark that led to
homelessness, and most of the youth described their childhoods and the
family "home" as emotionally charged, they nevertheless continued to have
contact with their mothers, fathers (to a lesser degree), and siblings (some
youth even had siblings who were already homeless or wound up on the
streets during the research). Some participants reported that their familial
relationships improved with their departure from the family home, and

they continued to visit their families on a weekly basis. Most youth continued to have sporadic or regular contact with family members, ranging from telephone or email contact to meals and visits, including sometimes sleeping over.

Some researchers have noted that experiences from early childhood help to shape homeless youth's perceptions of their lives on the streets (Colombo 2008, 2015; Gilbert 2004; Parazelli 2000, 2002). These early socialization experiences influence current-day expectations of interpersonal relationships and frame what is deemed acceptable or tolerable on the streets. What is important to highlight here is the significant threshold of abuse, violence, neglect, instability, and conflict these youth were exposed to and, arguably, became accustomed to prior to leaving home. Their risk perception was severely affected by these prior experiences. Annie's story at the beginning of this chapter highlights the complex relationship she has with her family and how this impacts her perceptions of street life and shapes subsequent decisions she makes. Youth's perceptions of risk on the streets are embedded in past experiences but are also constantly changing as they integrate new experiences that shift their perceptions of risk and the decisions they make.

CHILD WELFARE SYSTEM

The child welfare system plays a large role in the lives of many young people who experience victimization and eventually experience homelessness. Many young people who are victims of serious family violence are removed from their homes and placed in child protection services (in our case in Ontario, the Children's Aid Society). For these children, experiencing further abuse in "care" can be a strong push towards homelessness. Numerous studies show a link between youth homelessness and state care, and recent estimates indicate that roughly half of Canadian homeless youth have been involved in the child welfare system, with many entering the streets directly from group homes or foster care (Gaetz et al. 2016; Mallett et al. 2010; Novac, Hermer, Paradis, and Kellen 2006; Whitbeck 2009). This was quickly apparent in our research.

> *I don't know ... rough childhood, shit didn't work out ... went to Children's Aid in group homes, rebelled, criminal record, got into*

using drugs, and then ... shit just kind of went downhill. I fell out with my family, got kicked out of [a mental health treatment centre], and now I'm on the street. (Chad, age seventeen)

Chad described how he began to associate with criminally involved peers in the group home. He felt that he did not receive support when he began to get arrested:

The group homes? A bunch of kids who are all street smart put together in one room? It didn't exactly work out for the benefit of anybody. So ... this guy knows how to get drugs, this person knows how to rob somebody, you know how to make money quick, and the other guy is just there for support, so you all work together and look for ways to get high, rob people ... shit like that. And then your social worker is so busy that they don't even really know that you get arrested a lot. They're always, "Oh, I'm busy," and you're just like, "What the fuck, man?" So ... not very much support as a teenager in group homes.

Other young people, such as Jake (age nineteen), experienced severe emotional consequences stemming from sexual assault while living in group homes run by Children's Aid. Jake was particularly troubled by his perception that people were aware of the sexual assault he was experiencing and chose not to intervene:

My life in CAS [Children's Aid Society] was shit, and they knew that. A lot of the workers knew exactly what was going on, in my opinion. There were days where stuff would be going on to me, the staff would walk right past. They had to have seen something, but they would just pretend ... go on with their life like nothing had happened. It was so bizarre; they were like a statue ... they didn't know what to say or what to do about the situation so they'd just keep going, you know? The feeling ... I call it utter despair ... of your emotions running wild through you is kind of like taking the most powerful drug you could find. Because I can remember having been sexually assaulted and feeling so happy but yet so sad. And I'd be crying but laughing, trying to convince myself that it was all fucked, and like...I was just deluded in the head...maybe I just dreamed all of it.

Jake explained that sexual experimentation and assault was common in his group homes. His narrative shows how confused the abuse made him feel, as he tried to understand his feelings of sexual excitement and his sadness over being violated. He later explained that the sexual abuse he experienced continues to make him feel unsure about his own sexuality, since it was confusing to receive sexual attention from other males:

> *It's a common thing in group homes, I guess. I don't know if a lot of people are aware of that, but it is. I didn't even know how to react to that; they would just reach over and bam, their hand is in your pants, and there's nothing you can do ... or say. I mean, what do you say to that? Okay, I'm a boy, but yet another boy just touched me. So do I accept it or not?*

A similar case involved Marshall (age seventeen), whom Benjamin met several times in the drop-in centre when he came in for food and other available donations. The first time that Ben met him, they had a very open conversation with a staff member about injection drug use. On the day of his research interview, Marshall came into the office and slouched in his chair, laying his arms out across the desk; they were slashed with bright red marks from his hands all the way up to his shoulders. It was December, and Marshall explained that he was wearing a T-shirt because the cool weather outside helped him ease the burn of his self-inflicted injuries. Marshall had experienced sexual assault in his group home and found that the staff team was not able to understand what had happened or how it had affected him. "Recently, I was in a group home.... This was like three months ago.... I got raped. I ended up leaving ... running away from my group home 'cause nobody understood what was going on." Marshall described how he felt mistreated and misunderstood and how becoming homeless was a deliberate decision that he had made to escape the pain of living in the group home:

> *It was better to be homeless than to be in a house where everybody didn't understand. And every time I went back to the group home when I ran away, they would punish me and make me stay in my room. So I chose it.... Better to be on my own and be homeless*

and have nothing than to be in a house with stuff and feel like I have nothing. So why would I be in a house where everyone treats me like shit and I have nothing inside, when I can just go outside and have nothing without being treated like shit? So I would have rather been homeless than be in a house. I would have rather slept on the street than slept in a bed, 'cause of all the emotional pain that was going on.

Given his personal circumstances and the mistreatment that he experienced within a child protection agency, Marshall presented his decision to become homeless as a rational attempt to protect himself from further abuse and mistreatment. His description of the punitive response he received when he did return to his Children's Aid Society group home was echoed by Cheryl, a service provider with previous experience working for the agency. "When I worked at Children's Aid, if they took off, you had to strip search them when they got back … not complete strip search, but empty their pockets, do all this stuff. It went against how I wanted to work with youth," said Cheryl. Running away from child protection services seemed to be a common experience for a number of young people.

Some youth experiencing family violence deliberately waited until they turned sixteen to either become homeless or to report their abuse to authorities to avoid the involvement of child protection services. At the time of our research, the child protection legislation in Ontario mandated the involvement of child protection services when a child under sixteen was being mistreated; however, this is currently being reconsidered to align with other jurisdictions, where eighteen is the legal age of emancipation. Actively managing the timing of the disclosure of mistreatment demonstrates a deliberate decision by some youth, a form of negotiation with themselves, to wait until they reach an age when they will not be subject to the Children's Aid Society. In the case of Ella (age sixteen), she waited until she turned sixteen to leave home:

I told them … like a week before that I was going to leave and that this time I wasn't going to come back. And they didn't believe it because every other time I would always come back. When you're twelve and you're so little, they're not going to take you in a shelter, they're gonna send you to CAS [Children's Aid Society], and I didn't

want that. I didn't want to live in a group home. I would always
come back. So this time, I knew I was old enough to live in a shelter.
I just didn't know where it was.

Some youth did mention that they benefited from child welfare services, but stories of positive experiences were infrequent. Sadly, many young people continue to experience the profound contradiction of facing abuse within a system that is mandated to protect them. Some youth choose to leave care before they have acquired the skills to live independently; as a result, they become homeless. But as we see in these narratives, young people may feel that homelessness is the only alternative to living in group homes where they continue to be victimized. The articulation of choice regarding the child welfare system and the deliberate measures taken to avoid placement in child welfare demonstrates the significance of human agency and the effort that young people deploy to navigate their housing status on their own terms, allowing them to obtain a sense of control over their lives.

OTHER PATHWAYS INTO HOMELESSNESS

For some young people, the pathway into homelessness was eviction from the apartments that they were renting. This happened for numerous reasons. Max (age nineteen) was evicted from his apartment for having too many parties. Jake (age nineteen) nearly lost his social housing unit for hosting too many friends from the street who did not respect the building rules. Aaron (age twenty-three) explained how he and his girlfriend had so many fights over the past year that they were frequently evicted from their apartments. Ryan (age twenty-two) has experienced several reoccurrences of homelessness that have frequently been related to his drug use. However, at one point, Ryan was the victim of a home takeover when he was living in a downtown apartment with his father as the co-signer. Ryan allowed a young man to live at his place who was known to the police for dealing drugs. After the police were involved in an incident at his place, Ryan's dad refused to keep his name on the lease and Ryan was evicted:

I had an apartment downtown recently and ... I was addicted to
opiates at the time, but through sale and distribution I was able
to keep myself going. I met someone on the street, and he asked me
if he could stay with me for a little bit, and I wouldn't say I was

sympathetic, more empathetic 'cause I had been there, so I let him stay with me for a bit. Then ... a day turned into a week, and then he started selling crack cocaine out of my place. It was around that time that I was like, "Look, I think you should leave." That didn't go over so well. He was a bigger guy and basically took over my home. Within a month, my place was raided. No charges were pressed on me because I wasn't the perpetrator, but because my dad was the co-signer, he went and got me evicted because he found out what was going on at my place. So pretty much since then, I've been homeless.

Couch-surfing is another common experience for young people who are homeless and can occur at any point in the cycle of homelessness. Some young people manage to couch-surf for long periods of time to avoid living on the streets. Steve, a service provider, explained, "Some of them seem to have ways of finding a warm place to sleep or ... navigating other people they know, couch-surfing or whatever. Some kids arrive here and they've been couch-surfing for like eight months before they get to our services or find out about it." Many young people first turn to their friends for shelter when they leave home or the child welfare system. One young woman, June (age eighteen), bounced from house to house, and stayed on the streets periodically for several years. Others have friends with limited resources to help, and they quickly exhaust their social networks. Kristin (age eighteen) said, "And my friends, they can try as much as they can, but really? Couch hopping ... I can't stay at one place forever, you know?" It is common for young people to report crashing at a friend's place for several nights or weeks before eventually ending up on the streets.

ON BECOMING HOMELESS

Family conflict, family-related violence, mistreatment in the child welfare system, and eviction align well with previous research on pathways into youth homelessness (Aubry et al. 2003; Karabanow 2004; Mallett et al. 2010; Novac, Hermer, Paradis, and Kellen 2006). Themes of decision-making and human agency cut across the multiple narratives that the young people presented. For some, making the choice to be homeless was perceived as a matter of survival; for some, it was about asserting their independence; and for a few, it was a thrill-seeking adventure. For others, a series of negotiations with family members, landlords, and community services led to a moment where they were asked to leave their housing.

The thin line between choosing homelessness or having it forced upon them was not always clear in the narratives of the young people we met. On several occasions, youth indicated that they had been kicked out of their home, but later, when asked to clarify what had led to them being kicked out, they explained that they had actually decided to leave. The fluidity between the concepts of "being kicked out" or "choosing to leave" reflect how perceptions of violence, options, and choice can change with time or maturity or experience. It also highlights the process of negotiation that many youth are forced to engage in over their access to housing; these are complex interactions with serious consequences.

Mallett et al. (2010) explain that at times, young people minimize their own behaviours that may have led to them being asked to leave home, such as violence and drug use, and at other times the same young people may acknowledge that their behaviour left their parents with few options. This pattern of changing narratives was clear when talking with June (age eighteen), who initially said that she was kicked out of her home, and then later said that she chose to leave to get away from her mother. As she further reflected on her experiences, she emphasized the importance of taking the time to reflect honestly on the reasons for becoming homeless:

> *I guess there's a lot of decisions kids have to make when they're thrown out on the street. I think people need to come to the conclusion why they ended up there. A lot of people actually ended up there for really sad reasons, you know? And me, I was just a brat. And I think you'll find a lot of people like that ... but I think people need to be realistic and actually look at the situation and help themselves.*

Other young people, such as Kathryn (age eighteen), maintain that it was necessary to leave home, but still feel a degree of regret about severing ties with family, treating their parents poorly, and losing their housing. Kristin also expressed regret that she was not able to live with either of her parents but cast blame equally on her own mental health challenges and attitudes and what she perceived to be the shortcomings of her parents. We encountered a tremendous amount of ambivalence and mixed feelings about relationships with family when talking with youth. As we listened to young people share their stories, there was a sense that we were listening to accounts of unresolved situations and relationships that continued to exist in a state of flux. A few young people discussed how negatively they perceived their parents at the time of leaving home, but how they had developed a greater sense of appreciation as time passed. Others had made attempts to reconcile with family members, or had even moved home briefly, but found that their conflicts would reoccur. And yet others attempted to maintain a relationship with their parents, or gain support or closeness, but the parents were either unable or unwilling to provide what they needed, which also generated a lot of ambivalence among the youth.

Many young people also demonstrated a great deal of forethought and planning prior to leaving home. Examples include planning a safe time to leave home, arranging transportation into the city, observing how parents treated younger siblings to ensure their safety, tolerating violence until the age of sixteen to avoid placement in child welfare, and leaving a letter explaining the decision to leave home (even translated into Arabic for the parents). While some young people appear to have run away more spontaneously, these decisions were often shaped by responses to adverse living conditions. The way that young people perceive their initial departure may change with time, but it is common for young people to continue to reflect on the initial cause of their homelessness. For every young person we interviewed, leaving home was difficult.

3. PARADOXES OF STREET LIFE

I started coming downtown on the weekends when I was twelve. I was a real weekend warrior. My parents would kick me out for not listening to them or for not coming home for curfew or after school on time. I would hitch downtown on the weekends with my Barbie knapsack full of crack and coke to sell. I started to use, but I never got caught because I stayed outside on weekends, under the bridges and in parks with older friends I had made and who supplied me. And then during the week I went home and to school so CAS [Children's Aid Society] was never contacted. I remember hitchhiking downtown, and the cops would stop me and ask me my name and my age, so I would make it up and tell them a date of birth for a sixteen-year-old and would know the right year to say, and I was tall enough that I could pass for a sixteen-year-old even though I was only twelve or thirteen. (Ingrid, age seventeen)

After a few years spent being a "weekend warrior," Ingrid made the full-time move to the streets around age fourteen. She refused to stay in shelters, preferring instead to live on the streets with her friends. Looking back on these earlier experiences of homelessness, Ingrid remembered never feeling threatened or at risk when she was on the streets. She felt that her "new friends" were there to protect her and look out for her. The only fears she recalled were being caught by the police or child welfare authorities because of her age and drug dealing:

When I was twelve I didn't want to follow the rules. I came down-town. People downtown would get me high, but they also protected me. No one ever touched me, took advantage of me. My friends back home worried about me, told me they thought I was going to get killed. But I didn't feel unsafe.

Ingrid admitted that living this life "did not feel risky at that time." Even though she "witnessed crazy shit" and believed she "should be dead," she said, "I loved and still love being on the street." A few months after our first encounter, Ingrid rented a one-bedroom apartment with her boyfriend and six other youth. This was the first time in over three years that she had housing. She decided to get off the streets because her previous boyfriend had been murdered while they were partying under a bridge. Even though she had housing, however precarious, she continued to spend much of her time on the streets and reflected on how much she missed sleeping there. "Even now I miss the freedom of being on the streets with my knapsack and being able to take off at a moment's notice to Montreal or out west.... Now I have an apartment and responsibilities and I need to worry about paying the rent."

A few months later Ingrid disconnected from street life entirely for a variety of reasons: she had been evicted, she was tired of addiction ruling her life, and her boyfriend had assault charges that legally restricted him from living in the downtown core. She and her boyfriend made the big decision to move to her parents' home in the country, where she had not lived for over three years. She then secured a full-time service job in a hardware store. Speaking on the telephone with her one night, she revealed that she found her new life exceedingly boring. "It sucks. I have to be at work at 8 a.m. and I work 'til 6 p.m. It's so boring. I miss the life. I would give it all up to go back." After using morphine daily for several years — to the point where she would have to inject increasingly greater amounts to get high — and then deciding to quit and going through a very painful withdrawal process that she described as akin to "my insides tearing apart my skin," she admitted that "the worst thing is I just want to give up everything to go back."

After a year of living with her parents, her longing for the freedom and excitement of a nonconformist life and her urge to use drugs became too great and she returned to the streets. The monotony of her new life, she admitted, had become a real trigger for her return to street life. While her awareness of danger had grown, and her risk perceptions had changed in response to this consciousness, she was still drawn to street life and drug use. As such, perceptions of risk were not always rational ones. Choosing to live a certain lifestyle in the face of harmful consequences (e.g., relapsing, acquiring hepatitis C, experiencing violence and poverty) is not always rational and points to one of the many paradoxes of street life.

Turning to the literature, one of the central axes in discussions of risk among homeless youth is substance use. Rates of alcohol and drug use among street youth populations have been found to be substantially higher than those found in the general youth population (Benoit, Jansson, and Anderson 2007; Boivin et al. 2005; Haldenby, Berman, and Forchuk 2007; Tyler 2008). Some researchers emphasize that street youth are twice as likely to become injection drug users (Roy, Haley, Leclerc, Cédras, Blais, and Boivin 2003) and that there is a positive relationship between childhood sexual abuse and substance abuse (Haldenby, Berman, and Forchuk 2007). The focus on health risk behaviours, explored in greater detail in Chapter 4, in particular injection drug use and sexual practices, has been instrumental in constructing this population as "at-risk." Researchers have been proficiently documenting homeless youth's deteriorating health (Boivin et al. 2005; Ensign 1998; Gaetz and O'Grady 2002; Haldenby, Berman, and Forchuk 2007; Karabanow 2004; Kidd 2013), demonstrating that the longer an individual remains homeless, the worse that individual's health becomes (Karabanow 2004; Kraus, Eberle, and Serge 2001). Duration on the streets is also positively correlated with the amount of victimization experienced (Slesnick et al. 2008). The assertion that these youth are more likely to engage in high-risk behaviours the longer they are homeless (Slesnick et al. 2008; Tyler 2008), coupled with evidence of their worsening mental (Schwan et al. 2017) and physical health (Boivin et al. 2005; Karabanow 2004), demonstrates that there is a hierarchy of risks within this "at-risk" group. Those who are the most street-entrenched, alienated, or excluded, or have suffered the greatest childhood harms, are found to be at greater risk, a situation aggravated by the fact that they may be the least likely to ask for help. Yet despite the astounding evidence of risk factors from childhood and on the streets, little is understood about their viewpoints and experiences. The rather flattened images of youth gleaned from most research leaves little room for their own interpretations of their experiences. In our research we wanted to give youth the opportunity to speak to their experiences of getting by on the streets, and we found that the one common thread in their experiences was their paradoxical descriptions of street life, particularly with respect to drug use, freedom, relationships, and threat management.

CONSTRAINED FREEDOM

Young people's descriptions and perceptions of street life varied greatly. While some painted pictures of danger lurking on every corner, others described being on the streets as safer than living in their own homes or staying at shelters. Many youth portrayed themselves as highly adaptable survivors. Even though Annie stated that living on the streets was no more dangerous than living at home, she did admit that "the challenge is to stay alive," hinting at a survivor analogy. Many participants described the surge of excitement they drew from the backdrop of potential danger, and this double-edged nature of risk underlay many of the chances they took. For instance, several participants described the rush of sleeping outside and not being tied down to one place as exciting but sometimes dangerous, due to harassment by police and the threat of assault or theft. These examples illustrate the paradoxes inherent in the risks of street life.

Sleeping Rough and Travelling

When many of the young people first became homeless, they spent time "sleeping rough," looking for a place to sleep anywhere they thought they might be safe. They would often crawl into small out-of-the-way spaces to try and avoid public attention and to stay warm. Adam (age eighteen) shared, "I was pretty much sleeping in the stairwells.... Everywhere, stairwells, bus shelters — I didn't really care." Similarly, Marshall (age seventeen) explained, "I slept in an elevator, I slept in a parking garage, I slept in shelters.... I'd end up some nights just calling the city, 'cause I was just done." Several young people also reported sleeping in forested areas around the city or its outskirts. Chad (age seventeen) experienced severe health consequences after a period of camping out in the forest:

> I slept out in the forest for two months with one of my buddies, and
> then ... I checked into the [youth shelter]. I weighed eighty pounds,
> I was addicted to OxyContin, I had bronchitis.... I nearly died.

Young people expressed different sentiments about their first nights on the streets, but one of the most common reactions was fear; they often had trouble falling asleep. Jake (age nineteen) explained how he would look for a quiet place to sleep but that only slightly reduced his fear:

> *I found myself trying to sneak into buildings to try and get a place away from society, more or less. If I had to, I would sleep in little garbage areas or somewhere where I knew that for sure no one would be walking by. You know, this way I could ensure my safety. I could try to fall asleep, which was a joke.... You'd always be up every few hours, which is great because I like to get a sense of my surroundings again and reassure myself that I'm the only one there. Heaven forbid I wake up and there's a group full of people circling me. I used to stay in parks with people. We'd just stay awake all night.*

Pete (age eighteen) described his process for vetting a space to see whether it would be a good and safe place to sleep at night. His concern was finding a space where he would not be disturbed by law enforcement or private security:

> *It was hard being on your own all night ... doing nothing, trying to find a warm comfy place to sleep.... I actually had a pretty good system going where I would wait for a place for two hours, and then if I didn't see any [private security] or cops go by, I'd figure this is a good spot.... Not like a hard piece of concrete, I had to do that a couple of times, but one where you could lay your bag down and use that as a pillow and not be worried about being disturbed all night.*

Dustin (age sixteen) also experienced anxiety about being outside for the night and reported that he had trouble sleeping downtown because of all of the negative experiences he had witnessed:

> *Most of the time that I had to stay outside, I'd just stay up all night downtown, just doing whatever. I hate sleeping, especially when I'm on the street downtown. That just sketches me out. I've seen too much stuff. I don't like it at all. So if I'm downtown, then I'm awake no matter what. I ... can't sleep. It's annoying.*

In Sue-Ann's study, over half of the youth regularly slept outside and travelled, which they described as a way to seize freedom. They felt it was safer and less constraining than staying in a shelter. All of the youth that slept outside complained that shelter life was highly regimented. They disliked following the rules of the shelter, often felt that the staff was trying to control them, and believed that the dynamics of this form of group living encouraged in-fighting, theft, and assault. Youth were not oblivious to the risks of sleeping outside, but they did downplay them or portray them as integral to the thrill of sleeping outdoors.

At the beginning of the study, Olivia (age sixteen) loved the "freedom" of sleeping outside. "Even if I had my own place, I think I would still sleep outside. I like sleeping outdoors. Each day I like not knowing where I am going to end up." But she did not feel safe doing it alone: "It's too dangerous and lonely." One of the methods youth employed was a "safety in numbers" approach. Many of the youth who slept on the streets emphasized the importance of sleeping in a group or in pairs with people whom they trusted. However, sometimes circumstances did not permit them to sleep in groups, particularly when they travelled.

Youth described sleeping alone as "scary at first," which generally occurred when they were in a new setting. Jay (age seventeen) first experienced homelessness at the age of fourteen. He was terrified. When Benjamin asked him what it was like to be homeless at such a young age, he replied,

> *Pretty ... pretty ... pretty fucking devastating, man, like.... In all honesty, like it was pretty fucking scary. Like, it would get late, and I wouldn't have a place to go, and I'd wonder where to go. I'm fucking fourteen years old.... At this age I'm supposed to be put in a fuckin' foster home or something. I'm not supposed to be on the streets. I don't know where to go. My first night of being homeless, I ended up sleeping up on Major's Hill. No sleeping bag, no blanket, no nothing.... Just on the bench.*

Kristin (age eighteen) grew up in a rural area, so for her becoming homeless meant adjusting to urban life as well. Her fear of sleeping on the streets at night is linked to previous experiences of sexual victimization. When Kristin is not in a shelter or housed, she tries to find places in the city to sleep that are not in the downtown area:

> *City streets? That's a scary idea for me, but I have to do what I have*

to do, right? I've spent more than one night sleeping in my school's backyard, because it's better than sleeping downtown and getting raped again.

Several youth shared that they made sure they had a weapon to protect themselves in case of attack. The female participants in Sue-Ann's study also employed the buddy system in their hitchhiking experiences. Annie (age seventeen), who had hitchhiked out west to meet a girlfriend with whom she was supposed to return to Ontario, decided to purchase a plane ticket back to Ottawa when this friend abandoned her. Shane (age seventeen) teased her about not being brave enough to hitchhike back on her own, but Annie was adamant that it would not have been safe:

It's too dangerous to hitchhike back home alone. I've had bad experiences with guys always coming on to you. I always make sure I have a weapon. I had bear Mace. but I couldn't take it back on the plane with me.

Sleeping outside was generally described as appealing during the warmer months. During the winter, however, most youth sought refuge indoors or would travel out west until the spring. Annie stated, "When it starts to snow I have to look for a place to keep warm [i.e., a squat]…. I worry about freezing to death." The importance of knowing where to sleep outside predominated. Several youth complained of being hassled by police, other youth, or older homeless people when they slept outside in more visible places (e.g., under bridges). Many youth had places that they felt they had "first dibs on." This meant that they had found the site first, it was generally known that it was their territory, and only they could decide who could sleep there. Many arguments resulted from this form of territoriality, but the prevailing cultural norm was that one had to be accepted by the person who initially found the site in order to be granted the right to sleep there. Olivia (age seventeen) had been sleeping under a bridge with a friend but was evicted because another youth had claimed to have "found" the place first. She was told by her friend that she needed to respect this decision, even though she felt she was being unfairly singled out. She decided to try to get a bed at the shelter even though she did not relish the idea. "They [shelter staff] treat us like adopted children, always telling us what to do. But I would never sleep outside alone."

FREEDOM-DANGER PARADOX

Some youth revealed that the freedom of sleeping outdoors, hitchhiking, and hopping trains enabled them to party and travel as much as they wanted, unconstrained by curfews or shelter intoxication policies. This freedom meant that they could use substances as much as they pleased and with whomever they wanted. Sleeping outdoors and travelling were generally described as strategies that, while posing certain risks such as increased chance of assault or theft, also gave youth more control over their activities and allowed them to experiment with different forms of group living, even if their choices were constrained ones.

Similarly, hitchhiking, hopping trains, roaming, and travelling the country are experiences that play into this paradox of freedom and danger. The thrill of not being constrained by a schedule, a residence, or rules (whether imposed by parents, guardians, residences, or shelters) went hand in hand with the dangers of going hungry, battling the elements (especially winter storms), finding a place to sleep, and being assaulted or robbed. For many youth, testing their limits and being open to new experiences, especially experimenting with drugs and other nonconformist aspects of street youth culture (e.g., squeegeeing, panhandling, sleeping outdoors), formed a freedom-danger paradox. While Jay (age seventeen) was scared at first, he later enjoyed camping in a forest with a friend and loved the feeling of freedom that he experienced for a time. However, eventually the reality of his situation began to hit him, and he became quite distressed:

> So it was cool, it was fun, you know? I liked it. I liked being fourteen, no mom, no nothing, chilling with my friend, sleeping where I'm sitting. It was cool for a bit, but then like, you know, the reality set in. I didn't like it too much.

The lure of the streets as a default rite of passage represents another element of this paradox. D'Allondans (2005), Jeffrey (2005), and LeBreton (1991, 2003) have noted that in the absence of traditional rites of passage to adulthood and a predominant safety-at-all-cost approach to adolescence, youth have had to seek out other means, which often fall into the category these authors refer to as *conduits à risques* (risky conduct). This anthropological notion views the streets as providing a kind of rite of passage to test one's limits in an effort to feel alive by pushing the boundaries of one's existence. Many youth described the kinds of risks they would take and glorified the shared sense of danger. This camaraderie afforded a way to prove their ferocity and to highlight the kinds of risks they would take; in other words, their investment in "the life." And for some participants, like Luke (age seventeen), the streets represent the playground of possibilities that offer escape from what he hates: "conservatism and normal." For example, not abiding by parental or other authority figure's control and rules (e.g., shelters) meant that they could sleep outside or squat with other youth, party (experiment with different drugs), and engage in "mayhem missions" (Luke's words) — be generally mischievous by destroying public property, engaging in graffiti, stealing, and running away from the cops.

Laura (age sixteen) described street life as "equal opportunity risk":

> [I'm someone who] loves hitchhiking, and it is not dangerous once you figure it out [who and what is safe and not safe]. You see, people take a chance on you, but you are also taking a chance on them. That's why I think it is equal opportunity risk on the streets. It is easy to become addicted to street life, the lifestyle, because it is this excitement that drives you to take chances and try new things.

Annie shared this "excitement of living the life," stating that "travelling is like crack; once you start it's hard to stop." For many youth, especially those that were more brazen in their risk-taking, the excitement and danger of street life afforded opportunities in experimenting with who they wished to be.

It is important to bear in mind that not all of the participants went to the streets in search of excitement or freedom. Some youth were highly risk-averse, felt continuously under threat, and took steps to minimize perceived dangers; they also felt they had exhausted all their options and the streets were a last resort. Attitudes towards life on the streets ran the gamut from risk aversion to active risk-taking. Annie's experiences fell somewhere in the middle. While she recognized the danger inherent in such activities as sleeping alone outside or doing hard drugs and took steps to minimize certain risks, she also hitchhiked across the country several times, stayed in squats or slept outside, and experimented with different living situations. "I worry that a random crackhead may stab me," she stated. "I had my sleeping bag stolen the other day by a crackhead, but I wasn't hurt." She took steps to minimize these risks:

I don't like to sleep outside alone, but sometimes I have no choice. I generally stay with the same group of people when I am outside ... but a few times in Toronto I had no choice [but to sleep alone]. It's scary at first, but then you get used to it. I always make sure I have a weapon [knife].

This passage illustrates that Annie was not naïve to the various dangers of the streets but also embraced the unpredictability. "I am living each day as I want to right now. It's exciting. You never know what's going to happen.... You just keep moving on." Annie was invested in these experiences of freedom even though at times they scared her, but her willingness to take certain risks changed over time. These paradoxes of street life — whereby freedom entails risks, and danger breeds excitement — capture the essence and tensions of how many youth understand their lives on the streets. However, this drive to take risks in an effort to achieve autonomy or freedom, as described by other authors (Bellot 2001; Colombo 2008; Parazelli 1999), did change over time for several participants. In Annie's case, by the end of the study, her life had radically changed due to ill health and pregnancy, which severely altered her perception of risks and led to her disenchantment with homelessness (though she did continue to remain socially engaged in street life). This gradual shift in perspective is described in greater detail in the following chapters on the evolution of youth's roles and identities.

While youth often described risks on the streets as being overwhelmingly negative, they seemed in large measure to accept risk as part of street life and situated their experiences within a context of familiarity. They often characterized themselves as survivors and active agents shaping their own destinies, acknowledging that this was within an arena of constrained opportunities. Earlier childhood experiences significantly affected how youth perceived dangers and opportunities on the streets, and they were reflective about how these prior experiences shaped current-day decisions.

FREEDOM-CAPTIVITY PARADOX

Though less highlighted in the literature, many youth also described the complex relationship they had to their drug use. Laura explained that her relationship to drug use was both liberating and constraining, illustrating the paradox inherent to drug use. She was keenly aware of her dependency on drugs, and while she worried intensely about becoming ill if she quit, still she dreamed of freeing herself from this feeling of captivity. Others (Castel 1998; Colombo 2008) have noted this relational context of drug use, postulating that substance use constitutes a paradox of freedom and captivity. Laura's and Lucy's stories provide interesting case studies of this freedom-dependency paradox.

Laura's Story

Laura (age seventeen) is originally from a rural area just outside of Ottawa. She moved to downtown Ottawa with her parents and three sisters when she was six years old. Her parents had their children when they were young (starting at age seventeen) and had been on social assistance most of their lives. Laura described them as very loving and supportive. She was one of the few youth who did not leave home because of abuse or conflict. Her impetus for leaving home and being drawn to street life was that she "fell in love with a homeless boy." After spending a year and a half on and off the streets to be with him, she became addicted to morphine and "hooked on its effect." She developed a daily habit that she maintained because of her fear of the pain of withdrawal. She said she led a "double life," because she had never admitted her drug use to her parents, and she did not believe they suspected it even after her relationship with her boyfriend ended and she remained on the streets.

Even though Laura was very entrenched in street life, she continued to remain in close contact with her family and attended school during her first year on the streets. She felt that she lived "two separate lives" and had trouble reconciling them. In the first, she was very close to her parents, pretended she did not use drugs, held down a job, attended school, and had many friends connected with this more normative lifestyle. Her other life was her street life. She used injection drugs (morphine) every day, slept on the streets with friends, and socialized mostly downtown and in the areas where other street youth congregated (squats). She revealed that leading this double life was wearing her out and becoming too difficult to maintain. She worried intensely about her parents and school friends finding out about her drug use, especially since she had stayed on the streets after her relationship ended. Laura felt that her friends and parents would shun and disown her if they found out about her morphine dependency, particularly since she had an older sister who had gone through a similar dependency and it had been a painful experience for her parents. Because of the stigma associated with drug use, she worried about being judged or singled out as "different" or "tainted" (Goffman 1963) compared to her other siblings.

According to Laura, what kept her on the streets was not her ex-boyfriend or her street friends (although the latter had grown in prominence) but her addiction. While she described enjoying the effect of the morphine, she was also starting to recognize how it constrained her life. Her days were becoming increasingly organized around its acquisition, and her drug use had a negative impact on her relationships with family and school friends. She toyed with the idea of getting help and quitting. During her first few months on the street, Laura kept leading this "double life" and appearing to have some control over her drug use:

> I am not the kind of person who gets into this stuff. I've never partied a lot. I am responsible, mature, always held down a job, gone to school. I warn others not to try it [morphine] because the high is so good, the endorphin release so powerful, I know they'd get hooked like me.

She admitted, though, that the guilt of leading this double life and lying to her parents and school friends about her morphine use was too much for her to bear. She did eventually seek addiction treatment and support and revealed her dependency to her parents and friends.

Lucy's Story

Lucy (age seventeen) had a different approach to the paradox of drug use. Her life on the street revolved around maintaining her injection drug use, and she described herself as a "slave" to her habit, which sometimes placed her in dangerous situations. She described how older men often preyed on her by "constantly trying to give you free dope for sex." She stated that the "two greatest risks on the street are being a young woman and being street-involved and addicted to substances":

> Being a young woman, men are always after you for sex, trying to pick you up, offering you loaded needles to sleep with them, or they'll say they'll give you free drugs for a month if you sleep with them. Secondly, being a substance user means it's dangerous to get the drugs

you need and use them safely. I try to go to [a large adult shelter] to buy my drugs, but guys always stop us [her and her boyfriend], they threaten to beat up my boyfriend because they say, "Why are you getting a young girl hooked on dope?" They try to deny me access to the drugs I need.

Having a drug dependency was, according to Lucy, another element that put her at greater risk, since "it's dangerous to get the drugs you need and use them safely." She was dependent on her boyfriend because many of the dealers would not sell directly to her unless she agreed to have sex with them. However, when her boyfriend bought their opiates, these same dealers wanted to beat him up and accused him of getting her hooked on dope.

Drug use was a common theme, spanning a spectrum of choices and risk perceptions that are intimately tied to the binary of freedom and dependence outlined by other authors (e.g., Bellot 2001). While several youth described the feeling of freedom they experienced while using drugs, the downside was the constant preoccupation with the hunt for the "next hit." The constant need to acquire and use constrained and dominated their everyday activities and the circle of relationships they needed to maintain access to substances. Many of the youth used (or had used) hard drugs daily (often opioids) and described this push-pull phenomenon. Even those youth who were heavily invested in maintaining their drug use described the constraints of using and alluded to this paradox of freedom and dependence and their ambivalence about their continued use. Tyler (age sixteen), who purported to be a "hardcore addict" who was "using anything [drugs] I can get my hands on," also admitted that his "crack and dope use" was making him sick and he was hoping to get off crack and "get into more pot [marijuana] like I used to use, because I am tired of feeling sick all the time."

Youth were also not oblivious to the potential harms implicit in their continued drug use (e.g., poor health, risk of blood-borne infections, criminalization, low inhibition or diminished capacity to perceive threats, proximity to potential predators). Their ideas around drug use were diverse and suffused with ambivalence. While some, like Annie, had made changes to minimize the harmful effects of using (e.g., losing too much weight, getting sick) by choosing softer and arguably less harmful drugs (e.g., marijuana, alcohol), others, such as Daniel, chose abstinence, and yet others such as Laura and Lucy felt a certain necessity to maintain their drug use in the hopes of avoiding sickness. There were also perceived risks involved in accessing drugs and ensuring drug quality and clean instruments for administration. Lastly, there was a gendered dimension to drug use and staying safe. Young women revealed that sexual victimization was often part of drug use and their access to substances.

While there were common elements to their perception of dangers on the streets (e.g., being robbed, assaulted), young people's level of concern varied greatly. While some youth accepted dangers as part of street life and appeared to downplay them, others felt threatened and took active steps to minimize what risks they could. However, not all experiences on the street were described as harmful. For some, the streets were described as a method of finding excitement and freedom.

EXCITEMENT-BOREDOM PARADOX

Many youth described being drawn to street life because it was "exciting, thrilling, addictive and adventurous" (Annie) and provided a sense of belonging (Shane, Michelle, Olivia). Some young people missed this excitement when they transitioned out of homelessness and found it too enticing not to return to street life. For many of the youth we met, street life evoked feelings of excitement. Ingrid's (age seventeen) story reveals that the initial draw to the streets grew from finding her family home in a small town too restrictive and "boring." This notion fits well with anthropological ideas of risk as rites of passage, as described earlier. Ingrid described feeling stuck, constrained in her childhood life and needing to feel alive and "experience life." Unfortunately, this feeling persisted into adulthood even after she had left the streets, triggering several relapses that kept her entrenched in street life.

Many youth echoed these sentiments. Not being constrained by responsibilities and being able to pick up on a whim, sleep outside, and hitchhike with friends showcased the exciting and experimental sides to street life. Shane hopped trains from northern to southern Ontario and hitchhiked from coast to coast. He felt the most dangerous element of hopping trains and hitchhiking was keeping warm and fed. He liked having no responsibilities and no constraints on his movements, which he summed up by saying, "I can do what I want, when I want, where I want." He vowed never to stay in shelters because "everyone is too busy ripping everyone else off.

I would rather sleep outside with people I trust." The choice to sleep outdoors with friends and travel the country represented opportunity. These youth embraced a certain kind of lifestyle that they believed was founded on freedom, excitement, and the ability to experiment with different ways of living. The sense of shared trust between youth that Shane described was another element that bound youth together. As such, certain risks were seen as pathways to experimentation and liberation.

Several youth felt they were drawn to street life because of the excitement and unpredictability — that is to say, the risks and opportunities that street life afforded. They felt that they would have more control over their lives and power over choices that concerned them. A few youth disclosed that the streets were attractive precisely because their previous lives were rule-bound, constraining, and often boring, and because there was an expectation that they live a so-called normal life with which they did not identify. Conversely, and surprisingly, several youth said that once they had been homeless for a while and the initial thrill wore off, they began to find it monotonous and became tired of worrying about their daily survival. In this sense, boredom — both prior to and after becoming homeless — was a trigger for risk-taking, especially drug use, in the case of several participants.

Michelle's Story

Michelle (age seventeen) felt that she never "fit in" at school, and she would "hide" in the bathroom to avoid participating in the classroom. She said, "I would look in the mirror and think, 'I'm ugly and boring. Why would anyone want to be around me?'" She said that school made her anxious, so she stopped going. After being sent by her parents to live with her grandparents for a year to see if that would improve her poor attendance, she eventually just dropped out of school. After moving back in with her parents, her father told her she had to go back to school or leave their home. She hit the streets. Michelle travelled from time to time with friends, couch-surfed, and then eventually obtained housing and a part-time job. She remained socially involved with other homeless youth and requisite services and was very active in peer support work.

Michelle complained of the unrelenting boredom on the streets. "The days are so boring and long. I leave the shelter in the morning, walk around downtown for six hours looking for work, and go to the drop-in for lunch. All I do is hang out." A few months later, this same boredom drew her into a crowd that partied a lot using alcohol and ecstasy. Reflecting on the boredom of street life, she concluded that it was the primary cause for all the "drama downtown." She felt that her street friends were always "backstabbing each other or telling one another they owe them money and what starts out as $10 turns into owing $400…. This is what is at the root of most problems downtown." She blamed boredom for her personal misfortunes of getting into a "bad crowd" and "using too many drugs." In a more general sense, she also found boredom responsible for encouraging harmful interpersonal dynamics that ruined friendships and promoted violence.

Olivia's Story

Olivia (age seventeen) had been homeless for roughly two years. Her experience on the streets perfectly illustrates the binary of boredom and excitement. At times she loved the freedom of being on the streets, saying that it was not so bad: "Everyone always feels so sorry for homeless youth when they see us panning, but you know what, we have it really good, we are well taken care of." But a few months later, she described the monotony of street life as a "constant waiting game." She described long days spent panhandling, waiting for drop-in centres to open, and trying to find a safe place to sleep outside. Eventually, this routine propelled her to search for more excitement and freedom, and she decided to hitchhike out west. Friends she made in British Colombia encouraged her to join the carnival because she would be well paid, well fed, and well travelled. She worked for the carnival for three months as it travelled east but was sorely disappointed: "It sounded too good to be true and it was." Olivia described exploitative work conditions: standing for twelve hours with no food or water and being verbally abused by her employer. The worst condition of the job, she revealed, was that she was only permitted to stay with the carnival and return to Ontario if she had sex with her employer: "My boss said if I wanted to stay with them [the carnival] I had to sleep with him. So I did." After she returned to Ottawa and had been back on the streets for several months, she again became very tired and bored of street life. She became pregnant, began looking for a place to rent, and applied to return to school. Eventually she secured an apartment in subsidized housing and had her baby.

In Olivia's case, boredom was both a trigger for seeking excitement (travelling with the carnival) and normalcy (wanting to get off the streets). Street life and the search for excitement also signified nonconformity or a path different from the norm. In Olivia's earlier experiences, boredom triggered her desire to try new things, such as hitchhiking, sleeping outside, and experimenting with different drugs. But some risks engendered negative consequences, such as sexual victimization and exploitation, and altered her perception of risks. The monotony of street life, victimizing events, and her unexpected pregnancy led Olivia to mobilize the resources necessary to leave the streets. Her exit from the streets was a break from what it symbolized for her (different and "deviant") and led her to choose a more "normal" and conformist life for her and her baby. Her experiences affected her risk perception based on her changing desires and needs. For example, her pregnancy affected her perception of the risks of drug use. Prior drug use with friends was a great escape and brought excitement; once pregnant, she made the decision to quit using all drugs. She did not want her baby to be apprehended by child welfare authorities and declared, "My only vice now is cigarettes. I want this baby to be as healthy as he can be." Deciding to have and raise her baby also compelled her to conform to expectations regarding childrearing so that he would not be apprehended. She ensured that she had housing, took parenting courses, attended her pre- and postnatal appointments, and adhered to medical advice (i.e., nutritional advice, drug abstinence) in order to meet the expectations of both the child welfare authorities and other professionals she came into contact with who monitored her pregnancy and parenting habits.

At the other end of the spectrum of street involvement is Angela's experience of street life. Her story deserves special mention, because she always expressed feeling at risk while downtown.

Angela's Story

Angela (age sixteen) was a high school student originally from a rural area just outside of Ottawa. She had a part-time retail job and lived with her father, mother, and one sibling before going to the shelter. Prior to her initial experience at the shelter, she had never been downtown. She found it difficult living at the shelter, as she felt very frightened most of the time and did not feel comfortable being downtown alone.

As Angela was unfamiliar with the downtown core and how to access services for vulnerable youth, she described being quite fearful and rarely accessed the services downtown where many street youth congregated. She reported not feeling safe inside or outside the shelter, and often made excuses to shelter staff in order to stay in the shelter during the day when most youth were gone (generally, youth are expected to be engaged in activities during the day and are not allowed to stay inside the shelter, pending certain exceptions such as sickness, appointments, etc.). She left the shelter after two months and went to stay with a cousin in the suburbs before eventually moving back home. She never came downtown thereafter. Angela echoed many of Laura's, Daniel's, Lucy's, and Annie's sentiments regarding the dangerousness of urban life; however, her degree of street involvement was minimal. She left home because of conflict with her father, whom she described as physically and emotionally abusive, and said she felt scared and threatened when on her own downtown. Her conclusion was that "people are not safe, especially people downtown." She also described being offered drugs by older men and a general feeling of being preyed upon by older men at bus stops and in the downtown core. "Yeah, an older guy the other day at the bus stop in front of the YMCA asked me to go back to his room, smoke weed, and hang out. I told him that anything you want to do that's involved in hanging out is illegal 'cause I'm only sixteen."

Angela returned home after partially reconciling with her family. While she had experimented with drugs (marijuana, ecstasy) in her hometown with school friends, she did not consume drugs when she stayed downtown even though they had been offered several times. "It's just too scary taking drugs from people you don't know," she said. "You know they are going to want something in return, so I just say no and walk away." Angela reported that she never felt completely comfortable or safe in the city, even in the shelter, as she felt that other residents were often looking for fights. She was relieved to leave and move back to her small town.

Perceptions of street life thus ranged from dangerous to exciting to boring, and these perceptions shifted over time for street youth, affecting the kinds of risks they took. Boredom was often a trigger for voluntary risk-taking, whether it was engaging in volatile relationships, experimenting with more harmful drugs, or joining a carnival. Several youth also revealed that street life was no more dangerous than the situations they had left behind; however, the context of the dangers was quite different. While youth described violent and chaotic family situations, dangers on the street appeared more random and less predictable. Youth worried somewhat about being robbed or assaulted but also considered this an expectation of street life and shared similar stories that appeared to glorify street life to some degree. Their experiences were akin to rites of passage, and they demonstrated a certain acceptance of "the way things are" on the streets. Youth often described these risks in terms of a search for autonomy and personal power over decisions in ways that were not possible in their previous lives, forming part of their identity quests. Echoing findings of Parazelli's (1997, 1999) work, for many youth, the streets are a place of marginalized socialization, offering transitional spaces that serve as a forum in which to experiment and continuously reconstitute their identities.

Youth described a range of harmful experiences, including drug addiction, assault, and robbery, but most of them minimized the impact or described these experiences as rites of passage. They also framed these experiences within their expectations of street life. While some described actually being stabbed or beaten up for their drugs, money, or possessions, others worried about this possibility precisely because youth share stories and appear to emphasize the more titillating and sensational aspects. For example, Tyler (age sixteen), who was a self-proclaimed "drug hustler," was adamant about not seeking medical attention or informing the police a few days after being stabbed for his marijuana. A certain amount of bravado (i.e., proving oneself) and glorification of harmful experiences was evident in many of the stories shared by the youth; these stories formed the basis of street life folklore. Experiencing violence and threats of violence, acquiring and using drugs, and engaging in "deviant" acts intertwined to create elements of danger and excitement that affected and sometimes encouraged youth to take risks, often in relation to the identities they wanted to project. Stories appeared to be shared among youth in order to minimize the very real dangers that were present, relive the adrenaline rush that accompanied such dangers, prove their investment in "the life," and provide a commonality of experiences that gave them a sense of belonging. Many youth also described the positive aspects that street life offered, such as identity and role experimentation, camaraderie, and a sense of belonging that they had not experienced in their previous lives. This interplay between excitement and danger on the one hand, and freedom and captivity on the other, constitute central paradoxes of street life that youth articulated. They highlight the tensions in everyday homeless life amid attempts to keep themselves safe. These nuances of street life help to contextualize the next chapter, which examines youth understandings of keeping healthy and managing risks.

4. KEEPING HEALTHY, MANAGING RISKS

My whole day revolves around how we are going to make the money to keep going, for our habit. We [me and my boyfriend] need to make $20 a day to keep using so we don't get sick. We are very worried about getting sick.

I never share equipment. I've never had an abscess. We really need a safe injection site here in Ottawa. I have to try and find a place downtown that's out of the way to shoot up, but you worry about people jumping you for your stuff, or the cops taking your gear [instruments], or seeing you.... Sometimes I will go to the Site Van [community service that supplies drug instruments] twice a night to get clean gear. I've even stopped using a belt and now use a tourniquet. I don't even share [my tourniquet] with my friend who is hep [hepatitis] positive. I am a very careful user. (Lucy, age sixteen)

Lucy was living on the streets and couch-surfing at friends' places. She said she was a responsible injection drug user who started using drugs when her parents separated. Her father was emotionally abusive, and after child protection services intervened when she was thirteen, she was placed in her mother's care and not allowed to return to the family home. Angry about

---

Note: Parts of this chapter originally appeared in S.-A. MacDonald (2014), "Managing risk: Self-regulation among homeless youth," *Child & Adolescent Social Work Journal*, 31, 6: 497–520.

how abruptly her life had changed, she stated, "I wasn't given any notice. I never had the chance to go back to our apartment and get my things. I never saw my home again." Soon after, she started using opiates by pilfering friends' medicine cabinets and a local veterinary clinic for ketamine. It was not long before her mother lost their housing and they wound up in a family shelter. Lucy shuffled in and out of emergency shelters and foster homes, couch-surfed, and then made the move to the streets. There she met her boyfriend, who introduced her to injection drugs. Despite these challenges and instability, and also due to the key knowledge she acquired from these experiences, she became a vocal advocate for safe injection drug use and harm reduction and was given a position in a youth drop-in centre as a peer support worker. She hid her drug use and her risky homeless behaviours (such as sleeping in the streets) from youth service providers in order to maintain her eligibility for this kind of work and to serve as a "good role model" for other youth. She also employed various strategies to keep herself safe due to her strong desire to continue injecting drugs.

Lucy confessed that she made money in a number of ways: surveys, youth engagement work, and what she termed "ethical stealing" (stealing items from big stores that she viewed as serving the needs of the rich). She was very conscious about the risks inherent in injecting drugs, and she took actions to minimize the harms and was eager to engage others in conversations about drug policy. Lucy exemplifies Castel's (1998) findings that "addicts" often view their drug practices as a way of life, and their social identities are representations of the relational nature of these dependencies. Drug use, for Castel and Lucy, is not so much about the substance or chemicals involved but about the relational nature to the substance itself and the context in which it is acquired and maintained. Lucy was strongly invested in projecting her image as a "responsible" drug user.

Lucy's story demonstrates her awareness of the risks inherent in using drugs and the health messaging and harm reduction approaches carried out by public health institutions. She also endorsed a more individualized notion of responsibility and self-regulation. She was proud that she had not become physically ill from her drug use, as evidenced by her lack of abscesses, because she was a responsible and careful (self-regulating) user. Lucy was invested in projecting her image as a responsible drug user because of how injection drug users are viewed and she wanted strongly to combat this stereotype of deviancy and irresponsibility. Moreover, while she viewed maintaining her drug use as her primary responsibility, she also held it responsible for her estrangement from her family. In this sense, there was a triple-layered form of responsibilization occurring. Lucy felt individually responsible for her addiction and tried to promote her well-being by being a careful user, yet she also blamed it for creating distance from her family. This circularity of responsibilization was reinforced by her perception that her family blamed her for continuing to use drugs and for "choosing" street life.

Participants, particularly young women, described a range of health worries and self-monitoring and self-regulation practices related to sexual and reproductive health, mental and physical health, and drug addiction and withdrawal. While there were some commonalities in their self-monitoring, some youth were vigilant and responsible, while others appeared less concerned and did not employ active risk-management strategies. Indeed, experiences of risk were irregular, complex, and constantly evolving. Notions of the "responsible" self were evident in many of the narratives, but these frameworks were complex, involving internal and external layers of monitoring and regulation. However, they were not necessarily influenced by, and were rarely a result of, consultations with professionals, such as doctors or other health and social services providers. The most common thread unifying youth understandings of risk and self-regulation in relation to health was the reliance on self, encapsulated by situated knowledge based on intuition, experiences, and peer group advice. Perhaps this was in an effort to resist advice from experts and the constant normative messaging of institutions providing assistance. In general, public health approaches informing interventions assume actors are rational, atomized, and calculating, framed within a context of an array of options and free will. This *homo prudens* lens (Kemshall 2010) assumes rational choice framed within a normative context; however, this dominant orientation does not hold much merit for homeless youth who face limited options within contexts of survival. In this light, dominant expert messaging about keeping oneself safe and healthy — based on a growing healthicization approach (Conrad 1992), wherein "healthy" lifestyles are promoted and behavioural causes are the culprit for compromised health — underpin moral projects in which individuals bear the brunt of responsibility for their poor health and are judged for their inability to guard against risk. Indeed, youth often made choices based on experimentation, self-discovery, and survival in sharp contrast to health norms: constrained choices based on subsistence strategies that the streets provide, positioned within a context of marginality (such as have been described by Parazelli 1997 and Bellot 2001). However, scholarship has tended to be built on implicit assumptions about normative choices and free will, and the ability to keep oneself safe — thus reducing youth experiences to ones of risk and moral transgressions, and turning a blind eye to the context of limited and constrained choices in maintaining good health in extremely adverse contexts that tend to negatively impact and worsen it.

The literature demonstrates that deteriorating health is a common experience for homeless youth (Boivin et al. 2005; Ensign 1998; Gaetz and O'Grady 2002; Haldenby, Berman, and Forchuk 2007; Schwartz, James, Wagner, and Hart 2014). And the longer that individuals remain homeless, the worse their health becomes (Karabanow 2004; Kraus, Eberle, and Serge 2001). Higher incidences of HIV, sexually transmitted infections (Noell, Rohde, Seeley, and Ochs 2001; Schwartz et al. 2014), hepatitis B and C, tuberculosis, suicide, depression and other psychiatric disorders, substance abuse, poor nutrition, scabies, foot and dental problems, acute and chronic respiratory diseases, and viral infections have been found among the homeless population (Boivin et al. 2005). Indeed, the prevalence and incidence rates of many sexually transmitted and blood-borne infections are reported to be ten to twelve times higher in street youth than in the general youth population (Haldenby, Berman, and Forchuk 2007; Public Health Agency of Canada 2006). Despite the poor health of youth experiencing homelessness, many researchers have found that "these youth are the least likely to access the available health care services" (Haldenby, Berman, and Forchuk 2007: 1233).

Haldenby, Berman, and Forchuk (2007), Gaetz and O'Grady (2002), and Boivin et al. (2005) state that homeless youth are more likely to experience major mental illnesses, especially depression. In particular, Haldenby, Berman, and Forchuk (2007) point to the high rates of suicide among gay, lesbian, bisexual, and transgender youth. In Kidd's (2006: 413) research on suicidality among homeless youth, he found that although there was an overall high level of history of attempts (46 percent, with 78 percent of those reporting more than one attempt), there was a decrease in overall level of suicidality among participants after they left home and came to the streets. However, circumstances that increased risk included "feeling trapped" (e.g., victimization, poor health) and having friends who had attempted or committed suicide. This research points to the uneven mental health statuses of homeless youth. For some, detaching from their families or substitute care arrangements may improve their mental health but render them more at risk of developing physical health problems; for others, their mental health may worsen. Others have argued that being homeless is akin to being "psychologically traumatized" (Goodman, Saxe, and Harvey 1991). The interplay of physical and mental health and inherent risks in street life coupled with childhood histories of victimization forms a complex web of potential dangers, but there is uneven evidence about the potentiality of further harm.

Rates of alcohol and drug use among street youth populations have been found to be substantially higher than those in the general youth population (Benoit, Jansson, and Anderson 2007; Boivin et al. 2005; Haldenby, Berman, and Forchuk 2007; McMorris, Tyler, Whitbeck, and Hoyt 2002; Tyler 2008). Similar to physical and mental health problems, alcohol and drug use forms one of the central axes of risk within this population. A study of street youth in Montreal found that almost half had injected drugs, and they were eleven times more likely to die of drug overdose and suicide than the general youth population (Public Health Agency of Canada 2006: 2). In fact, suicide and drug overdose are the leading causes of death among Canadian homeless youth (Roy et al. 2004). Several researchers have found that a history of childhood sexual abuse increases the risk of substance abuse among homeless youth (Haldenby, Berman, and Forchuk 2007), with one study finding that youth were twice as likely to become injection drug users (Roy et al. 2003). Substance use has also been described as a method of coping, often referred to as a form of "self-medicating" in response to isolation, loneliness, and negative life events, in particular, early childhood abuse (McMorris et al. 2002; Tyler 2008).

SEX AND SELF-REGULATION

A particularly gendered dimension of risk that emerged from this study was young women participants' concern regarding their sexual health and, in particular, the risk of pregnancy, sexually transmitted infections, and sexual violence. Most of the female youth in this study were self-monitoring and self-regulating their sexual and reproductive health practices. While most female youth reported they were self-monitoring and had an awareness of their reproductive cycles, the risk of pregnancy, and the risk of contracting sexually transmitted infections, their knowledge and strategies were intimately tied to their own situated knowledge based on intuition, experiential knowledge, and advice from within their social networks, in contrast to reliance on professional advice or expert opinion.

Olivia believed she had reduced her risk of becoming pregnant by monitoring her menstrual cycle. She described how she did not use condoms or other forms of prophylaxis because she knew when she was most fertile. She claimed she was not worried about contracting a sexually transmitted infection because her boyfriend had not "slept with many girls" and she was "tested a lot." Midway through the study, however, she was devastated when she tested positive for three sexually transmitted infections and worried about revealing the news to her boyfriend:

> I am worried my boyfriend is going to break up with me. I feel really ashamed about how many guys I have slept with. He's only slept with three girls, so I know I didn't get any infections from him.... I know who I got it from. He [another youth] had chlamydia and I slept with him anyways without a condom. Now I have probably given it to my boyfriend. How am I going to tell him? What a stupid mistake.

A short time later, she became pregnant and decided to keep the baby. These two events, contracting sexually transmitted infections and becoming a mother, forced her to reconsider her earlier practices. Both outcomes urged her to adopt two new regimes, contraception and prophylactic use, in her future sexual relationships. However, what is interesting here is that she made these changes not on the advice of a medical professional, though she did frequently visit sexual health clinics, but based on her direct experiences and discussion with friends.

Most female participants worried about becoming pregnant, and many revealed they took active precautions to reduce the risk. Indeed, of the twelve young women in Sue-Ann's study, two had babies during the study, one had a two-year-old prior to the study, and two revealed they had abortions during the study. The remaining seven young women did not divulge whether they were or had been pregnant. More generally, the risks inherent in sexual activity were commonly described as fears: the fear of getting pregnant and the fear of contracting sexually transmitted infections. The self-protection strategies commonly employed were being in a monogamous relationship and knowing the sexual history of one's partner.

The fear of sexual violence and rape was especially prominent. This threat generated sharp discussion among female participants, as most described it as a common occurrence during the first few months on the streets. Most young women revealed that they had been sexually assaulted, raped, or both within their first few months on the streets. They distanced and contextualized these experiences as akin to a painful rite of passage, an unfortunate and common experience of being a new arrival — "fresh meat." Some participants mentioned that after their first experiences of rape, they confided in friends and learned from others how to "keep safe." One strategy to ward off situations that made youth vulnerable was to acquire protection from peer group membership and to use a buddy system in order to never be alone or use drugs alone. Others relayed feeling betrayed when peers did not believe that they had been raped, or feeling blamed because they were not consoled and instead told by their peers that it was their fault because they "were too high to know any better," did not "keep their guard up," or "got high alone."

Many young women openly discussed their practices and strategies to minimize the risk of sexual violence. Lucy (age seventeen) said,

> I never go buy [drugs] without my boyfriend. It's a recipe for rape. For too many girls, it happens that way. When I shoot up, I do it discreetly, away from the action, like under a bridge, away from traffic and people, and I make sure my boyfriend is with me.

In research by Bungay and colleagues (Bungay, Johnson, Varcoe, and Boyd 2010), young women who used drugs described using secluded locations, such as alleys, in order to avoid detection by police and also other users. However, for women who found themselves alone, these locations often increased their vulnerability to sexual assault.

Other participants in our study echoed Lucy's thoughts, stating they always carried a weapon and were never alone (using a safety in numbers approach, particularly when sleeping outdoors, buying drugs, or partying), strategies they gleaned from street friends with similar experiences. Rape was unfortunately a common event that was more or less normalized and trivialized, and it differentiated newly arrived youth from the more seasoned veterans.

Marie (age sixteen) became pregnant during the course of the study and elected to start a family with her boyfriend. Prior to becoming pregnant, however, she was very conscious of the risks associated with sexual activity. She said that she had practised abstinence before she met her current partner. Once they started to have sex, she relied on birth control pills, condoms, and the pull-out method to reduce the risk of pregnancy and sexually transmitted infections. She admitted that she worried about getting infected and becoming pregnant, and these were her considerations for remaining in a monogamous relationship using safer sex practices. Midway through the study, however, Marie was baffled about how she had become pregnant when she felt they had taken all necessary precautions, stating, "I don't know how this happened. But we are going to keep it. I don't believe in abortion. Anyways, most of my friends are pregnant now, too." After the initial shock, she and her partner were excited about having a baby and started making preparations, such as moving into his apartment and acquiring things for the baby.

Unlike Olivia, Marie was acutely aware of sexual risks before hitting the streets, and she employed active strategies to minimize those risks. Marie's story also alludes to the importance of group membership in normalizing behaviours. Her pregnancy became validated and normalized by her peer group (whom she identified as not street youth). For Marie, it also became a way to distance herself from other homeless youth on the street, whom she perceived as not trying as hard as her to exit street life or set life goals, as evidenced in the previous chapter. Pregnancy for Marie became a way to reposition her identity and distance herself from a street identity by accepting a new responsibility (i.e., a baby) and building her life around this new identity as a mother.

There was a wide range of responses regarding participants' perceptions and practices with regards to safer sex. Some participants acknowledged that they always practised safer sex (e.g., birth control, condoms) and that they were fearful of becoming pregnant because so many of their friends were. According to Sadie (age seventeen), who was living in the shelter and looking for an apartment for herself and her two-year-old son, becoming a mother at her age was somewhat of an expectation. Most of her girlfriends either had children or were expecting. According to Sadie, the responsibility of child-rearing always disproportionately fell on the women:

It's all on us [young women] to raise the kids, and they [the children]

need you in the morning, 24/7. There is never a break. As soon as
we have the kids, the guys are gone. They aren't reliable. My ex has
only seen my boy four times since he's been born, and now he's fight-
ing me for custody because he's trying to control me, get back at me.

The perception that young women assume the risk of pregnancy and responsibility of raising children was a predominant theme. There was a spectrum of experiences and strategies that young women employed to reduce the risk of getting pregnant and acquiring sexually transmitted infections. Most female participants, however, were conscious about the risks inherent in sexual activity and took steps to actively minimize them by surveying their own habits and ensuring they had appropriate protection, such as condoms and birth control pills. Most female participants viewed themselves as responsible for their own sexual and reproductive health, but they also blamed sexual partners for not being forthcoming about their sexual histories, not having adequate protection, or abandoning them once they became pregnant or gave birth to the child.

Self-regulation occurred not only in relation to sexual and reproductive health but also in relation to participants' physical and mental health. Female and male participants alike revealed that they often struggled with mood swings, in particular feelings of depression, which they often attributed to drug use and/or emotional issues stemming from relationships with their families, peers, or partners on the streets. Interestingly, several youth reported feeling more emotionally stable once they left their homes and lived on the streets. Several youth also reported that their drug use, and withdrawal from substances in particular, negatively affected their mood. Some youth revealed that at these times they accessed, or attempted to access, mental health services. Again, there was a wide range of responses in terms of self-monitoring with regards to participants' mental and physical health.

The literature on homeless youth often categorizes young men's and young women's experiences of victimization differently, arguing that women are much more vulnerable to sexual violence (Haldenby, Berman, and Forchuk 2007; Noell et al. 2001; Whitbeck, Hoyt, and Yoder 1999). Young women are at an increased risk for sexual victimization and exploitation, while young men are more likely to experience physical victimization and exhibit aggressive behaviours (Whitbeck, Hoyt, and Yoder 1999).

GENDERED DIMENSIONS OF HEALTH

O'Grady and Gaetz (2009) contend that the culture of the streets is male-dominated and thereby places women at greater risk for victimization. "The streets are a social and economic arena where men have more power and control than women" (O'Grady and Gaetz 2009: 5). They also point to the fact that until very recently, research on

> public youth cultures (and, indeed, much of the research on street youth) has rendered young women practically invisible. Female involvement in such spaces, however, should not be considered as marginal to that of men; rather, it is structurally different in terms of how young women exercise independence, nurture friendships and attachments, and explore youth cultural options and economic opportunities. (O'Grady and Gaetz 2009: 5)

A central feature of this phenomenon, they argue, is that homeless young women are detached from their families and situated within a male-dominated arena. Haldenby, Berman, and Forchuk (2007: 1239) found that there was a common perception among homeless youth that young women living on the streets were more vulnerable and not as able to take care of themselves as young men were, and thus needed to adopt a more aggressive approach in order to make themselves feel safer. Lucchini (2001: 77) argues that due to the prevalence of resource shortages on the streets (conceptualized not only as material but also symbolic and affective resources), a spirit of competition and dominance tends to predominate, which pushes street youth to take on more of an aggressive masculine identity. This impacts where young women sleep, eat and socialize, and use drugs. It affects how they access resources and keep safe, and the kinds of relationships they need to create and maintain in order to survive.

Researchers have found that homeless youth engage in risky sexual practices, including low rates of condom use, and have numerous sexual partners, high rates of sexually transmitted infections (Haldenby, Berman, and Forchuk 2007; Noell et al. 2001; Tyler 2008), and high rates of pregnancy (Boivin et al. 2005; Haley 2007; LaBoy 2018; Novac, Paradis, Brown, and Morton 2006, 2009). Rates of trading sex for items such as money, drugs, or shelter, also referred to as "survival sex" (Greene, Ennett, and Ringwalt 1997; Haldenby, Berman, and Forchuk 2007), have also been found to be high, ranging from 11 to 46 percent (Tyler 2008: 674), particularly among young women. In Greene, Ennett, and Ringwalt's (1997: 1408) study,

> the odds of engaging in survival sex were increased for youths who had been victimized, those who had participated in criminal behaviours, those who had attempted suicide, those who had an STD [sexually transmitted disease], and those who had been pregnant. Survival sex was strongly associated with all recent substance use indicators and with lifetime injection drug use.

According to the Public Health Agency of Canada's (2006) vast study on street youth, approximately one-quarter of street youth reported having traded sex at some point in their lives, and a high proportion of them reported not having used condoms during their most recent episode of sexual intercourse, with most reporting having had no fewer than seventeen partners in their lifetime (Public Health Agency of Canada 2006: 5). Furthermore, street youth did not seem to modify their sexual behaviours after being diagnosed with a sexually transmitted infection (Public Health Agency of Canada 2006: 6).

Becoming pregnant is a reality for many young homeless women and a common occurrence (Haldenby, Berman, and Forchuk 2007; Novac, Paradis, Brown, and Morton 2006, 2009). In a study conducted with homeless youth in Calgary, half reported having been pregnant or having been responsible for getting someone pregnant (Worthington et al. 2008: xxiv). Similar results have been found in Montreal (50 percent; Boivin et al. 2005) and Toronto (more than 50 percent; Novac, Paradis, Brown, and Morton 2006), and in another study 5 percent of female street youth had had more than one pregnancy (Haley et al. 2003). In a study in the United States, youth living on the street had the highest lifetime rates of pregnancy (48 percent), followed by youth residing in shelters (33 percent), while youth living in stable households had lifetime pregnancy rates of under 10 percent (Greene and Ringwalt 1998: 370). According to Novac, Paradis, Brown, and Morton (2009: 1),

> homeless pregnant adolescents are a vulnerable group. Both homelessness and pregnancy are risk factors for poor health among youth. Pregnancy among homeless young women is associated with earlier

and more severe abuse during childhood, earlier onset of drug use, and poor mental health.

Moreover, in another study, young women with a history of childhood sexual abuse were more likely to report incidences of sexual victimization (Noell et al. 2001).

MENTAL HEALTH, SELF-REGULATION, AND GETTING HELP

Many of the young people that we spoke with had struggled with mental health in multiple capacities. Young people reported symptoms related to depression, bipolar disorder, multiple personalities, post-traumatic stress disorder, and schizophrenia diagnoses. Several youth we met had spent time hospitalized for suicide attempts or treatment programs, and the actual number may be higher than reported. In Jean-Olivier's (age twenty) case, his ongoing mental health challenges were the cause of considerable tension in his family home. In his view, these challenges were not understood until he became homeless and service providers were able to identify his symptoms and refer him to mental health resources, where he eventually received a diagnosis of bipolar disorder. Trying to cope with his symptoms at home had generated tension to the point that his mother did not want to keep him and he was kicked out. He lived with a friend for a while before returning home and then choosing to live with his grandmother. Eventually, Jean-Olivier's mother and grandmother dropped him off at a youth shelter:

> *Finally, my mother kicked me out when I was fifteen. I was staying at a friend's house, and she calls my friend's mother, and was like, "I don't want her anymore [Jean-Olivier's mother did not accept his trans male identity]. Can you adopt her? Just keep her. I don't want her." It made me hate my mother even more. Then finally, I went back home. And again, I chose to leave because I was like ... I live in this house and it makes me want to kill myself, so I don't want to stay here anymore. So I went to stay with my grandmother, but things were not much better because you can't just run away from your issues, right? I wasn't in school, I wasn't doing anything, I wasn't eating, I wasn't talking to anybody. I was just in my room all day.*

And my grandmother comes in one morning, wakes me up at eight in the morning, and she's like, "Pack your stuff, we're leaving." And I'm like, "Where are we going?" And she says, "We're sending you to this place." And I'm like, "Okay." So I pack my stuff and they drop me off at the [youth shelter]. It was a little after I turned sixteen. My mother, she wanted to give me a hug, she met me there.... And I was like, "Don't even talk to me right now." And I left. I didn't say anything to anybody. I didn't see this coming.

Jean-Olivier felt that his family was not equipped to handle his mental health challenges and this contributed to the escalating conflict in his home. In the end, without communication or negotiation, his family dropped him off at a homeless shelter. It is likely that some of the conflict other young people experienced in their families was also related to mental health challenges. Kristin (age eighteen) explained how spending time at her mother's house exacerbated her multiple personality disorder, and other young people spoke more generally about the challenges they experienced coping with mental health disorders at home. While mental health disorders on their own may not be a direct pathway to homelessness for young people, they may be understood as a powerful risk factor that applies pressure on pre-existing challenges in the family home and complicates family conflict.

Luke (age seventeen) attempted suicide twice. However, he downplayed the significance of these events and, in fact, laughed about them, blaming their occurrence on his withdrawal from morphine. He had recently decided to abstain from injection drug use and revealed that he now only used "chemicals and pot." For him, the switch from injection drugs to what he perceived as safer drugs was an effort to mitigate episodes of suicidality and promote mental stability. Hence, Luke actively monitored his mental health status by employing a risk-reduction strategy (e.g., not using injection drugs and choosing ones perceived to be safer) that was driven by his personal experience and insight, not expert advice. He made the decision to do "softer drugs" because he viewed them as safer. His self-monitoring and self-regulation were not due to the advice of authorities or expert systems, nor were they strategies that he felt subjugated by, as some theorists have hypothesized. His interpretation and understanding of the urgency to abstain was spurred by intuition, personal experience, and will.

Similarly, Annie had made the switch to softer drugs because she had found her physical and mental health suffered when she was using harder drugs, such as methamphetamine. She revealed that at the height of her use, she had lost a significant amount of weight and had been "down to 107 pounds." Her perception was that her physical health was at its worst and she never ate; she said she never wanted to "look that unhealthy again." Moreover, she felt that her mental health and her self-esteem were negatively impacted: "I didn't like who I was on meth [methamphetamine]. I wasn't myself. I was all nasty and uptight. I was a real bitch." She stated that her decision to quit using methamphetamine was also inspired by her fear of getting "bad drugs." She said, "[You] never knew what you were getting, what kind of trip [drug reaction] you are going to have," adding that "meth is made in bathtubs, you don't know what the hell it's mixed with." Annie's story demonstrates that not only did her risk perception change in relation to her drug use and its impact on her physical and mental health, but also she was acutely aware of these changes and constantly monitoring her body and mental reactions to promote her well-being. Her decisions were based on her own situated, local knowledge of her body and her understanding of what was healthy for her. Annie admitted that until she left the streets, she was "oblivious" to the dangers around her:

> I was aware there were risks being on the street but I didn't think it applied to me.... I can't believe I didn't get hep C or HIV. I mean, workers told me not to share needles, but I didn't listen. I feel very lucky nothing bad happened.

Marie admitted that she struggled with depression and was very depressed when she lived with her parents and foster family before hitting the streets. When she was fifteen years old, she attended a "suicide party," in which she and a few of her friends attempted suicide. She ended up at the children's hospital and had her "stomach pumped." She explained that "nobody talked about what happened"; the event was never discussed within her family. Shortly thereafter, she began seeing a psychiatrist, but her family remained silent about the depression. At the time of the study, she revealed that she no longer had suicidal feelings and was no longer on antidepressant medication (though she did admit that she still struggled with symptoms of depression), but she did continue to see her psychiatrist. She also revealed that she tried not to consume alcohol and rarely smoked marijuana, because she found it affected her mood and caused her to be more depressed. During the study, her psychiatrist urged her to reconsider starting a different antidepressant because she was still depressed, but Marie stood by her conviction that she did not like the way the previous medication had made her feel. Marie's perception was that she was very sensitive to medication and was not interested in experimenting with a new one. "My doctor wants to switch me to Paxil [antidepressant], but I am really sensitive to medications and I don't find they work. That's why I stopped Prozac [another antidepressant] last year. I do feel down most of the time though."

Marie also did not have the funds to purchase the medication. She had been denied benefits that would cover her prescription medication through welfare in the past, and she was not interested in trying to apply for these benefits again. While Marie was acutely aware of feeling down, and was very open to discussing her feelings, she did not think medication would be beneficial, nor did she believe it would be paid for by social assistance. The possible benefit did not outweigh the risk and the work involved. While she monitored her mental and physical health status, and openly discussed mental health symptoms, she did not take "expert" advice and start a new medication, instead following her intuition, including cutting down on her substance use.

Like many youth, while Marie was self-monitoring her health, she preferred to try and deal with these issues in what she perceived as a non-invasive and self-controlling way. She admitted that she found counselling, setting goals, and engaging in productive work (e.g., attending school, working under the table at a restaurant, babysitting) more beneficial to her mental health than following expert advice (e.g., taking prescribed antidepressant medication). "I just prefer to deal with things on my own. When I keep myself busy, get out, and dress well, put myself together well, I feel better," she said.

Indeed, many youth were fearful of taking prescribed medications for mental health symptoms and did not follow professional psychiatric advice, instead preferring to try and deal with symptoms on their own and in their own ways, such as talking to friends, using herbal methods (over-the-counter alternative medicine pills and marijuana), and engaging in artistic expression.

NAVIGATING RISKS TO WELL-BEING

Luke was living intermittently between an emergency shelter for young men and the streets but was actively looking for housing. He claimed that he employed a risk-reduction strategy that was driven by his personal experience and insight. He rejected expert advice that he had been given in hospital emergency departments when he had overdosed, stating, "They don't even know what it's like."

Tyler (age sixteen) claimed not to take active measures to reduce potential harm and was rather glib about the risks involved in street life and drug use. His story also illustrates the difficulties youth have accessing harm reduction programs that are designed to promote health in the adult population but ignore parallel pressing concerns among youth. For example, while Tyler claimed to like to use any substances, his drug of choice was crack. At the time of the study, free crack pipes were being given out in the community to reduce the risk of infection (e.g., hepatitis) from sharing pipes. But unlike needle exchange programs, which are funded provincially and can be accessed by individuals under eighteen, the crack pipe program was targeted for the adult population (i.e., eighteen years and over). Tyler revealed that he smoked crack daily and shared pipes "all the time." When he tried to access the free crack pipes, he was turned away because he was not eighteen years of age. Sometimes he would send a friend to get a free pipe, but then he would have to share his drugs and the pipe anyways, so he stopped trying because he figured it was not worth the cost of sharing his drugs. Tyler explained that he knew he could contract infections from sharing pipes but that it was "worth the risk." He wanted to project an image of prowess and carelessness, stating he did not care what he used nor how much. He prided himself on being able to handle any kind and amount of drugs, and gave the impression that he did not monitor the quantity of drugs he used or care about the methods of administration. Tyler challenges the intertwined notion of internalization of blame and individualization of responsibility. He acted like he was not invested in policing himself and denied engaging in any form of self-monitoring. Moreover, he enjoyed experimenting with different modes of living and admitted to taking any opportunities that street life afforded him (e.g., drugs, partying, criminal opportunities). Tyler portrayed himself as deviant and as a "hustler," able to buy, sell, or rob anything. He downplayed giving much thought to living a more "normal" life, principally because his childhood had a similar character of survival, adaptation, instability, and delinquency. He appeared to resist conformity and expert messaging about keeping himself safe, even though he was well versed in the potential harms of his lifestyle.

A different dimension and complexity in the continuum of self-regulation can be found in Laura's (age eighteen) story. Laura was a heavy morphine injection drug user and had been searching for a community outpatient methadone treatment program to assist her with quitting. After several attempts to access these services, she decided that she needed a more intensive residential program to fight her addiction. She wanted a program with medical detoxification, as she was fearful of the pain associated with withdrawal and the concomitant risk of relapse. Initially she was embarrassed about her addiction and concealed it from her family — what she called living a "double life" — she finally turned to them for help once they discovered that she was using:

> *My mom and her best friend are pushing me to go to detox right away, but I want a program with a med detox. I feel like if I go to detox for a few days, it's setting me up to fail, to relapse, because I'll have to wait to get into a treatment centre [long-term residential facility]. They don't seem to understand, and they think I am copping out, looking for an easy fix because of the meds they can prescribe you in a med detox program. I am scared of getting very sick, and I don't want to relapse. I tried to quit cold turkey on my own for three days before, and I got really, really sick. I am never doing that again.*

Laura's perception of successful recovery was intimately tied to her constructions of risk and was competing against her family's notions of risk as well. Her family monitored her abstinence and developed a "list of rules and conditions" that she had to abide by in order to return to live at home: "no drugs, no needles, shower every day, eat a healthy lunch, and be respectful of others." Her mother reviewed these rules and said it was now up to Laura to "mother herself" — that is, to monitor her behaviour by adhering to her mother's list of rules. Laura's story illustrates a complex arrangement of surveillance. While she was told she needed to monitor her abstinence, her family also monitored and regulated her behaviour as a condition to receiving their help and support. There is also a third element to this interplay between their risk discourses, regulation, and responsibilization. While Laura did feel responsible for her recovery and wanted to make her family "proud," she also felt that the system was responsible for not providing the requisite services in a timely manner. She searched for months before finding a program that could adequately meet her needs.

Indeed, many youth complained about the wait for methadone maintenance program services, the lack of medical detoxification programs, and the difficulty accessing supplies to reduce the potential harm involved in drug use. For instance, Lucy admitted that she had looked into the methadone maintenance program, but there was a two- to three-month wait, and she did not want to "take that spot away from someone else who is worse off than us [she and her boyfriend]." While many youth held themselves responsible for their drug dependency and its consequences, they also indicated that they held the system responsible for not providing adequate, accessible services when they needed them most.

While some youth actively self-monitored symptoms related to their health or their substance use, others were free-spirited and experimental, testing different roles, relationships, and substances. While some youth did mention the messages about risk they received from frontline workers (e.g., dangers of hepatitis, sexually transmitted infections, pregnancy, drugs, and violence), the relevance and importance of authority figures did not predominate in their risk consciousness, nor were their practices greatly impacted by these conduits of advice and intervention. Self-regulation was fashioned from individual experience located at the heart of identity and experience. Indeed, while many homeless youth experience health issues, they rarely access professional services (Bournes and Meredith 2008; Novac, Hermer, Paradis, and Kellen 2009; Novac, Paradis, Brown, and Morton 2009). Those who do seek help report that they frequently do not heed medical advice (Bournes and Meredith 2008; Haldenby, Berman, and Forchuk 2007). In this study, many youth described their struggles with mental health problems and drug use but preferred to use their own methods to manage difficulties, including talking to friends and sharing solutions, making art, playing music, and using herbal methods (mostly marijuana but also over-the-counter medications). The importance of informal social networks in the construction of lay knowledge and in the management of these kinds of problems was paramount in this study, but the impact of these social networks is little studied (Tyler and Melander 2011).

Less than half the youth felt quite fearful of risks and as a consequence of this were self-monitoring, while others reported being quite cavalier or seemed to reject forms of self-regulation. Moreover, with the passage of time and the accumulation of street experiences, some youth actively changed their risk practices to reduce potential harm. Indeed, this study revealed the heterogeneous, temporal, irregular, and dynamic nature of risk discourses. Participants projected blame and responsibility for their misfortunes onto family members, peer influences, system barriers, and the environment, disproving elements of simple causality, responsibility, and self-blame (i.e., the privatization of risk). Moreover, in some cases living the "double life" meant that some participants not only monitored their own behaviours but were monitored by others as well. Notions of self-regulation and responsibilization were not simple, discrete, and linear but were embedded in a context of interaction and directionality in which youth rejected social representations of themselves as immoral and reckless and others embraced them. While much internalization of responsibility was evident, it was not an absolute, as many youth rejected full responsibility and cast blame outward.

Young people's analyses of their capacities and ways to overcome challenges, negotiate risk, and resist expert and authoritative systems were diffuse, creative, and very much embedded in their ontological understanding of themselves and their environment. In this light, there was a wide spectrum of image projection in relation to self-regulation. Some depicted themselves as extremely self-monitoring and responsible, while others wanted to project an image of disinhibition as "crazy motherfuckers" (Luke), "warriors" (Ingrid), and "survivors" (Tyler). Perhaps this was an effort to resist a "safety at all cost" zeitgeist (Furedi 2006), hinting to the anthropological notion of taking risks in the pursuit to feel alive. A common thread of survivability was evident in their understandings. Many viewed themselves as resourceful and creative survivors, who were not passive but were active agents who frequently and actively resisted expert advice and others who tried to exert authority over them (e.g., police, other youth). Instead of the common stereotype that pervades adolescent literature (as described by Becker 1963), in which youth are deemed as impulsive, rebellious, and cognitively stunted, this study found that many youth were thoughtful about their lives, their identities, and their relationships with others, and they were very conscious of social stigma. Many youth did not characterize their experiences as ones of victimization or deviance but equated harmful or exciting experiences as character testing and shaping.

Some researchers have noted the importance of building relationships with youth in intervention work (Kidd, Miner, Walker, and Davidson 2007) as a springboard for developing trust and more effective work. Others (Bellot 2001; Levac 2005) have put forward the idea that frontline workers, in general, occupy little space in the lives of homeless youth. Even those youth that were connected to mental health and addictions services and sought regular support ultimately determined their own treatment plans and frequently bucked professional advice. Themes of creativity, survivability, and resistance were common in their narratives. The assumption that expert knowledges are paramount to individual understandings of risk was certainly not proven for this risky and at-risk group, which raises many questions about the efficacy of risk-based interventions. There is a mismatch between the risk logics disseminated by and orienting professional practices and the understandings and lived realities of homeless youth. These differing standpoints and interpretations translate into a faulty application and a lack of relevance for homeless youth, as their situated knowledge and constrained options are not taken into account. Acknowledging a more diminutive view of the influence of expert systems, Furedi (2006: 7) attests that "peer pressure is a far more powerful influence on individual behaviour than the workings of formal institutions." However, peer influences are rarely discussed in these social theories of risk (Sharland 2006). And this is all the more true for a group deemed at-risk or risky, wherein peer networks play a determinant role in survival or exploitation.

5. SURVIVING AND KEEPING SAFE

I used to be such a pushover when I first hit the streets. Everyone pushed me around. But now I've made my place. Everyone knows not to mess with me 'cause I'll fuck them up [beat them up]. Everyone knows not to fuck with me. I'll just beat them with my longboard [similar to a skateboard] or my eight balls [pool balls in a sock]. (Luke, age seventeen)

Luke was staying at a youth shelter but was actively looking for housing. He explained that he was kicked out of his mother's house last year because she had caught him looking at pornography on the computer. She did not let him wear women's clothing, something he frequently liked to do. He said his mother was very poor and had received disability income support for as long as he could remember. When he was a baby, his father left, remarried, and started another family. Luke had not kept in contact with his family and had no desire to do so. It was challenging to build rapport with him. Over the course of several years, he moved in and out of different living arrangements, including private and subsidized apartments, shelters, and sleeping outside. Throughout the study he continued to attend a part-time school program in a drop-in centre. When asked about time spent on and off the streets, Luke said that his experiences only made him "tougher." For example, he stated he was "jumped" by a gang the year before for a small amount of weed in his possession. Luke said this was the most frightening thing that had happened to him since hitting the streets, but he also felt that it helped him learn how to stand up for himself. He emphasized that he did not seek medical help or contact the police, even though he knew the attackers. He denied being concerned about it happening again, even though he felt that being stabbed and robbed was the greatest danger on the streets. Luke liked to think of himself as a "crazy motherfucker," in contrast to his "conservative and preppy family." Despite his investment in a nonconformist identity and desire to gain respect and street credibility so others would not "mess with him," Luke also dreamed about the future, thought about pursuing a career in engineering, and stayed in school for several years.

The streets are characterized as intensely dangerous places for youth. Rates of violence and victimization are greater for street youth than for the general Canadian public (Gaetz 2004, 2009), and victimization is likely to increase with the length of time spent homeless (Boivin et al. 2005). Not only are the streets defined as dangerous or risky, but the activities associated with street life appear to increase the chances of youth becoming victims of violence (Hoyt, Ryan, and Cauce 1999). Ironically, these youth are the least likely to seek help, adding another layer to their vulnerability (Gaetz 2004, 2009; Karabanow 2004). Many youth in this study described the importance of peer networks for their survival. Others, however, described peer groups as a source of victimization, which leads to another paradox of street life. While peer groups provided some measure of protection, they were also known to victimize outliers or oppress members within the group by forbidding the emergence of individual opinions and differences. Youth also had to contend with social representations of and the stigma associated with being young and homeless, and often had to engage the informal economy in order to live.

VIOLENCE AND VICTIMIZATION

Young people experience high rates of victimization both prior to becoming homeless and once they are living on the streets or in shelters (Aubry et al. 2003; Baron 2003; Bassuk, Perloff, and Dawson 2001; Novac, Hermer, Paradis, and Kellen 2006; Tanner and Wortley 2002). They often become involved in the criminal justice system and in general have very negative experiences with police officers (Barnaby, Penn, and Erickson 2010; Gaetz 2002; Gaetz, O'Grady and Buccieri 2010; Larouche 2010). They are physically and sexually assaulted, robbed, threatened with a weapon, chased, shot at, stabbed, beaten up, and exploited at rates greater than the general population (Boivin et al. 2005; Sleegers et al. 1998; Whitbeck, Hoyt, and Ackley 1997). They are five times as likely to be victims of assault, five times more likely to be victims of theft, and ten times more likely to be robbed by force and be victims of sexual assault than domiciled youth (Gaetz 2004). There is overwhelming evidence that these youth live in precarious environments where the threat of victimization is ever present, and this is further supported by the fact that youth often employ safety strategies to reduce these risks (e.g., change their routines and activities, avoid certain places, carry weapons and possessions, alter their appearance; Gaetz 2004).

Physical Violence, Robbery, and Theft of Belongings

Life on the streets can be extremely violent, and young people are frequently assaulted and are the victims of robbery and theft. Vince (age twenty), who had spent three to four years on and off the street, reflected, "I see some people get robbed for no reason … for money and stuff like that, for iPods." Young people reported having their laptops, iPods, cameras, phones, clothing, and other personal belongings stolen, and three reported having someone "borrow" money from their credit card that was not paid back. Ella (age sixteen) had saved over $1,000 to use once she left home. She met a young man at a drop-in centre who befriended her, then stole her bank card and used it to commit several acts of fraud. As part of recouping the damages, the bank withheld Ella's original $1,000 and would not return it.

Many young people maintain high levels of caution about whom they trust, and they are careful to manage their relationships to minimize "the drama." In a focus group with young people, one young woman spoke about the dangers of trusting the wrong person:

> You've got to be careful who you trust. You trust the wrong person, you could get really fucked over and you're in jail. I have so many frenemies, it's not even funny. Everyone is such a big backstabber. You've got to be really careful who you trust when you're homeless, 'cause a lot of the other homeless people will try to get you hooked on drugs. Or stabbed! Like I did!

Young people reported being especially vulnerable to violence and theft when they were using drugs or sleeping. Chad (age seventeen) experienced a life-threatening stabbing when he spent time with the wrong crowd and became too drunk to take care of himself:

> *I got stabbed a couple weeks ago because I blacked out when I was drinking. I probably said something to someone, so they stabbed me, and like ... you start thinking, what if? Like what if someone hadn't carried me back to the shelter? I would have died, you know? You start thinking about what can actually happen to you. For me ... it made me realize life is worth living, you know? Like this isn't what I want with my life. I guess it's smartened me up a bit because I want out, but ... easier said than done.... I've been stabbed three times, shot four times.*

In Chad's case, much of his violent victimization is tied to earlier gang involvement, where he was caught up in a cycle of retaliatory gang acts that resulted in the murder of two of his closest friends. He relocated to Ottawa to maintain a safe distance from his gang; however, without housing, he continued to be victimized. He tried to be very careful of how he treated others when he became upset, and he tried to think everything through to avoid acts of retaliation:

> *Impulse decisions fuck you over on the street, like.... okay, I don't like that guy, he robbed me, and you go beat him up.... Well then, all of a sudden, all of his friends are coming to beat you up, and all 'cause you just got angry over five bucks or something.*

Dustin (age sixteen) shared a similar sense of caution about his peers and provided a rationale for why some homeless young people target others in the same situation:

> *I've hung out with a lot of people who seem really chill, and then in the end, they're just like, "Give me your shit." That's happened to me a couple of times.... Its really hard to explain, but street kids, they like to rob street kids 'cause it's easy. I'm not gonna tell the cops, and I probably have something on me, you know? That's just the way it goes. You always have to watch who you're gonna hang out with, where you're gonna go with somebody.... Always have to keep your eye out.*

Dustin believed that the vulnerability of young people who are homeless and the likelihood that they are involved in drugs or criminal activity makes them easy targets, since they are unlikely to contact the police. He said he carefully watched his peers and was careful about where he would go with people. He explained that he was very unlikely to join peers in a dark alley if they offered him drugs, because he would be unprotected and worried that they might turn on him. Marshall (age seventeen) deliberately chose not to deal drugs even though he used them, because he felt particularly vulnerable to robbery. He felt it was safer to use and not sell. For Pete (age eighteen), however, his choice to abstain from drugs overall had gotten him into trouble with his peers. He had been beaten up several times by other young people on the street who suspected that he might be working with the police because he would not use drugs with them.

Young people may also actively confront victimization by making significant life choices such as relocating to a new city or confronting other youth. Paul (age eighteen) said that after being beat up continually while living in a shelter on the East Coast, and having people try to stab him, he decided to move to live with his grandmother in Ottawa. He tried to escape the victimization by rebuilding ties with his family members in another part of the country. Unfortunately, his living situation with his grandparents deteriorated quickly, and he chose to leave their house and became homeless in Ottawa.

Even though homeless youth remain one of the most victimized groups in Canada, they are one of the least likely groups to seek help from authorities (Gaetz 2004; Karabanow 2004; Novac, Hermer, Paradis, and Kellen 2009). According to Karabanow, Clement, Carson, and Crane (2005), the majority of street-entrenched youth have negative relationships with the police and feel that police treat them badly. Consequently, they are less likely to go to the police when they have concerns for their own safety. Similarly, Novac, Hermer, Paradis, and Kellen (2009) found that respondents rarely reported criminal victimization to the police because they did not trust the police to be fair or to protect them, they felt the police would be disinterested or ineffective, or they believed the police were the principal offenders. Moreover, the "code of the street" was cited as a reason for not contacting the police:

> Street people may protect other street people (for example, by not "squealing" on a homeless person). If loyalty is not a sufficient reason

to keep quiet, fear of retaliation is generally effective. Violations of street culture can result in reprisal from other homeless people. (Novac, Hermer, Paradis, and Kellen 2009: 9)

Gaetz (2004: 440) found that street youth rarely reported incidents of criminal victimization to members of their family or to adult authority figures (e.g., teachers, social workers, or counsellors), "reflecting the estrangement of young people who are homeless, their weak guardianship, and their limited social capital." Karabanow (2004: 42) argues that violence needs to be understood within a larger cycle of repression

as a means for some disenfranchised youth on the streets of gaining control, or self-empowerment.... Street youth are frequently both perpetrators and victims of street violence. The streets for homeless adolescents shape a constantly changing subculture that is often animated by a dynamic of lawlessness.

In one of the incongruencies in the literature though, Kipke et al. (1997: 366) found that despite the high rates of exposure to violence, a large proportion of youth reported that they felt "not at all afraid" of being beaten up (60 percent) or sexually assaulted (54 percent). According to these researchers, the discrepancy may be explained by the

subjective perceptions of fearlessness because they have failed to acknowledge their risk of victimization to themselves, to avoid the cognitive dissonance that would result from continuing to subject themselves or be subjected to the dangers of life on the street. (Kipke et al. 1997: 366)

Baron, Forde, and Kennedy's (2007: 412) research reveals that "violence often evolves from 'character contests' where each participant attempts to save face" and that "expressive acts of violence typically begin with a dispute over relatively trivial matters." Moreover, "many who seek redress and justice through violence end up as the victims in the conflict" (Baron Forde, and Kennedy 2007: 412) and "the more violent incidents that street youths are involved in, the more likely they are to report being victimized" (Baron Forde, and Kennedy 2007: 422).

Indisputably, homeless youth experience higher rates of violence and victimization than their housed peers, and if this violence was transposed

onto another social group, the moral panic and outrage would be immediate. However, despite this disturbing evidence of victimization and
violence, youth perceptions and reactions to these phenomena remain
largely unknown.

Peer Networks and Safety

Several researchers (Haldenby, Berman, and Forchuk 2007; Parazelli 2000)
have noted that street youth commonly perceive themselves as different
and have a general feeling of awkwardness, which drives them to look for
a sense of belonging on the streets. Gilbert (2004) notes that homeless
youth with childhood histories lacking warmth and nurturing search for
"affective compensation" and a place to belong. While most participants
in our study wanted to belong to a peer group as a way to reduce harm
and provide a sense of belonging, the peer group also had its drawbacks
and its victims. Olivia's story is a testament to this paradox, introducing
us to a young woman who was lonely and yearned to belong to a group,
whatever the risks involved.

Olivia's Story

Olivia had been homeless for roughly two years when she met Sue-Ann. She
initially stayed at a shelter but grew tired of the constraints of shelter living.
She opted for living on the streets with her friends and visited her family
frequently. During our first few encounters, Olivia described her loneliness
and her efforts to gain entry into a street group:

> *I have to meet them [street names of other youth] to see whether they
> are going to accept me into [their gang]. I am gaining higher status
> because I lift [steal] things they tell me to.... We take care of our
> own; we help each other out.... People think I am stupid, but I am
> really smart. I have to know seven cards [playing cards from a deck
> of cards] by tomorrow and know what they mean — that is my first
> test. [She shows the seven cards that she is trying to memorize and
> recites their names and meanings.] After that I have to be "raped"
> by the [female] leader.... I don't know what that means, but I am
> sure it's not rape. I really miss these new friends [the gang] when I
> am not with them.*

Olivia admitted to committing several criminal acts over the ensuing months to gain entry into the group, tasks she was instructed to perform to earn their loyalty. In consequence, she was charged with shoplifting, trespassing, assaulting a police officer, and breaking and entering. She confessed that she knew that she should stay away from this peer group because it meant trouble, but she was very lonely and wanted to belong. Olivia felt the risks of participation were worth the benefit of belonging. As the negative experiences accumulated, her investment in this peer group diminished, particularly once she learned of an unexpected pregnancy (which she viewed as a positive turning point in her life). She became more preoccupied with finding housing, returning to school, and preparing for her baby than meeting the group's expectations for membership. Thus, her initial preoccupation with securing her place in this group lost its potency over time. In addition, the demands of child protective services required her to find housing and stop using drugs if she wanted to keep her child.

Michelle's Story

Engaging in criminal activity and remaining silent about sexual victimization were not the only drawbacks of group membership mentioned by youth. Michelle (age seventeen), who had been on the streets for a year, described the lack of privacy or individuality that stemmed from the need for conformity to maintain cohesion within the group:

> On the streets everyone is your friend, and nothing is just yours. What's yours is everyone else's too. You have to share everything and if you don't, someone will pick a fight with you.… If you want to feel rich you buy a pack of smokes, but you have to open the pack when you are alone, because if you don't, everyone who is your friend wants one and they think they are entitled to them.

Over the course of the next year, Michelle grew tired of what she called "the drama downtown." She moved back home and came downtown as little as possible:

> I try to avoid coming downtown. I try to avoid the drama. There's a girl who wants to beat me up because she thinks I stole her laptop, and she sent a girl after me to beat me up, but I just explained to

her that I didn't steal it and now I've been left alone. Everyone is
always backstabbing each other. You can't trust anyone.

Michelle felt that the supremacy of group cohesion and proscription of divergent opinions negatively affected her identity. She described feeling caged in by the expectations of other youth. In some instances, she was forced to go along with her peer group's course of action against her better judgment, because she knew that if she openly disagreed, she would be excluded and possibly victimized. The peer group's actions included victimizing others to get what the group desired (i.e., robbing or assaulting strangers or other street youth). Bellot (2001) likewise found that as the heart of identity shifts to the group, individual identity tends to become subsumed and diluted by the group's identity.

Claire's Story

Claire (age seventeen) illustrates an extreme example of peer group victimization. She reported being marginalized by a group of homeless peers who limited her access to services and friendships, even falsely accusing her of sexual harassment and attempting to have criminal charges laid against her. Claire was an elusive young woman that service providers had a hard time connecting with. She frequented shelters or services in a very sporadic manner, often disappearing for long stretches of time, then reappearing but remaining aloof. She revealed finally that her abrupt "in and outs" were the result of her movements being constrained by a group of young street women who disliked her.

Claire was of Eastern European heritage and adopted into a Canadian family at age three. She had no siblings. She explained that she left home because her parents were emotionally and physically abusive. She said that child protective services were contacted once when she was six or seven years old for suspected abuse, but when she denied the abuse, they never intervened again. She described her parents as very controlling and conservative. They limited her phone and internet use, decided which friends were acceptable to associate with, and did not allow her to date. If she disobeyed, there were physical repercussions. Claire still had contact with her parents and visited them from time to time but found it difficult to maintain a relationship with them. She had recently started taking some college courses and was finding it challenging to meet the demands of her course work without a stable place to live and work on her school assignments. She often slept at the college library overnight to do her course work because she had nowhere else to go.

Claire cycled in and out of shelters, couch-surfed, and slept on the streets. She also frequented the drop-in centres that serve homeless youth. She had recently been accused of sexual harassment by another young woman who belonged to a group that disliked and harassed her. A member of this same group had beaten Claire up twice and said she would do it again if she saw Claire downtown:

> I ended up getting barred from the shelter because this girl accused me of sexual harassment and even contacted the police because the group leader told her to lie. They wanted to charge me with sexual harassment, but they had no proof. They [the agency] also barred me from using the drop-in because she had lied to the police and told them I was stalking her. So for "safety" reasons the staff at both the drop-in and the shelter barred me, inside and outside. Like, I couldn't even hang around the area. We [Claire and the girl] used to go to the same support group at the hospital, and I just tried talking to her on the bus, but then she turned it around and told them I was stalking her.... She hangs out with this group that hates me.... They've beaten me up twice and won't leave me alone, and no one wants to hang out with me because they are scared of them, especially the group leader, "the queen." She wants to be the queen of downtown; she has a lot of people scared. But I don't believe in violence, and I let her hit me. I don't fight back because violence doesn't solve anything.

Claire admitted that when she slept outside, she slept alone because everyone else was too frightened to associate with her. She was also instructed by the group not to access the agencies that serve homeless youth downtown. Claire wound up spending more time drifting in other parts of the city because of this marginalization and victimization. She relied on her school friendships and college resources to eke out a living and maintain a social life, and she was somewhat philosophical about the group's impact on her life. She described herself as a survivor and did not want to be bothered with these "trivial" matters:

It's fine, it's okay for now, it's not such a big deal. I mean, what more can I do? Everyone downtown is too scared to be around me. I just stay in the west end, mostly at the college library, and I see some of my old school friends from my old 'hood. Sometimes they will come downtown and pan [panhandle] with me outside of McDonald's. I always make do, get by, survive.

Claire described choosing different friendships, frequenting different areas of town, and generally adapting to the constraints set by this group victimization. She considered this response reasonable since she always felt "different" as a child anyway. These experiences solidified her belief that she was adaptable, a survivor, and somehow different from other people.

Peer networks thus present another paradox uncovered by this study and likewise noted by other authors (Bellot 2001; Haldenby, Berman, and Forchuk 2007; Parazelli 1997). While they provided protection and belonging for some members, youth also reported feeling oppressed within a group, and still others experienced direct victimization.

SOCIAL REPRESENTATION AND INTERACTIONS WITH POLICE

Young people's identities were not only influenced by their peers via peer network membership but also affected by stereotypes and friction with authority figures. Many youth described feeling targeted by the police, and felt unfairly treated because of their appearance, age, and identification with street life. Previous research on youth homelessness and interactions with the police demonstrates that young people on the street have more interaction with police officers because of a lack of access to private space, the use of social profiling, the stigmatization reinforced by business owners who do not want youth loitering, and youth involvement in criminal activity, most notably the sale and exchange of criminalized and prescription drugs (Avila, Campbell, and Eid 2009; Barnaby, Penn, and Erickson 2010; Gaetz, 2002; Hagan and McCarthy 1997). Furthermore, young people have both positive and negative interactions with police officers (Barnaby, Penn, and Erickson 2010; Gaetz, O'Grady and Buccieri, 2010). In our study, a few young people indicated that they had not really had many interactions with the police, and some also mentioned positive interactions, but the majority spoke very negatively about police interactions. Young people expressed a tremendous amount of anxiety about these interactions. They reported feeling intimidated, shaking, distrusting authority, being embarrassed in front of their peers by the way that police treated them, experiencing threats of physical harm from police officers, being hurt physically by the use of force, and having their experiences of victimization dismissed by the officers.

The youth had their own understandings of social representations and the stigma associated with being young and homeless. Laura explained that she and her friends felt singled out by the police because of how they looked and where they hung out (under a downtown bridge):

> The other day we were sitting under the bridge and the cops came along and searched us all. They started searching my bag.... You know, people don't know their rights, and they had no right, we were just hanging out. I was embarrassed so I asked them to take me over to the side because I didn't want my friends to see my syringes and know I had been using.... At first they took me to the side, then they thought I was resisting so they threw me down. I started freaking out. I told them I was scared. They handcuffed me and made me sit in the grass while they searched my stuff.... Another guy, they pulled his pants down and looked for drugs.

Many youth echoed these sentiments of fear and powerlessness when faced with police who targeted them for the way they looked, the public spaces they were occupying, and the people they were hanging out with. Olivia described a similar event:

> Yesterday, me and my friend were walking in the [the mall downtown] when the cops stopped us. They said that we fit the description of two people that committed an assault recently. They took my friend's survival knife, his grinder with a little crystal meth in it, smashed his pipe on the ground for no reason ... I threatened them, asking for their badge numbers and supervisor's name. They had no reason to stop us, we were just walking, minding our own business ... but you know it's 'cause of the way we look. They let us go after questioning us for ten minutes and barred us from the mall.

The perception that authority figures saw youth as deviant simply because they identified with street life was a common theme. When youth were victims of crimes, they felt particularly judged and were often revictimized by systems that they felt were supposed to protect them, a phenomenon that has been described by other scholars (Gaetz 2004; Karabanow 2004; Kidd 2009). For example, Laura (age seventeen) had been assaulted by a homeless man and tried reporting the incident to the police but felt that her concerns were not taken seriously because she was young and homeless. She was told to come back a few months later to look at mug shots because they were too busy to follow up with the incident at the time:

> I am going down to the cop shop [police station] to try and identify who jacked [assaulted] me, but it was before I went away [to an addictions treatment centre] so I can't exactly remember what the crackhead looked like. I just saw his silhouette. Too much time has passed. The cops were too busy until now to give me an appointment. They don't take you seriously when you look like I look [punk]. They figure it's your fault for being in the wrong place at the wrong time.

Hagan and McCarthy (1997) wrote that young people who have been abused by people in positions of authority may be especially sensitive to mistreatment by police officers. When Benjamin conducted his feedback group to share his findings with young people, they were very vocal about mistreatment from police officers. One young woman reported that she had been tasered when a police officer found her sleeping in a parking garage. She was upset about the incident and claimed that she told the officer that she would file an official complaint. She reported that the officer asked, "Who are they going to believe: a police officer or a dirty street kid?" She decided not to file an official complaint about the incident.

Young people who had experienced being searched in public or being arrested in front of their peers frequently reported feeling embarrassed. This seemed to be connected to the use of force by police officers. When a young person felt unsafe because of a police intervention and began to fight back, only to be physically subdued by officers in front of their peers, they felt a loss of power that was experienced as profoundly embarrassing. Young people reported being concerned with how others perceived them following the intervention. Chad (age seventeen) is relatively short with gang-related tattoos on his neck. He reported that his tattoos were an identifier and that he was stopped and searched by police constantly. His description of one police search shows his efforts to resist the use of force by police officers and his embarrassment in front of his peers:

> It's embarrassing when they search you like they do.... They're really rough ... like, they smash you around and shit, and you're just like, "Fuck man, like leave me alone." When you get arrested, they don't pull you aside; they do it in the middle of the street. Smack! Pull your pockets out, slam you against the wall ... both hands on the wall, and then they yell at you. They're angry too. They're like, "Keep your fucking hands on the wall! Don't move! Stop resisting!" And you're like, "What the hell? I'm standing here." Like ... I'm sorry, you're shaking me around. I'm gonna be like, "Yo, what the hell are you doing," you know? You're coming at me from behind. I'm kind of gonna sketch here. I don't know, they're just like ... aggressive and rude ... the whole time. They make a scene about it so everyone looks at you, and you're just like, "Man ... everyone thinks I'm a piece of shit now."

In this story, Chad rationalized his resistance to the police with the phrase "I'm kind of gonna sketch here," indicating that he found the experience frightening. Later in the interview, Chad also expressed disappointment that the police might detain young people for a night, without considering that this may cause them to miss curfew and lose their bed at the youth shelter.

Ezra (age eighteen) was laughing when he told a story of how he unknowingly tried to break into an undercover police car to steal a phone. Like Chad, he was upset by the degree of force used by the officer and how the physical force occurred in front of his peers:

> I got tackled to the ground like no tomorrow, like ... this guy was crazy. He just gets out of his car.... Well, first of all he slams me with his door, and I get like knocked over, you know? So I was just like, "What the hell!" and then like, I was gonna get ready to punch him in the face. And he gets out and starts tackling me. He's like, "I'm a cop." And I was like, "Bad idea to hit him," and so I just like gave up, and he just pinned me down. Everybody was looking at me, and I was just like, "What are you all looking at?"

Feeling Targeted by Police Because of Homelessness

Service providers and young people noted that sometimes young people who are homeless may be targeted by police officers. This aligns with the findings of an inquiry by the Quebec Commission on Human Rights and the Rights of the Child into the discriminatory practice of social profiling (Avila, Campbell, and Eid 2009). In a focus group with service providers at a youth shelter, Bob described "harassment from police" as one of the challenges of homelessness: "Just because they live in a shelter, they're all under this negative, 'Do you do drugs? Do you sell drugs? I'll stop you every time I see you.' They've got a radar for them almost … which is unfortunate." Chad (age seventeen) expressed a similar sentiment: "With cops, they treat you like shit. If they know you're a street kid … automatically cops are all over you."

Young people also expressed anger over how they perceived officers treating others who were homeless. Talking about older homeless men around the adult shelters, Chad (age seventeen) said, "They harass crackheads like no tomorrow … which sucks 'cause you're trying to make money and cops are harassing some poor bastard, and you're like, man, give this guy a break, you know? He's smoking crack and eating out of a garbage. Like … why are you busting him?" Paul (age nineteen) also felt like police treated young people who were homeless in a discriminatory manner:

> The cops are ruder to homeless people than needed. If we're standing outside in front of McDonald's having a smoke and talking, we're automatically selling drugs … automatically.… That's what the cops think. And they'll charge us for loitering, they'll charge us for possession if we have even our own personal shit that we smoke ourselves. And they try to get us thrown in jail as fast as they can.… That's what it's like … in my eyes. Because a lot of my friends have been getting put in jail because of what they do to help themselves survive.

Chad also spoke about the use of ticketing in a discriminatory fashion:

> So let's say I'm kickin' in front of McDonald's and I see cops.… Automatically, if I don't leave, I'm going to be getting ticketed … just 'cause I don't look like someone who has money. So it's automatic. "Oh what? You're a street kid and you live at [the shelter]? Here's a

$65 ticket." There's a lot of undercovers who give tickets, like, "Oh, you're within three metres of a bus shelter, you're supposed to be nine metres. Here's a $65 ticket." 'Cause they ask you where you live first, right? They take down all of your information. "Oh, the shelter? Awesome. Let's fuck you over nicely."

Chad and Paul were the most outspoken on these issues in Benjamin's study; however, the use of ticketing and the perception of police targeting of homeless youth was a sentiment that was widely shared among youth, particularly those that were more street-involved. During a focus group, three young women reported that they had been red-zoned from Rideau Street in Ottawa — meaning that they were not allowed to be on this street, which is an area that also covers much of the downtown and the resources available to homeless youth, such as drop-ins, clinics, and shelters, but also social spheres where youth congregate. They reported that a breach could result in their arrest. This was a fairly common experience reported by youth in our interactions.

Chad expressed concern that police officers may lack understanding about the issues surrounding youth homelessness and that the well-being of young people may be compromised by a police objective of keeping them off the streets. He was also frustrated that he was often caught up in the clash between the mandate of public health initiatives that provide free needle exchange services and the police who conduct drug enforcement

If you're a street kid, they make it seem like it's all your fault that you're on the street.... I've seen kids get arrested for being runaways, but there's obviously a reason they don't want to go back to where they came from. They just haul you back there. They don't really care for you personally; they just want you off the street, that's it. So charges, restrictions, anything they can do to keep you bound up.... They're not very lenient with anything. So let's say I get caught with a needle in my pocket. Paraphernalia charge.... Even though you have an unopened needle in your pocket, you're getting arrested if they find it. You're like, man, I get these from the shelter so I don't get AIDS!

Frequently, youth complained about how they were perceived and subsequently judged by other authority figures and "street-level bureaucrats"

(Lipsky 1980), whom they felt exercised a lot of discretionary power over the choices offered, creating a conditionalized offer of service. A few participants revealed that they told service providers what they wanted to hear in order to maintain access to necessary services. For instance, Tyler was in a drop-in centre when his girlfriend became agitated by the presence of another young woman. He responded to her agitation by saying, "Shut up and tell them [frontline workers] you aren't going to do anything, that way you can still come to the drop-in." Tyler encouraged her to settle their dispute outside of the agency and to hide it from the workers, because agencies often restrict a client's access if they are aware of an assault on another client. Youth were keenly aware of the identities they were assigned by frontline workers and authority figures, and used them to their advantage, in particular to diminish harmful consequences (e.g., criminal charges, loss of access to services).

Young people expressed resentment about the social exclusion they experienced. In one of the youth focus groups, after discussing barriers to finding employment, Paul (age nineteen) passionately explained why he rejected mainstream society:

> *They judge us for going to drugs, and going to alcohol, yet how can they expect us to rely on anything else when we constantly get rejected for who we are when they don't even know us? Of course we're going to turn to the only shit that seems to give comfort to everybody else around us. Nobody else supports us. They reject our potential, they reject our capabilities, so we reject them. What do they expect?... Fuck the system!*

For some young people, the perception that they had been deliberately rejected by society encouraged them to reject social norms and the expectations that others might have for their behaviour. Youth were very conscious of how their appearance affected opportunities, judgments, and treatment by others. When dealing with opportunities in the non-street world, many youth tried to soften their image to appear more socially acceptable. For example, Olivia changed her hair colour to one tone and Laura cut off her dreadlocks before important interviews to increase their chances of landing a job or an apartment. Adjusting their image to appear more "responsible" and "normal" involved simple changes to their outward appearance. When looking for a part-time job, Michelle pretended to be in school full-time because she felt that she would have a better chance with employers if they believed she lived a more "normal" life. Luke dressed as a young male when looking for housing even though he preferred to wear women's clothing: "I like to wear women's clothes.... But when I am looking for housing, I make sure to make myself look presentable and responsible-looking, look more like a guy." Youth were keenly aware of the multiple roles they needed to play in order to access services or resources, or to start the process of disengagement from street life.

THE INFLUENCE OF THE INFORMAL ECONOMY

Researchers argue that youth do not have access to legitimate means of self-support, and as a result, a significant number of youth are drawn into illegal activity as a method of survival on the streets, which further increases their chances of victimization (Gaetz 2004; Kraus, Eberle, and Serge 2001). Homeless youth are more likely to engage in deviant acts such as drug dealing, trading or selling sex, phone sex solicitation, theft, panhandling, and squeegeeing. Gaetz and O'Grady (2002: 437), in their study on the informal economy, found that young people who are homeless use a flexible economic strategy, symbolizing "an adaptive response to an inherently unstable life style." They revealed a pattern to the ways in which youth made money that was intimately tied to experiences prior to becoming street-involved and to the current situation of homelessness. They argue that differing street cultures coexist regarding how youth make money. This in turn profoundly shapes their different experiences of survival and their identities pre- and post-homelessness (i.e., paid employment vs. squeegee, sex trade):

> Money-making activities of homeless youth are patterned, in varying degrees, by our selected background characteristics. It is also evident that those youth who earn most of their income by working in the sex trade are the most disadvantaged group of youth in our sample. At the same time, those who reported earning most of their money from paid employment came from relatively less deprived families. (Gaetz and O'Grady 2002: 445)

Gaetz and O'Grady (2002) argue that we need to move away from dichotomous representations of homeless youth as either employed or unemployed and instead broaden the concept of work to include the diverse economic strategies that youth employ to survive. Interestingly, they noted that the level of power and control that youth had over their work was strongly associated with risk. That is to say,

> those youth who are the most '"advantaged" tend to work in relatively socially acceptable lines of work. Conversely, those who have to contend with more negative "baggage," and currently find themselves in difficult circumstances, are more likely to be engaging in "riskier" money making activities that occur in the context of the less reputable sectors of the homeless economy. (Gaetz and O'Grady 2002: 452)

In their more recent work, O'Grady and Gaetz (2009) point to the gendered dimensions of street-related work and its impact on identity construction:

> Space, place, and identity thus are bound in a way distinct from more structured family, community, and institutional spaces under the greater control of adults … much of the informal economic work that young people engage in — begging, squeegeeing, sex work, or dealing drugs — plays a role in helping homeless youth stake out urban space not only for economic activities, but also for recreation, eating, and sleeping. Such space is also used tactically in the negotiation of gender identities. (O'Grady and Gaetz 2009: 4–5)

O'Grady and Gaetz (2009) are also among the few authors to highlight the "cash in hand" benefits of such forms of street-related work that naturally fit the ebb and flow of street life and the immediacy of survival needs (food and shelter). They caution though that "while this form of payment means that they [youth] do not pay taxes on income, it also means that they typically are paid at rates below minimum wage, and that they are otherwise vulnerable to abuse by employers" (O'Grady and Gaetz 2009: 9).

Moreover, some authors have noted that many youth would like to find paid employment but have difficulty doing so (e.g., due to the barriers to getting and keeping a job, such as inadequate housing, higher incidence of illnesses and injuries, and inability to give potential employers an address or contact info). In fact, they have fairly conventional attitudes about work

(Gaetz and O'Grady 2002; Karabanow 2004). O'Grady and Gaetz (2009: 8) found that an overwhelming majority of their sample wanted to find paid employment. And this was certainly echoed in our research.

Experimentation and Making Money

Surviving on the streets required youth to be creative and engage in different forms of work. These creative enterprises often had a large bearing on their evolving identities. Work in the informal economy included but was not restricted to panhandling, squeegeeing, buying and selling items, drug dealing, participating in surveys and doing work for agencies (including internships and acting as resources for agencies involved in community engagement work), babysitting, sex work (including telephone solicitation), working in the service industry (getting paid under the table or in kind), and working for family members or friends. Some youth even described "ethical stealing" as a form of work they undertook. Attempting new forms of work in the informal economy came with its own risks, as has been explored by other scholars (Gaetz 2004; Gaetz and O'Grady 2002). Due to the many constraints imposed by welfare and the job market, many youth found creative ways to make money or find work in exchange for food, drugs, or shelter. Most youth engaged in some form of work in the informal economy. Karabanow and Kidd (2014) underscore the importance accorded to work by homeless youth, stating that it is not only a means of survival but also a means of feeling good about oneself and preserving one's self-esteem.

Lucy identified herself first and foremost as an injection drug user. She stated that her main preoccupation was to make $20 a day so that she could maintain her drug use and not become sick from withdrawal. Her ability to articulate issues around responsible drug use made her attractive to agencies that served youth struggling with addiction, and she was hired as a peer support worker. She performed different tasks, sharing her knowledge on harm reduction and substance use with other substance-using youth. She described this knowledge sharing as especially helpful to her self-esteem: "Because I have been there, I know they really listen to me. It helps to know that I am making a difference." Lucy was also extremely resourceful in the different kinds of work activities she participated in. She had participated in numerous surveys and she knew which ones were taking place in the community and how much participants were remunerated. She admitted that when she could not make enough money through these means, she resorted to stealing with her boyfriend, but only when she felt she had no other option:

> *We will steal if necessary but only from big franchises like Walmart. We are very ethical in who we choose to steal from if we have to. I don't like doing it and don't feel good about it, but it's when we have no choice and we don't want to get sick [from withdrawal].*

While Lucy was quite open about her drug use and passionate about issues related to safe injection use, she admitted that she had not revealed her continued drug use to her family and workers, fearing that it would negatively affect her relationships. In this light, Lucy shifted her identity in multiple ways, ranging from a responsible and creative injection drug user navigating the unfair constraints that the streets impose on young women to a highly politicized peer advocate projecting the image of a former drug user in recovery.

Many young people offered a similar perspective, expressing a sense of systemic injustice that limited their ability to make "respectable" choices. Ella (age sixteen) explained, "Well, when you don't have any money and you're starving, you steal food ... and clothes too. But I only stole stuff when I needed it, not when I just wanted it. You know ... I wasn't a klepto." Ella described her theft as a necessity but seemed proud that she exercised restraint and only stole when she perceived it to be required. Pete (age nineteen) shared a similar rationale for stealing food. He found the decision difficult but experienced a sense of pride in taking care of himself:

> *It did get really desperate sometimes, where I was having to steal to eat because nothing was available. I felt really bad afterwards, but it's like that sort of good guilt that you get ... where you know you did something wrong and you don't like it, but it was for the better.... Like if you didn't you would have probably been up all night reeling over 'cause your stomach hurts so bad 'cause you haven't eaten anything in a couple of days. So it's kind of like, "Okay, good. I'm not going to do this again, it's the last time." It's sort of that desperation mode that you go into. I think everybody who has gone homeless knows the feeling of being that desperate*

to do really anything to get something. Yeah, they were really hard
decisions to make, and I didn't really like them, but it got me
through to where I am.

Ella and Pete rationalized their choices based on their perception that
engaging in criminal behaviour was necessary given the disadvantaged context of homelessness. Most of the young people who thought in these terms
also seemed to think about homelessness as a temporary condition, which
helped mitigate their feelings of responsibility for the criminal behaviour.
They might also neutralize their guilt about the theft by telling themselves,
as Pete did, that it would be the last time. Pete even expressed pride in having done what was necessary to survive, believing that it helped him get to
where he was at the time: housed, employed, and self-sufficient.

Ryan disclosed that he did steal, but that he exercised some constraint
when he made that choice. He had a series of rationalizations that he used
to deny the injury caused by his actions, such as targeting corporations:

I won't ... I can't steal from people. Like, if I see the person, I can't
steal from a person, but stealing from a store ... like a corporation,
I'm able to kind of rationalize why that's okay. "Oh, they're running
all these mom-and-pop shops out of business.... It's all the corporate
businessmen profiting from it." You kind of make these excuses in
your head.

This Robin Hood logic of stealing from the rich to help the poor effectively
neutralized the sense that his theft caused harm.

The experiences of victimization on the street combined with the dis-
advantages inherent to homelessness create conditions that can lead to
criminalized behaviours. For many young people, experiences of victimization and marginalization are linked to the types of illegal behaviours that
they engage in, such as petty theft, drug dealing, or sex work. However, this
discussion has focused on the perceptions and rationalizations entertained
by young people in making decisions around these behaviours, and many
of the case studies have shown that young people wrestle with their values
and engage in a series of personal negotiations that attempt to balance the
idea of the people they want to become with the realities of homelessness.
The struggles highlighted in this section demonstrate the importance of
human agency, recognizing that individual actors, although situated within

broader structures of disadvantage, still retain the capacity to interpret their circumstances and make choices about how to respond.

Most of the young men in this study gravitated towards deviant identities, self-identifying as hustlers, drug pushers, and thieves, reinforcing the commonly held notion that males occupy more deviant roles in society. Many young men engaged in selling and dealing items to other youth, often lying about the origins of the product or its condition. Young women and men alike were often victims of one another's sales pitches, and when faulty items were sold, verbal and physical arguments often ensued, with peer group members rallying to the side of either the claimant or defendant. Outside a drop-in centre one morning, Olivia reported that she had spent her last $10 on a music player that did not work. She was visibly upset and said, "My friends will deal with him [the seller]." The seller, however, happened to be another youth that Sue-Ann knew, and he felt that he had earned the money because he had worked hard to hustle his product. He was proud of this part of his identity: "I was a door-to-door salesman when I was fifteen. I used to make $500 per day. I can sell anything, even if it is broken." Youth used their street-savvy skills to survive, whether it was selling weed, panhandling, or squeegeeing, or other occasional activities reported by youth such as selling stolen or second-hand items or working under the table in various capacities, as servers, babysitters, phone solicitors, flyer distributors, carnival workers, and performers (e.g., transsexual impersonator).

It would be inaccurate, however, to situate all of the participants' work experiences within the informal economy, as several denied ever engaging in any informal, under-the-table, or black market work. However, many were involved in invisible or illegal forms of work on a daily basis. Roughly half of the youth were also active in the formal economy at some point over the course of the study. Much of this work was in the service industry and was described as insecure and temporary, hinting at a labour market that is increasingly precarious. Chris explained that he sometimes worked for one or two weeks at a time, typically in fast food chains, but the jobs never lasted. He admitted that he was fired because he was caught stealing. He decided that he did not want to be constrained by a work schedule, particularly when the financial rewards were minimal, so instead, he made money through a combination of petty thefts and panhandling:

Yeah, I worked at Lone Star and Mickey D's [McDonald's] for a few *weeks, but I ended up getting canned 'cause I stole stuff.... I tried to leave with a keg from the Lone Star and I took other stuff.... I had to steal the CHEO [children's hospital] charity bottle out of the Beer Store yesterday. There was about $25 in it. I don't feel good about it, but you got to do what you need to do to survive.... I stole a car and drove to Montreal last year, but they caught me and now I am on probation for five years. With my record, no one wants to hire me.*

Daniel, on the other hand, had several part-time service sector jobs while living at the shelter, but they lasted only a few weeks at a time. "I got this job at the slaughterhouse, but it only lasted a day because the boss said I wasn't strong enough.... I think he thought I was too young." A few weeks later, he worked at a fast food chain for a couple of weeks. "I lost my job at Subway for being late too many times.... I have been smoking up more lately, I am not dealing anymore, but I need to cut down.... I need to find another job." Daniel was not entrenched in street life and decided that he wanted to exit the streets. A few months later, he had his own room in a supportive housing complex. He was working full-time in a bakery and had been promoted several times, which came with higher wages and more responsibility:

I have been promoted to overnight baker. I like it because I work on my own, I am fast, and I get most of the work done by 4 a.m., one hour ahead of schedule. It pays $14 an hour.... I don't hang around downtown or with the same friends from my past. I don't even smoke up anymore or drink that much. I am living the straight and narrow. I've been to hell and back. I don't miss that life, and I want to move forward. Me and my girlfriend are getting a place together.

He then moved in with his girlfriend and disengaged from street life entirely. In Daniel's case, work played an active role in his exit from street life, and he made a conscious choice to steer away from previous street-associated activities (i.e., drugs, certain friends, dangerous places).

Youth performed many different roles in relation to work. Typically, the more street-involved youth engaged in work embedded in the informal economy, as substantiated by other scholars (Gaetz 2004; Gaetz and O'Grady 2002). Youth attempting to disengage from street life, on the other hand, chose more recognized forms of work in the formal economy and gradually slipped into more socially acceptable roles. Working in the formal economy had a great influence on their identities and the kinds of risks they took, leading many to search for housing (Karabanow 2004). However, this path was not universal. Some youth were heavily invested in street life and managed to maintain jobs in the formal economy. Most youth experienced barriers to employment in the formal economy because of their age, appearance, and lack of experience and education. Structural constraints (e.g., insecure and low-paying work, lack of education, difficulties accessing social assistance) often pushed youth into the informal economy, where they engaged in high-risk and stigmatizing activities (i.e., squeegeeing, panhandling, selling drugs, stealing). Other youth indicated that these were the kinds of choices street life presented or the kinds of activities they wished to experiment with. Whether the reasons were structural or individual, or a combination thereof, their work experiences had a significant effect on the evolution of their identities.

For the most part, young people's identities shifted over the course of their trajectories through homelessness in light of new roles, activities, or responsibilities. Elements common to the stories of many youth, from the very street-entrenched to the relatively mainstream, were the twin notions of adaptability and creativity in overcoming obstacles, whereby they attempted to adapt positively and make the most of very complex, demanding, and adverse circumstances. This dimension has been explored by Lucchini (1996), who was one of the first to view street children as actors in their own lives and not merely as victims or deviants. In fact, many youth appropriate these images of victimhood and use them to their advantage, resisting authority in both covert and overt ways. Youth use aspects of their multiple identities to cross over into the mainstream by assuming socially appropriate roles (e.g., students, employees, tenants, service users) in the search for social recognition and survival.

In sum, youth described a range of harmful experiences, including drug addiction, assault, and robbery, but most of them minimized the impact of these risks or described them as rites of passage. Many also described needing to build up sufficient "street cred" in order to be taken seriously and reduce their chance of being victims. Many youth reflected on their lack of control over certain risks (e.g., being robbed or assaulted by a "crackhead") and the random nature of their occurrence. They also framed these experiences within their expectations of street life. It is critical to place these experiences within a framework of risk consciousness that involves violence, neglect, and abandonment, and the instability that pre-existed street life for most of the participants. While some described experiences of being stabbed or beaten up for their drugs, money, or possessions, others worried about this possibility precisely because youth share stories and often emphasize the more titillating and sensational aspects. Story-sharing among youth appeared to serve a few purposes: to minimize the very real dangers present, to relive the adrenaline rush that accompanies them, and to provide a common framework to their experiences that offer a sense of belonging.

The threats and constraints posed by street life prompted youth to take steps to minimize risks in a number of ways, including being hypervigilant, both physically and emotionally. The drama of street life was seen by many as harmful and in some cases more unsettling than the threat of physical assault. The need to belong to a group for protection from physical and emotional harm was a strong and recurring theme and formed another survival strategy employed by youth.

6. EVOLVING ROLES AND IDENTITIES

It made me who I am. You can't deny that. And if I hadn't been homeless, things would have been different. Whether it would have been better or worse, I don't know. It would have just been completely different. (Jean-Olivier, age twenty)

As highlighted in the previous chapters, most youth arrive on the streets with pre-existing histories rife with violence, conflict, instability, and neglect. Youth revealed that their childhoods and their relationships with their families had an enormous impact on their identity and the subsequent choices they made on the streets. Here we draw on theories of adolescence and identity construction that underscore the importance of experimentation and self-discovery. These ideas stand in sharp contrast to traditional views of adolescence as a time of turmoil and growth, in which youth have developmental deficits that need to be overcome in order to form a coherent sense of self (e.g., Erikson 1968; Hall 1904).

Like Bajoit (1999, 2000), we believe that identity construction is continuous and complex and that identity is tied to the past, to the present, and to future aspirations. In this sense, identity is in constant flux, evolving and interacting with different dimensions of life. In the context of this research, identity construction refers to the changing nature of one's identity as it interacts with one's perceptions of childhood, current relationships, daily activities, differing roles, and future goals. We also take up Parazelli's (1997, 1999, 2000, 2002) analysis (borrowing from Winnicott's 1971 theory) that many street youth use the streets as transitional spaces that allow them to continuously reconstitute their identities by engaging in active role experimentation. It is important to note that this experimentation often takes place within an arena of constrained choices. For many youth, adolescence is a time of heightened risk and sensation seeking. As outlined in previous chapters, street youth are confronted with many paradoxes, such as the search for excitement in the face of danger and the search for freedom within a context of captivity. These constraints all have an impact on the risks youth perceive or are willing to take. Young people's identities were shaped by the multiple roles they played and the accumulation of experiences that street life offered. For some youth, it was also tied to their attempts to disengage from or exit street life, as noted in previous research (Bellot 2001; Colombo 2008, 2015).

RESHAPING IDENTITY

One pattern that emerged in the discussion of personal change was the notion that experiencing homelessness and disconnecting from pre-existing social networks allowed some young people to experiment with their personal identity or to recreate themselves. Pete (age eighteen) described himself as very shy and withdrawn prior to becoming homeless. He explained that his introverted nature had caused him to be bullied in school. During his first night of homelessness, he made a calculated decision to change aspects of his personality that did not seem to be working for him:

> *And then I'm homeless, and I kind of just changed my ways of doing things overnight. So rather than being that secluded, cocooned person, I was more ... the one that's always out there, just doing stuff and having fun all the time, and trying to keep a positive outlook on everything ... rather than being depressed all the time.... 'Cause making friends wasn't my forte, and interacting with people wasn't my thing, so it was kind of a new test ground for me. I thought for a little bit, and then decided, "What the hell?... Why not try it?" And then eventually, I just started realizing, "Okay this actually does work, and I'm actually making some decent friends, and people actually like me for what I am." So I was just like, "Alright, let's do this instead." I felt like I had actually let what was inside come out, and ... you know ... just be myself, and be energetic, and I actually*

enjoy life rather than sit in a corner and hate it.... So a lot of stuff
changed, and I actually like it, and I still feel that it's me ... 'cause
the person that I was, I don't think... wasn't me. I think it was just
like an outer shell that I had to break out of.

Pete described how "everything changed," including the way that he dressed and the music that he listened to. He said that he started wearing brighter clothes that fit him and that made him feel like he looked good, and he started listening to more upbeat and inspiring music. Pete believed that the positive changes he experienced in his life and his ability to more fully embrace his self-identity developed as he adapted to becoming homeless.

Queer/Gender Identity

A few other young people had a similar experience in relation to their gender identity. In their family home they had to repress who they felt they were, but once they were on the street they were able to experiment and discover who they really were without fear of judgment from the people who knew them well. They had space to re-create their identity and present themselves to people in the way they had long wanted to, as who they felt they were. Several of the youth we met were transitioning. Jean-Olivier (age twenty) first came out as a lesbian, but later, after learning more about sexuality through a sexual health education seminar, came out as a transgender man. Thomas (age nineteen) experimented with life as a transgender woman, moving from a shelter for young men to a shelter for young women, but following some disappointing experiences decided to return to identifying as a gay male or genderqueer. Syrus (age twenty-one) described his gender as "fluid," recognizing that his self-identity seemed to be male but could change in the future. For Syrus, leaving his strict Middle Eastern family provided him with the opportunity to explore how to express his sexuality. He explained that at first he wore "flamboyant" clothing but later chose to dress a little more conservatively as a sign of respect when he was accepted by his family and able to move back home. Luke liked to dress as a woman, though not all the time, but did not state that his gender identity was female, preferring instead to experiment and remain gender-fluid. However, this was a big reason for being kicked out of his mother's home, as is the case with so many non-cisgender youth.

IMPRESSION MANAGEMENT AND NEGOTIATION

The way that young people who were homeless described themselves in interviews, periods of observation, and focus groups ranged from expressions of powerlessness to expressions of strength and capacity; it also became apparent that in certain circumstances young people would behave in a way that did not actually reflect how they felt about themselves. We explore this dynamic using the metaphor of theatrical performances to examine how human beings relate to one another and attempt to manage the impressions of their identity that they allow others to see (Goffman 1959, 1961; Scott 2016). Drawing on a dramaturgical perspective, Goffman (1959, 1961) makes a distinction between how people present themselves backstage and front stage: the backstage represents what is hidden from others when there is no pressure to perform and most accurately reflects what people believe about themselves, while the front stage represents a performance presented to a particular audience. Goffman recognizes that at times people want others to perceive them differently than how they perceive themselves and will put on an act to make themselves more appealing to their observers. People want to be perceived as authentic, even when they believe something different about themselves than what they are portraying to others (Scott 2016). Even so, there may be a difference between the impression that people intend to give and the impression they actually give off. According to Goffman, these subtleties shape human interactions. In this discussion, we explore the impact of these performances on negotiation. The young people we interviewed were conscious that they staged performances, and several of the interviews felt like frank discussions with actors backstage as they described the work that goes into staging their performances.

Backstage Reflections on Acting Tough

As identified earlier in the findings, young people reported that they often felt the need to "act tough" on the streets, a perspective that aligns with a front stage performance of identity staged for a specific audience. Acting tough was a common strategy to try and avoid being perceived as vulnerable, which young people felt could lead to being targeted for victimization, such as theft, physical assault, or sexual assault. Chad (age seventeen) explained his perception of the danger of showing emotions to other young people on the street and described how he tried to keep a very even demeanour:

When you're with your friend on the street, [if] you portray any emo-
tion ... it's a weakness. Like ... you cry? And you're a guy? You're a
pussy. You don't fight? Me ... I'm like this all the time, just mellow,
you know? 'Cause like ... you show happiness, sadness ... all that
does is get you hurt on the street. (Chad, age seventeen)

Chad confessed that performing this role on the street for so long had
caused him some confusion, and after reaching a point when he was considering transitioning off the street, he was trying to rediscover who he was,
and who he could be, apart from the character he played on the streets:

So I have to learn how to separate myself from the street to who I
really am. 'Cause on the street, you can't always be yourself. Like
when you're with a crowd of people you don't know, you're a tough
guy, like ... nothing bothers me, nothing gets me shook. When
you're with your friends, that's when you express it. But you have
to learn to express emotions all the time apparently [when you're
off the streets], or so I've been told. So I have to learn to accept ...
everything, emotions and shit.

In this narrative, Chad made a strong distinction between who he was
backstage and the character he played on the street, and he described the
challenge of keeping these two identities separate. Kristin (age eighteen)
maintained a stronger distinction between who she believed she was and
the identity she tried to perform on the street, arguing that most people she
knew on the street were terrified but tried to appear strong to others. She
also questioned her ability to perform a tough persona in a way that others
would accept as credible:

I'm not a confident person, I'm not generally a violent person, and
I can't defend myself.... I can't. I'm not big, I'm 5'2" and 100
pounds.... I'm not big. And I think most of the kids I meet, as
confident as they are, as loud as they are, as friendly as they can
be ... I think inside, they're terrified, and ... they won't admit it
to themselves. And even if they admit it to themselves ... hell no,
you don't admit you're scared when you're living on the streets. You
admit you're scared to someone else on the streets ... that's when you
get the crap beaten out of you and all your stuff taken. You have

to be as tough as you can be ... and I mean, I'm 5'2" and 100
pounds. If I'm not acting tough, if I'm not watching my back 24/7,
I guarantee one day some guy is going to come up to me, knock me
up, and take my shit.

Kristin believed that everyone she knew on the streets was putting on a performance to try and protect themselves. In the short comment provided above, she referred to her small size twice, and given her belief that she was not likely to scare anyone off, she relied instead on allying herself with others on the street who appeared tough. "I associate with a few fairly well-respected people, and ... that keeps me safe. And [if] I piss someone off and I didn't have tough people around me, or weren't tough myself, I'd have three or four people coming after me to kick my ass, and I wouldn't be downtown ... you know? So that's it.... Survival ... survival of the fittest." Kristin believed that portraying a tough image or being associated with others who appeared tough was a matter of survival, and performing this identity was part of how she negotiated a sense of personal safety in her surroundings.

Similar to Chad, Kristin also expressed that playing a tough role has the power to change a person, although she reflected on a friend she had seen change since becoming homeless:

I know a guy who's down here, and he's this big beast of a guy, and
he was the sweetest guy. When he ended up on the streets, he chose
to start dealing drugs, and he took on that role ... this "I don't give
a fuck" attitude and this "You get out of my face or I'll knock your
teeth out" attitude. That personality ... that person is now him. He's
not who he was, he's not the nice guy that he was.

Kristin explained that her friend had alienated everyone around him and had run into trouble at school with his teachers and principal. She questioned where he would ever find a place to live or get a job. One other young man, Dustin (age sixteen), also appeared to have adopted a tough personal identity, rather than conceiving of it as a role that he played, although it is possible that the interview with him could also be understood as a performance rather than a backstage discussion. Contrasting many of the other narratives, Dustin actually thought of himself as tough but felt that his physical appearance might not be adequate to convince others. He described himself as having a "young face" and explained how that would take people by surprise when he robbed them on the street. To be taken credibly, Dustin explained, he robbed people with a small group of guys who were bigger and more intimidating than him, and he also used a knife to intimidate others. Dustin did not think of his behaviour as harmful, but rather as a temporary act of intimidation to convince people to hand over whatever valuables they might be carrying.

Appearing strong on the street is not just a matter of protection; it can also be a matter of personal dignity. Max (age twenty) experienced embarrassment in a homeless shelter when he discovered that some of the service providers and volunteers were previously peers at his high school. He described this as the most challenging aspect of homelessness that he had experienced:

> *They're working behind the counter, and then there's me … and they're like, "I know this guy. He's a fuck-up. Look at him." You know? They say it doesn't matter what people think about you, but it really does … because if everyone thinks of you as shit, then you're not really going to get anywhere.*

Because of the previous relationship that Max had with the volunteers and service providers, he felt judged and believed he was perceived as a failure. His connection with these people made it difficult for him to portray himself in a position of strength, and his concern for his future actually served as a motivator to get off the street and move away from Ottawa, to a place where he could have a fresh start and people did not know him. When we spoke, he was days away from moving into a new apartment and was eager to get away from downtown Ottawa, where people might recognize him.

Backstage Reflections on Acting Vulnerable

In the narratives that have been presented, young people have discussed how they often feel vulnerable but try to appear strong. However, there are also times when young people bring their vulnerability to the front stage and present themselves as weaker than they feel as part of their negotiations to meet their needs. In the interviews, young people described these interactions as being predominantly staged for service providers, but they were also staged for parents, teachers, and police officers. Jake (age nineteen) was the most articulate about playing this role. When he turned sixteen years old, he left the child welfare system, and after a falling out with his family, he went to his bank to withdraw $10,000 in savings for education that was held in a joint account with his father. When he requested to withdraw the full amount, the bank clerk tried to decline the transaction and referred him to the bank manager:

> *They're like, "Wait a second, let's just talk to the bank manager." And I started freaking out, and I was like, "Well I need the money, because I just got out of CAS [Children's Aid Society], and I need to get a house for myself, I have nowhere to go." And it turned into the biggest sob story you have ever heard, but I had to do it.... I had to lie to them, and I had to make the situation as far-fetched but as believable as possible, right? 'Cause I'm protecting myself, it's my money, fuck you, you know? Give me my money.*

In reality, Jake was scared and angry and felt like he had limited options; however, he did not intend to use the money for housing, and he played up his vulnerable position as a form of bargaining power to manipulate others into letting him withdraw his money. After providing a written statement to the bank manager, he was able to withdraw the full amount without having the bank contact his father. Jake then described with regret how he spent the full amount in the months that followed, ending up with no money and staying in a barn near a friend who he knew through the child welfare system.

Following that incident, Jake was housed again, but had another experience of homelessness following a violent incident in his family home. When he accessed support at a youth drop-in centre, he learned that his history of violent victimization in the child welfare system and his homeless status would grant him priority status on the social housing registry. He described in a playful manner how he tried to encourage young people to use any history of victimization to gain priority status as he did:

> *I tell a lot of people who walk into the drop-in, "What brought you?" I try to find something, any priority I can think of in my head: safety priority, medical priority.... I just want to jog people's memories. "Did anyone ever hit you? Did anyone do this or that? Were you ever wronged in any situation? So you left because of this, right?" I'm trying to find it for them ... trying to get them thinking. But people are too honest. The reality is that it's on a big trust system here.*

Jake recognized that these priority areas of vulnerability provide leverage in the negotiation for social housing. He encouraged young people to find any area of vulnerability possible and present it to service providers to support their application to the social housing registry, even if they needed to embellish their experiences. At the same time, his motivation was rooted in a deeper belief that young people should not be homeless. "I feel like being homeless should be illegal," he said. "No citizen should have the right to be out on the street in my opinion, because there's too much wrong that can be done to them." Based on this belief, Jake was willing to use vulnerability and a history of victimization as a tool of negotiation to meet his needs. While the experiences he described might be real, he was aware of the power of presenting this image to service providers. He was very open about this aspect of his self-advocacy and also described how he would present a similar vulnerable image in negotiations with his social assistance worker. Service providers also spoke in depth about their perceptions of young people intentionally "playing a victim role."

"Acted Upon" vs. "Acting On"

Returning to the central theme of human agency and Giddens' (1984) theory of structuration, when young people present themselves to others, they select between narratives that prioritize the power of either structure or agency, portraying themselves as being "acted upon" by their circumstances, or as "acting on" their circumstances. An "acted upon" presentation of the self implies that human agency is limited and prioritizes the power of social structures in determining personal outcomes. An "acting on" presentation of the self prioritizes the capacity of human agency to affect social structures and shape personal outcomes. In the narratives presented above, there were often contrasts between what young people believed about themselves backstage and what they presented to others on the front stage; these contrasts can be understood through the lens of being "acted upon" and "acting on." With their peers, young people who feel unsafe and limited in their personal power (acted upon) often convey an image of being powerful and strong (acting on) as a way of negotiating for their security. Conversely, when seeking help from service providers, sometimes young people intentionally portray themselves as more vulnerable than they feel (acted upon) because they believe this will help them to get what they are looking for. The narratives show a reflexive use of these two identities, and the way that these roles may be played as part of the negotiation process.

At the same time, young people may also experience changes in their backstage beliefs about themselves and transition between states of feeling powerless and feeling powerful, perceiving themselves as "acted upon" or "acting on." This became apparent as we heard young people discuss their choices when they left home and became homeless. At least two young people in Benjamin's study said that their parents had kicked them out of their home but later discussed their own choice to leave home. Others who had been homeless for a longer period explained that the time they had spent homeless had given them more opportunity to reflect on the events leading to being kicked out, and they explained that they consequently took a greater degree of responsibility for their own behaviours. This is consistent with Mallett et al. (2003), who found that many of the young people they interviewed reported that their understanding of how they had become homeless changed over time and with distance from the other people involved, and they gained a more mature perspective based on greater life experience.

The most dramatic shift in narratives Benjamin observed occurred in an interview with Kristin (age eighteen), who attended the focus group for young women and then participated in a one-on-one interview the following day. During the focus group Benjamin asked the young women to draw a picture of what they relied on to help them when times were difficult. Almost all of the drawings in the focus groups with young women and young men depicted drugs and alcohol, so Kristin's drawing stood apart (see Figure 1).

Figure 1. Kristin's drawing from the focus group with young women.

Kristin's drawing included references to close friends, her "street family," music, and a glass of wine with an arrow pointing towards a picture of a strong arm inside a box, which was intended to represent inner strength.

During the one-on-one interview, Kristin spoke about her life in a disempowered manner, describing her challenges and repeatedly asking questions like, "What do you do? What am I supposed to do? What do you do when you have nowhere to sleep?" She spoke at great length about how afraid she was on the streets and presented a narrative that emphasized the obstacles in her life, portraying a limited view of human agency that could be understood as "acted upon." After thirty minutes of Kristin presenting this type of narrative, Benjamin asked her to say more about the drawing that she had said represented inner strength. A distinct and immediate change occurred in her narrative that emphasized her human agency and personal capacity to overcome obstacles:

> *I believe I'm capable of completing my high school education, finding somewhere to live, becoming successful. I ... I think I'm capable of that. I think I'm capable of getting sober. If I can do two weeks, I can do six months, I can do a year, and so on and so forth. And I'm capable of getting past this.... I'm capable of taking that first step, and the second one, and getting out of here. And ... I ... I think that I can get somewhere with my life if I put my mind to it and put my talents to it.*

At this point in the interview, Kristin continued to elaborate on her personal strengths and her determination to transition off the streets. She acknowledged again that since the death of a friend, she had managed to remain sober for two weeks, overcoming her addiction to alcohol and OxyContin for that period of time. Her demeanour changed, and she began to speak with confidence. Having stayed clean for two weeks following the death of her friend was a significant personal victory, especially since earlier in the interview she had described how she would typically use drugs to deal with emotional pain. She also indicated that she had been able to avoid self-injurious behaviour in the previous two weeks.

Kristin's narratives reflected both perspectives of being "acted upon" and "acting on." Combining this example with the others presented in this chapter leads to three observations:

1) Young people experience temporal shifts in their belief about their capacity to affect their social structures and circumstances.
2) These beliefs are influenced through interactions with other actors, in
   ways that can reinforce both feelings of powerlessness and feelings of
   strength and capacity.
3) Young people also consciously play the roles of being "acted upon" or
   "acting on" to negotiate with other actors to achieve a desired outcome.

The temporal nature of these perceptions is particularly important to
understanding a constructivist model of resilience. Young people are continually reflecting on their lives and at the same time being influenced by
others. While adults also experience temporal shifts in their beliefs about
their capacity to affect their circumstances, young people passing through
adolescence are constantly navigating the expectations of adults and systems
that fluctuate between treating them like children who require adult intervention and like adult decision-makers with responsibility for managing their
own lives. Youth perceptions and beliefs about personal capacity are in a
constant state of flux, which may be further influenced by the rapid changes
created by "drama" on the streets. A young person may describe himself one
month as being connected with a "street family" that provides support and
helps him through difficulty, but then have a falling out the next month and
come to perceive the same people as a threat. In this example, the supportive
peers could be understood as a protective factor one month and a risk factor
the next. Other young people may experience constant tension in how they
perceive and value their peers. This is why Ungar (2004a, 2004, 2005, 2008)
advocates a model of resilience that explores how marginalized young people
navigate and negotiate the multiple tensions in their lives. A young person
on the street with a desire to feel acceptance and belonging from peers has
to navigate a large number of rapid changes in the social environment to
achieve acceptance into a group, and also has to continually negotiate for a
sense of belonging. These rapid changes also affect how young people think
about themselves, and the highs and lows of street life influence, to some
extent, when young people perceive of themselves as being "acted upon" or
"acting on." However, individual capacity to respond in unexpected ways
cannot be overstated, and many of the young people we interviewed demonstrated a tremendous capacity to maintain a positive outlook and sense
of personal capacity despite experiencing significant adversity.

MEANING GIVEN TO FAMILY HISTORIES

Young people's evolving identities in relation to their early origins affect they way they understand themselves and how they make decisions on the street. There was a wide spectrum of meanings; some youth accepted the great influence of these early years on their identities and the decisions they made, endorsing a certain affinity or fatality approach, whereas others rejected these influences and acted in direct opposition to these associations, as if to disprove the influence of family histories on their lives.

Acceptance

Several youth felt that they had inherited certain character traits and inclinations from their parents. Many youth described their roles (e.g., drug dealer, drug user, hustler, protector) and behaviours (e.g., stealing, using violence, using drugs) as within the realm of normal experiences for their family. A few youth in particular ascribed their identities to their parents' influence and used this link to rationalize their behaviour.

Tyler's Story

Tyler (age sixteen) said he was a hustler and a drug addict. He believed that these roles were predestined and attributable to the environment he was exposed to growing up. He said his mother was a drug addict ("crackhead") and a hustler who became involved with wealthy men to keep a roof over their heads and maintain her cocaine addiction. He described growing up with his mother as chaotic and punctuated with frequent moves across the country whenever his mother would strike up a new intimate relationship. He also felt that his mother was vulnerable because of her drug dependency and tended to be drawn to abusive men. He recounted many early childhood experiences growing up in the notorious Vancouver Downtown Eastside, which is well known for heavy drug use and sex work. Tyler and his mother eventually fled to Ottawa for a "fresh start," leaving behind his mother's string of abusive boyfriends. He admitted that he rarely attended school, but his frequent uprooting meant that child welfare authorities were evaded. These early experiences shaped him into a tough and street-savvy young man, allowing him to "earn his stripes" on the street. These early experiences moulded his present-day understanding of his roles on the street and his assessments of danger and opportunity.

Tyler was very entrenched in street life. He admitted that he smoked crack every day and would "do anything — ecstasy, pot, powder." He revealed that he had always been heavily involved in street life, even as a child. "She [Tyler's mother] started smoking me up when I was nine. I was using crack by the time I was thirteen." Tyler cycled in and out of detention centres and the streets and had previous charges stemming from small robberies, breaking and entering, and drug dealing.

Tyler described the different facets of his identity in an exuberant, larger-than-life way. He described himself as a drug addict first and foremost, and further identified as a hustler, a role necessary to satisfy the needs of his primary identity. As a self-identified hustler, he admitted to committing criminal acts that included theft and drug dealing and employed several innovative entrepreneurial strategies. He identified strongly with both of these roles, which he attributed to his mother's influence and his early exposure to a deviant lifestyle, stating, "There are drug addicts who do criminal acts to get drugs, and there are criminals who do drugs. I am a drug addict like my mom." Tyler described his ability to hustle as a gift:

> I am really good at hustling and ripping things off. I really like to rob safes. I am really good at it, and I almost never get caught. But last time, I missed covering one camera and they picked me up four hours later. It's great being only sixteen, because I usually get let off [do not have to serve time] and only have conditions to follow. I am also good at hustling drugs. I walk over to the [youth shelter] and everyone starts saying, "You have, you have" — I take their money, and within half an hour and a six-block radius I get the rock [crack] to them. I have a lot of older suppliers because of my mother's connections. Because of my age and my looks, I get away with it. If I hustle crack, I can make $300 in a morning if I move fast.

Tyler said his goal every day was to make enough money to get a hotel room for the night. He supported himself by dealing drugs, committing small thefts, and panhandling:

> Every day I try to make $56.50 for a hotel room at the Concord [downtown hotel]. If I haven't made enough, then I spend it all on drugs. I also pan [panhandle] ... not regular panning, but I cruise

the mall and ask everyone for one dollar for the bus. Every third
person gives you a buck, then in an hour you've made $30. I can
make hundreds [of dollars] a day.

Tyler believed he was a masterful artist of street life and exuded confidence and knowledge in the twin roles of drug addict and hustler. He prided himself on his ability to evade and outsmart police (e.g., after a robbery) and perceived himself to be powerful because of his street knowledge and skills. Throughout most of the study, Tyler lived on the streets and used substances daily. However, after a couple of years, he was convicted of several criminal charges and the court ordered him to attend an addictions treatment centre for one year. His age no longer served as a buffer.

Marie's Story

Marie (age sixteen) was forced out of her home by her father when she was fifteen years old, following which she lived with a foster family on a military base. She was told to leave her foster family's home because they were unable to cope with her behaviour, which included fighting, using drugs, vandalizing school property, and truancy. When Marie was evicted from the foster family, her father refused to let her return to their family home.

When Sue-Ann first met Marie, she had been suspended from school for fighting and subsequent assault charges. She was working on her high school diploma through correspondence. "There is too much violence at school. I worry about losing control and hurting people. I am a lot like my father that way. My dad is very violent. I am a lot like him. He hates me because he wishes I were a boy." Her father's temper was the reason that child welfare authorities removed her from the family home. Now this same anger had manifested itself in her, resulting in assault charges that prevented her from attending secondary school. During the course of the year, she was arrested twice for assaulting other young women. She stated, "I am not trying to get into fights, but I feel as if people are always trying to pick them with me." Upon reflection, Marie recognized that the conflict with her father and her own violent outbursts affected her self-concept in a negative way.

A few months later, Marie became pregnant, and she and her boyfriend decided to start a family. She left the shelter and moved into his apartment. She revealed that a visit to her family home with her boyfriend opened her eyes to how much she had changed since leaving:

My dad started calling me names, giving me a hard time. My boy-friend wanted to do something, but I told him not to bother even talking to him. I feel healthier not living there, and I can see now how much it affected me. I feel more in control of my emotions now. I know my father still hates me and treats me differently than my brother, but it doesn't affect me as much now.

Marie's circumstances changed radically during her first year on the streets, and her identity underwent a similarly radical evolution. She had learned how to detach herself emotionally from her father, and she felt more in control of her emotions and behaviour. She also acquired a new role as an expectant mother and took on the responsibility of preparing for her baby. By the end of the study, Marie was attending an alternative school and attempting to avoid conflicts downtown. She had stopped consuming drugs and alcohol, which she admitted would not only be damaging for her baby's health but also make her more prone to behaving in a violent or unpredictable manner. She was proud that she had no new assault charges and had turned her attention to finishing her high school diploma and preparing for the arrival of her baby.

While Marie initially looked to her father's anger and violence as an expla-nation for her own behaviour, this rationalization became insufficient over time and she began to reject this identification. In so doing, she engaged in less risky activities and described feeling more in control of her life.

Rejection

At the other end of the spectrum, several youth flatly rejected their parents' identities as determinants of their own, and in so doing, they hoped to build a better life on the streets. For instance, more than half the youth Sue-Ann met witnessed domestic violence growing up, and all of them vowed not to become abusers or victims. Many youth described their conscious efforts to detach themselves physically and emotionally from their families. Withdrawing from the family environment became an act of self-preservation that made room for their own identities to evolve. These youth rejected the notion that drug use and violence were hereditary behaviours, and they fought hard to be different and better than their parents. Consequently, their risk frameworks were constructed around their negative perceptions of their parents' behaviour.

While Chris had a criminal history similar to Tyler's, involving car thefts, small robberies, and uttering threats, he vowed never to use hard drugs such as crack because his father was a "crackhead" and he did not want to become subservient to his drug use. Shane also led an entrenched street life and described a childhood that revolved around his mother's drug use and her short-term and precarious intimate relationships. Chris and Shane, in contrast to Tyler, actively chose to use less harmful drugs, such as alcohol and marijuana, than did their parents. Shane described his trajectory into homelessness and how his perception of his mother's lifestyle and drug use affected his choices.

Shane's Story

Shane (age sixteen) was sitting in a drop-in centre. Originally from a town in Northern Ontario, he described how the draw of street life was liberating, allowing him to "hop" trains and travel from coast to coast. He claimed that he had left his mother's home because he was tired of her boyfriends and chaotic lifestyle and wanted to leave the remoteness of Northern Ontario. He lived on the streets during the first half of the study, hitchhiked out west, and then returned to Ottawa and obtained housing and began labouring full-time. He remained street-involved through his social contacts and frequently used youth services:

> I left home because my mom is a ho [whore]. She finds guys through internet dating sites, then moves in with them, and it only lasts a year or so.... I got tired of having to move around. I ended up renting an apartment with my brother [thirty years old] and selling drugs [weed], but we ended up getting into a fistfight and I trashed the apartment. I hitched a train to Sudbury and almost froze to death, then hitched to Ottawa.... I only use alcohol and marijuana. I hate chems [chemicals]. I have seen what it does to my mom. Crystal meth is dangerous. People make it in big bathtubs and you don't know what the hell is in it. I don't touch the stuff.

Chris's and Shane's rejection of aspects of their parents' lifestyles shaped their own perceptions of risk regarding drug use and intimate relationships, and ultimately affected the evolution of their identities and the decisions they made.

Betrayal and Abandonment

While many youth described the abuse and instability they suffered in their own homes before leaving, equally prominent were themes of abandonment and dishonesty in their relationships. Several youth felt that they had been the family scapegoat. At least half of the participants reported feeling like the primary targets and victims of sexual, physical, and emotional abuse. They also felt strongly disliked and rejected by their families. As Tanya's story demonstrates, many youth revealed that they felt less loved than their siblings or their parents' partners.

Tanya's Story

Tanya (age sixteen) was adopted into a Canadian Jamaican family as a baby from Jamaica. Her identity was strongly rooted in her perception of being different from her siblings. Tanya explained that she "always felt different and didn't quite belong," even before she found out at age twelve that she had been adopted. When one of her foster sisters revealed to her that she had been adopted, Tanya felt betrayed by her mother. This discovery confirmed to her that she was different from her siblings and explained the differential treatment she received. She explained that it was not only the physical and emotional abuse she endured that forced her to leave; she was tired of "always feeling different," being blamed for events that were not her fault, and feeling unloved.

Tanya revealed that she had suffered abuse but child welfare authorities never intervened:

> When I was nine I used to hide my lunch in my knapsack because I did not want to eat. One time, I forgot all about the lunches I hadn't eaten in my bag, and I left my bag on the porch.... When my mom found all the garbage collecting in my bag, she beat me with the cord of the vacuum cleaner and told me she was going to beat me again when I got home from school. I was scared all day and let it slip to my teacher that my mom beat me and was waiting for me to get home from school to do it again. Instead of phoning CAS [Children's Aid Society] the teacher phoned my mom, so when I got home she was twice as mad and beat me twice as hard.... I was always the one beaten on by my brothers and sister, and my mom never did anything to stop it.

Two years prior to becoming homeless, Tanya had experimented with body alterations (e.g., piercings, tattoos) and began partying and using drugs. When she came home with her lip pierced, her mother was furious and sent her to live with her biological family in Jamaica. What her mother had anticipated would be a punishment, Tanya saw as a reward. She described feeling much closer to her biological family in Jamaica than her adopted one in Canada:

> *My mom gave me a one-way ticket and told me not to come back until the lip ring was removed. I really enjoyed meeting my biological family and felt closer to them than my own back at home. When my lip got infected, I had to take out the ring, and my mom sent me a return ticket home. But I didn't really want to leave.*

Despite her residential instability, Tanya remained in high school, maintained a good academic record, held down a part-time job, and planned to go to college. When she became pregnant, she tried unsuccessfully to conceal the pregnancy from her family. Tanya and her boyfriend decided to terminate the pregnancy and her family was furious:

> *I know it's the right decision [getting an abortion] even though my family is really upset with me.... I don't know how to take care of a baby, and I am not ready for the responsibility. My boyfriend and I want to get our education and careers first.... My mom wants me to have the baby and give it up for adoption, but I can't go through the whole pregnancy and birth and then give it up. I was adopted, and I don't want the baby to go through the same things that I went through.*

Tanya admitted that terminating the pregnancy was the most difficult decision she had ever made, and she felt immense guilt that she and her boyfriend had not used protection. "It's a stupid mistake that I will never forgive myself for," she said. By the end of the study, Tanya was estranged from her family, and her boyfriend was supporting her financially. She stood steadfastly by her goals, despite not having a place to live or financial or emotional support from her family. She vowed that she would finish high school and apply for a pre-medical program at college. She wanted to prove to her family that even without their support she would be successful in life.

Her career goal was to become a doctor and "prove my family wrong, that I can make it and that I'll do better than all of them."

Many youth described themselves as the scapegoat of the family. They perceived themselves to be less loved, treated unfairly and differently, and blamed for many things that were not their fault. While Colombo's (2008, 2015) study found that youth who experienced a greater degree of rejection by their parents developed more fragile identities and tended to have more difficulty exiting street life, this correlation was not found to hold unequivocally in this study. While youth were profoundly affected by their relationships with their parents, especially ones based on rejection, they often questioned these dynamics and their influence. In Marie's case, for example, she did not continue to engage in self-destructive acts and instead chose to examine aspects of her behaviour that were damaging and make necessary changes. In Tanya's case, she accepted the fact that she was different from her siblings but rejected the ascribed image of deviant for which she felt persecuted by her family. She set goals for herself and wanted to be successful in life despite the lack of support from her family. While both of these young women felt victimized by their families, they placed great emphasis on how they overcame obstacles and ultimately chose paths that diverged from their families' trajectories or beliefs.

Leading a Double Life

Some participants in this study mentioned leading a double life. These youth struggled to reconcile aspects of multiple identities in order to remain connected to their families, friends, or service providers. Laura, Lucy, and Olivia all revealed that they were living a double life, concealing aspects of their drug use and street lives in order to keep family, friends, or workers engaged.

Laura's story, which was outlined in the previous chapter, demonstrates the double life that many youth led to maintain their families', friends', or workers' trust. Laura felt that she had to lie to her non-street-involved school friends and hide her morphine dependency:

> *Street life sucks. I feel like I am living a double life. I see my friends from school downtown, and I am embarrassed if I am with my street friends. My parents hate street life. I can't tell them about my addiction. I am too ashamed — they would never forgive me.*

Laura's oldest sister had also become street-involved, heavily addicted, and estranged from her family. Laura worried that she would be compared to her sister, and her family would become ashamed and resentful of her:

I can't tell my family about my morphine problem. I am too ashamed. My oldest sister left for the streets when she was fourteen.... I didn't see her for four years and because of this I hated her. I resented her because she missed all of my accomplishments [graduation from junior high school]. I don't want them comparing me to her.

In this case, Laura identified with her older sister's street lifestyle but worried that her identity would be conflated with her sister's. She was relieved when her parents found out about her drug use but did not compare her to her sister, and instead helped her access a drug treatment program.

Similarly, Olivia lied to her family about sleeping on the streets to preserve her relationships. She would tell them she was staying at a shelter because they considered that more acceptable than street life. At one point, her sister denied her access to her home because she was living on the streets. Her father judged her for having too many sexual partners:

I would like to go home [in a small town] for a visit but not to stay. My dad is really upset with me because he says I've been with too many guys [starts counting how many sexual partners she has had since hitting the streets]. My dad is worried that I am being taken advantage of, not just sexually but financially and emotionally.... I don't have a good relationship with him. He used to beat us when we were young. CAS [Children's Aid Society] never found out and neither did anyone else because he always hit us on our chest or backs so no one could see the marks. I would like to see my sister too, because my niece is turning three, and she [the sister] is expecting again, but my whole family is upset with the life I am leading. They tell me I will never amount to anything. So my sister won't let me see her daughter.... I have to lie to them and tell them I am staying at the shelter just so they'll let me visit. They ask me why I don't do something with my life.

Eventually, Olivia's family allowed her to visit because she told them what they wanted to hear. "I just tell them I am at the shelter even though I don't plan on it because of all the rules. That way, they let me see my niece and they are not worried about me." Olivia and Laura admitted that this double identity, which involved downplaying their entrenchment in street culture, was stressful and anxiety provoking. They worried that the deceit would cost them their relationships with their families, and they felt pressured to choose which kind of life they wanted to pursue.

Young people's narratives about their shifting identities were strongly rooted in their stories about childhood and their perception of their families' identities. Scapegoating, betrayal, and abandonment by family members were strong and recurrent themes. While some youth considered their street lives to be unavoidable because of their parents' involvement in a similar lifestyle, others rejected this hypothesis and worked against it, actively making different choices from their parents to distance themselves from their origins. In this light, many youth saw themselves as survivors. In Colombo's (2008, 2015) study, youth who experienced parental abandonment were more likely to appropriate the streets in the quest for autonomy. In contrast, those whose relationships with their parents were defined by control and denial of their needs tended to have more fragile identities and engage in more self-destructive activities. This finding was relevant for some participants in our study (Michelle, Olivia, Shane, Luke, Annie) who felt particularly abandoned by their parents and sought excitement and freedom on the streets, but this did not hold true for all participants. For example, Laura and Ingrid did not feel abandoned by their parents but were very invested in street culture and the perceived freedom it brought; in their words, they were "living the life."

7. NAVIGATING OBSTACLES AND NEGOTIATING WITH SERVICE PROVIDERS

Casey (age sixteen) had recently arrived from Toronto. She grew up mostly in the child welfare system but was contemplating leaving child protection and striking out on her own, starting a new life in Ottawa. When she arrived at the shelter, she began the process of applying to Ontario Works for income support and found out she would receive only $520 per month. She knew this would not be enough to live on, even if she were deemed eligible. She decided to remain with child protection, which meant she had to be in school, and the family home back in Toronto had to be deemed unfit.

"I get $882 per month from CAS [Children's Aid Society] until I am twenty-one.… So why would I leave [their care] when I'd have to struggle to get on welfare and they'd be pressuring me to get a job and to get off the system?" After looking for an apartment, she said, "No one will rent to a sixteen-year-old. If you are sixteen, you are discredited. Landlords told me I need to get a co-signer and to ask my social worker to co-sign. But my social worker told me to find someone else to co-sign.… Who *am I* going to find?"

Young people who are homeless manage and negotiate the expectations of numerous adult decision-makers as they access and pass through community services. Armaline (2005) identifies that young people living in emergency shelters engage in continual negotiation of rules, power, and social control with service providers. Many youth do not want to sleep on the streets, but there are many barriers to finding housing. There is a very limited number of shelter beds for youth, and many youth do not want to live with the restrictions that shelters demand. Private and public housing offer their own problems as well, with high rents, stigma, and the mistaken belief that you must be eighteen to rent all contributing to the difficulty youth experience when attempting to secure shelter. Based on our interviews and interactions with youth, we found that some social services, like youth shelters, are more youth-friendly and have developed their service framework specifically for young people, while other services, like social assistance or adult shelters, have more rigid regulations. In Benjamin's study, for the most part, young people expressed appreciation for the youth services they received in the community, and their description of their experiences accessing services were generally aligned with the values that service providers tried to emulate in their work.

At the same time, Sue-Ann's research grew out of an observation that homeless youth, particularly the younger youth (sixteen- and seventeen-year-olds), face extraordinary challenges compared to their older counterparts. The structural constraints that make it very difficult for younger people to access resources (e.g., housing, income) are very pronounced. These obstacles may in fact encourage risk-taking behaviours and put youth at greater risk for victimization or engagement in deviant activities. This structural discrimination constitutes another paradox acting on homeless youth: those considered the most "at risk" (as defined by their younger age) are often pushed and pulled into more dangerous or "risky" situations in order to survive. These issues are rarely examined for this distinct category of homeless youth, especially those under eighteen. The system (e.g., social assistance, supportive and/or transitional housing, shelters, child welfare authorities) poses enormous challenges for youth, particularly for sixteen- and seventeen-year-olds residing in Ontario. One of the most significant barriers is the narrow eligibility criteria for accessing social assistance, particularly income assistance (welfare), known as Ontario Works, but also with various kinds of public and private housing systems.

OBSTACLES TO ACCESSING SOCIAL ASSISTANCE

In Ontario, one of the criteria needed to apply for social assistance is proper identification, whether it is a driver's licence, health card, or some other form of identification. Many sixteen- and seventeen-year-olds do not have the requisite ID cards before hitting the streets, and if they do, it is often not long before they are stolen or lost. It is a well-accepted fact that IDs are frequently stolen or lost among the homeless generally, as evidenced by the growth in "ID clinics" run out of many shelters, drop-in centres, and community health centres that help people apply for new ID cards. Chris, a seventeen-year-old who had cycled in and out of juvenile detention centres for several years, stated, "I can't get OW [Ontario Works]. I am not eighteen and I have no ID." He admitted to committing petty crimes to support himself. Other researchers have likewise noted that youth are less likely to rely on social assistance than their adult counterparts.

Some of the other constraints imposed by social assistance eligibility criteria for sixteen- and seventeen-year-olds, as described by youth, included needing to prove that their previous home was unsafe (as determined by the Ontario Works workers after consulting with the parents or guardians) and that they were enrolled in school full-time. This requirement to contact family members was a risk that some participants were not willing to take, as they were fearful their location might be disclosed to their families. In addition, the determination of whether the home was unfit was made by the frontline worker, and many participants felt these workers were biased and could relate better to their parents. Workers' judgments of eligibility was a common complaint among youth. Participants perceived these determinations to be laden with strong moral undertones that made them feel that they were failures for not living at home and attending school regularly. O'Grady and Gaetz (2009: 9) state that "young people under the age of 18 who are not 'legally emancipated' are not eligible to receive welfare benefits unless they are enrolled in school full time and with the permission of their parents." In some instances, in the Ontario system, exceptional circumstances permit a youth to be enrolled in some form of treatment (e.g., addictions or mental health counselling) as an alternative to being enrolled in school, but it is within the discretionary authority of the Ontario Works worker to refuse this option.

Annie did not pursue an application for welfare because she felt it was too difficult to obtain. "When you are sixteen or seventeen, you are in limbo.... It is impossible to get.... How are we supposed to manage being in school when we don't have a place to live?" Roughly half of the participants echoed her opinion. Annie also said, "I got tired of waiting on the phone for hours for the intake. I called back so many times that eventually I just gave up." Claire cancelled her application when she found out that her parents would be contacted. "I was really worried they [parents] would find out where I am or share my information with them. I just want to be left alone. I'll make money another way. I can always pan or sell my art." Michelle was told that she would have to go back to her old high school, but she protested, "I just can't go back there. I was cutting class all the time and hiding out in the bathroom. I had no friends. I felt like I was suffocating." Like many other youth, she eventually decided to try the alternative school in a drop-in centre so as to be eligible for social assistance. Many youth did not apply for social assistance because they did not want to be forced to go back to school or told what to do by a social assistance worker, nor did they want to be dependent on the welfare system. Only 15 percent of O'Grady and Gaetz's (2009: 9) sample relied on social assistance, which "reflects the barriers to obtaining and maintaining such benefits for people who are young, out of school and without shelter." Only four participants in Sue-Ann's study were successful in obtaining social assistance at sixteen or seventeen years of age. More participants were able to access income assistance once they turned eighteen or had children to care for.

OBSTACLES TO ACCESSING SAFE HOUSING

Unfortunately, youth identified just as many problems with the different kinds of housing systems. Supportive and affordable housing systems, as well as the private housing market, posed many barriers to access or involved too many constraints to be considered appealing. Olivia had applied for a room in supportive housing, but she needed to prove to the housing provider and Ontario Works that she had already attended school for two weeks. For Olivia, who had been homeless for roughly two years and had not attended secondary school in as much time, meeting this requirement was simply not realistic. Supportive housing was also perceived by several youth as imposing too many rules, such as curfews and bans on overnight guests, pets, and alcohol and drugs.

Many youth also described the immense difficulties they encountered trying to access the private housing market. With long waiting lists for public housing (five to ten years at the time), many youth searched aimlessly for private housing, with little success. Without a prior rental history, renting a private room or an apartment was an insurmountable challenge for most, compounded by landlords' common misconception that they could not rent to individuals under eighteen. When youth made rental inquiries, they were frequently told that they needed someone to co-sign the lease.

Sadie (age seventeen) was a college student with a two-year-old son and lived at the shelter. She explained that she had been apartment hunting for the past eight months. She was repeatedly told by prospective landlords that in order to rent an apartment, she had to be eighteen years old or have someone co-sign the lease. When she reluctantly applied for subsidized housing, however, she was informed that she was eligible to rent an apartment despite her age. To make matters worse, Sadie was routinely denied assistance from Ontario Works because she had not yet found an apartment. Homeless youth her age were often caught in this ridiculous situation: unable to find a place to live because landlords refused to rent to them, and ineligible for income assistance because they could not find a place to live.

When youth did find a landlord who would rent to them, the housing was often substandard and precarious. Tyler revealed that he had recently rented an apartment in a more dangerous part of town and was only able to do so because he gave the landlord $1,200 in cash upfront. "The landlord told me 'you look a little young,' but after I flashed him the $1,200 he went to get the keys." The apartment did not last long, however, as Tyler subsequently spent his money on crack and defaulted on his rent payment. Many youth like Tyler wound up renting apartments in more dangerous parts of town with limited rental security. They were often evicted from these apartments, and many were uninformed of their rights as tenants.

Informal rental arrangements are often the only means street youth have of breaking into the rental market. The downsides to this type of housing are significant: their tenancy is often insecure and subject to the whims of the landlord, and the places tend to be located in more dangerous areas of the city, particularly in rooming houses where younger people are vulnerable to sexual victimization, sex work, or rampant drug use. Similarly, Krüsi and colleagues (Krüsi, Fast, Small, Wood, and Kerr 2010) found that landlords would typically not rent to youth who are on welfare, and the only other option available to youth were single-room occupancies (such as those found in rooming houses), often viewed as an undesirable option by youth because they are considered a last resort and occupied mostly by older, typically male, adults.

Daniel revealed that once he moved to his father's place in the city, he began partying, drinking, and using ecstasy. He stopped going to his classes and his father kicked him out "to teach me a lesson but then I just dropped out of school." Eventually, Daniel rented a room in a rooming house that he described as a "big setup":

> *Everyone in this rooming house was doing crack. I mean, the dealer lived in the building and he knew when it was cheque day [when people receive their social assistance cheques]. You wouldn't even see your money, it would just be handed over to the crack dealer…. There was no way you were going to pay the rent or stay clean.*

Daniel admitted that he spent all his money on crack, was evicted, and ended up in the shelter. He described how the most accessible places for sixteen- and seventeen-year-olds were located in rooming houses, where the most danger lurked. He explained that not only did these places serve as gateways into harder and more addictive drugs, but the level of violence and criminality (theft, sex work, drug dealing) was such that the tenant never felt safe.

Another major obstacle for youth trying to access housing in the private market was the cost. Research points to a number of housing-related reasons for increases in homelessness: discrimination by landlords, low incomes that render housing difficult to access and maintain, and low vacancy rates (Aubry et al. 2007; Falvo 2016). Rents have continued to rise, and renters thus spend more on housing than they can afford or is generally considered acceptable. Several youth in our study did manage to secure a place but always beyond what they could reasonably afford. As a result, they would let several friends stay with them to split the rent, but this overcrowding often led to eviction. Results from Aubry et al.'s study (2007: 8) indicate similar findings: youth who could not afford market rents and were forced to share accommodation were particularly vulnerable to losing housing because of conflicts with roommates. Ingrid revealed that a one-bedroom apartment that she had rented with her boyfriend soon housed eight people. They were spending most of their money on drugs and were being evicted at the end of the month. Despite having paid the rent for the month, she and her boyfriend were no longer living there because there was no privacy and the place was constantly being burglarized.

Even youth who were not looking for housing had to exercise creativity in order to access a bed in a shelter, because shelter options for sixteen- and seventeen-year-olds are limited (to one shelter for young women and one shelter for young men). Chris described how he had been barred from the only young men's shelter because of racial slurs he had used around staff members. As he was only seventeen years old, he had to lie about his age to stay at another shelter, which required clients to be eighteen years old. "I told them I was twenty-one. I have no ID so they couldn't check. I told them I just came up from Montreal and had my ID stolen." Chris also tried to rent a room in a rooming house with his friend. They told the landlord that they would split the cost but the landlord would not consent, stating "one room to one person." Without ID or a source of income, "no landlord would look at me," said Chris.

Structural factors intertwine with symbolic ones, such as social stigma and discrimination, creating a double barrier to young people's efforts to access resources. Youth felt discriminated against because their appearance was associated with deviance or marginality, which carries a social stigma. Appearing to strongly identify with goth or street culture (e.g., dark clothes; piercings; body markings, alterations, or tattoos; dreadlocks; hair dyes) or being transgender decreased their chances of breaking into the housing and labour markets. Many youth would purposely tone down their image by dyeing their hair a uniform colour, removing piercings or gages (earlobe-stretching ornaments), or dressing in a gender-conforming manner. Their perception was that they had to transform themselves into more "presentable" people by projecting a more responsible image.

ACCESSING ADULT SHELTERS

There is some overlap of clientele between adult and youth shelters, since adult shelters will accept young people who are age eighteen or over, and youth shelters will accept young people up until the age of twenty-one. Ten of the twenty-four young people Benjamin interviewed mentioned a previous stay in an adult shelter in Ottawa, and a few had spent several months to more than a year in adult shelters. With the exception of two young people who had stayed in adult shelters and did not mind the experience, every other young person who mentioned adult shelters was apprehensive. Young people conveyed fears about interacting with older people who were homeless, particularly those with mental health disorders or those heavily addicted to substances, since they were perceived as unpredictable and dangerous.

In youth focus groups, four young people shared the following experiences about adult shelters. One young person said, "I'm only eighteen, and these are like fifty-, eighty-year-old guys.... They're aggressive, they're dangerous. I've had people put knives to my throat." Similarly, another shared, "They smashed coffee cups and held it to my throat." And another young person added, "You get robbed when you go to the [adult shelter] too. They go through all your shit, even the staff." One young woman reported that she almost stepped on a needle in the shower and was frightened that she could have been infected with a disease.

When discussing adult shelters, young people talked about fighting, drug dealing, police interactions, and the overall sentiment that adult shelters were unsafe and frightening places where they did not want to be. Three young people even indicated that they would rather sleep outside than in an adult shelter. This fear of adult shelters and the negative experiences that some young people have had appeared to lead to a greater appreciation of the youth services and youth shelters offered in the city. The young people expressed gratitude that there were youth shelters that were accessible to them. A few young people also cited adult shelters as a motivator to get off the streets, since they did not want to age into using adult services.

NEGOTIATING WITH SERVICE PROVIDERS IN YOUTH SHELTERS

The young people in Benjamin's study conveyed that the youth shelters made them feel safer than other alternatives such as sleeping rough or spending time in adult shelters. The overall sentiment expressed by young people was that the majority of service providers in the youth shelters were caring and understanding most of the time. Chad (age seventeen) found the service providers in the shelter helped him deal with his emotions when he found out that his ex-girlfriend was pregnant and continued drinking and using drugs. "I was like ... this girl is killing my kid. And they were able to sit down and have a conversation about how I was feeling and like ... things I could do instead of going out and getting high." Without parents to provide mentoring through difficult circumstances, youth may find adult service providers offer a listening ear away from the drama that might be going on with peers on the streets:

With the staff, you can have a connection with someone who's not on the street, like someone who actually cares and knows what you're going through but isn't living it with you. So you can talk about it, and you know it's not bringing them down, because it's not adding to the drama that they have on the street ... a safe place to talk. 'Cause ... I know guys who ... they won't cry on the street, but they'll cry at the shelter. So you're like ... alright, you know? People just got respect there. Just having people to talk to makes it so much easier, because that way you're not stuck in your own head all the time.

Residential programs for young people, as well as adults, involve a set of expectations for clients that are governed by agency policies and legislative requirements. They are generally funded on a per diem basis, and young people entering a youth shelter are stepping into a pre-existing structure where adults are paid to provide supervision and supports, in addition to ensuring the safety of all residents. In the delivery of services, it is inevitable that some conflict will arise, since people may have different perspectives on many of the daily decisions that need to be made. Some residential programs for young people may be characterized by rigid environments that prioritize the decisions of adults, while other environments seek to be client-centred and try to adopt a flexible case-by-case approach tailored to the strengths and abilities of youth to ensure they all have opportunities to succeed (see Finlay 2007; Kalke, Glanton, and Cristalli 2007; Roebuck and Roebuck 2013; Whittaker 2000). In either case, young people are often in a position where they feel they must self-advocate in order to have their needs met. In the interviews, young people and service providers identified the three primary aspects of the shelter environment that are most commonly negotiated:

1) the requirement to return by curfew or risk losing the shelter bed,
2) the requirement to participate in chores at the shelter, and
3) the requirement to leave the shelter during business hours.

Curfew is one of the policies that has the most direct impact on the trajectories of young people who are homeless, and more study of this area would be valuable. Young people staying at a youth shelter are required to return to the shelter by a set curfew or they will lose their bed. This is a common practice in services for people who are homeless and is related to both the desire to provide services as well as the vested interests of the agency.

From a service delivery standpoint, having an empty bed when there are so many people who need shelter is unacceptable. From an agency standpoint, shelters are generally funded on a per diem basis, and shelters that function at maximum capacity will receive more government funding for services. Statistics on occupancy are also a powerful advocacy tool for demonstrating the usefulness and need for the service, which helps to ensure the continued operation of the shelter.

Chores are also mandatory at shelters, and youth who refuse to participate will lose their beds. From a service delivery standpoint, chores are a way for young people to give back to the shelter and to contribute to the environment where they are staying. They are also framed as a form of life skills training, since many of the young people in a shelter may be learning to live independently for the first time and need to learn how to care for their property. Cheryl (service provider) indicated that young people who participate in the care of the facility develop ownership and pride for the building, which she believed was demonstrated through the cleanliness and lack of vandalism at the shelter. From an agency standpoint, this work also reduces the burden on staff to care for the facility and saves on the costs of cleaning staff.

Finally, day access to the shelter is another area of negotiation for youth and service providers. When the morning comes, young people are asked to leave the shelter for the day and to return again in the early evening. Cheryl (service provider) explained that in the past the shelter she worked at was available to young people 24/7, but a significant number of young people would stay during the day rather than attend school or look for housing or employment. Now the policy requires young people to leave the shelter and spend the day "working on their goals," according to Cheryl. Since the agency also provides a drop-in centre, in addition to another youth drop-in centre serving the same clientele in the city, young people who prefer not to "pursue goals" still have access to a safe place to spend time and access many resources. The limited day access policy also allows the agency to reduce their staffing needs during the day and avoid a duplication of services, since the youth shelters provide similar services to the drop-in centre, which is funded through the same agency.

These three policies generated a lot discussion with young people and service providers, and people shared mixed opinions about the effectiveness of these approaches. In the focus group with young men, one young person indicated that he was proud that he had been able to respect curfew, and that it reflected one of the important decisions that young people have to make on the street. When Benjamin asked the question, "Is there anything else that you think I should know about the decisions you have to make when you're young and when you're homeless?", the young man responded:

> *Are you or are you not going to make curfew at shelters? That's the main thing. Nobody ever makes curfew, man. When I got here, I stayed in the shelter for only two and a half months before I got transitional.... Never once missed curfew. That's what saved me. Dang. Would you rather have a warm place to sleep or get drunk? 'Cause that shit can happen any day.... If you miss curfew, you lose your bed. You're not allowed to go back there until there's another bed, and in the winter time it's so hard to get another bed.*

This young man's comments reflected his view that meeting curfew was his choice to make, and that he was choosing to prioritize shelter over other things that he could have been doing with his time. While she does not question this policy, Kristin (age eighteen) felt that the policies around curfew and chores had negatively affected one of her friends who was also homeless:

> *If you mess up, you're back on the streets again. And they're strict. And if you're living on the streets, you're not used to having curfew. You're not used to having to do chores, 'cause you have no chores to do. You're not about to wander around and be told, 'Okay. You don't get food 'til you clean up the block.' That doesn't happen. You're used to not having food, so ... you try ... but then she gets told that if she screws up on something one too many times she has to spend three days out on the street. You're not helping her by saying, 'Okay. Get out.' You know? That's not helping her, but that's what they do every time. And where do you go from there? Back to phase one.*

These two comments show the contrast that we saw in response to shelter rules; some youth felt that the rules were a reasonable exchange for accommodation, while others felt the rules were rigid and could introduce harm to young people. The dangers of losing a bed are most pronounced for shelter residents who are sixteen or seventeen years old and therefore not old enough to access adult shelters. Some of the young people in the focus groups felt that it was unreasonable to be expected to consistently return before curfew and that the policy interfered with their social lives and connections with their peers.

Youth shelter polices are clearly documented and articulated to young people at intake; however, in practice they are frequently negotiated, and to some extent, service providers may encourage negotiation. Yanick, a service provider, explained that negotiation is an expected part of providing services, and that this informal expectation is also communicated to shelter residents:

> *Extended curfews, staying in the morning because they're not feeling well, accessing [the shelter] during the day for X, Y, Z reason…. I think that's a message that all staff give out to youth, "Negotiate it, and maybe we can work with it on an individual [basis], depending on what the negotiation is." We'll have a youth who says, "I really need to be on a computer and not disturbed to do housing research. Can I stay today?" Well, we'll meet as a team, we'll review that and see what the rationales are, and then it's rare that we'd say, "No, you can't do housing research today." But we'll also give them other resources to access that. So it's day to day.*

The young people in Benjamin's study shared that service providers were generally accommodating and respectful and that it was often possible to negotiate flexibility in the delivery of services. However, they also recognized that their own attitude had a role to play in the negotiation. Chad (age seventeen) and Jake (age nineteen) both spoke about times when they were able to achieve some flexibility based on how they approached the issue. Chad talked about how the youth also had to act respectfully in order to be given respect and accommodation by the staff:

> *So if you're nice with the staff, they're nice with you, right? Do your chores and it's good. But if you have a bad day, and you know the staff well, and you talk with them, you can get a day off chores. Let's say you flip out on somebody in the shelter, right? Like you give them beef for something. If you go talk to the staff about it, you can save your ass from getting kicked out. You just have to build relationships with them.*

Jake found that he needed to negotiate more sensitive matters with service providers that related to his personal sense of safety. When he first arrived at the youth shelter, he described himself as being in a "paranoid state from homelessness," convinced that he would be assaulted or get into trouble in the shelter in a way that would spill over into the streets during the day. During intake, Jake disclosed that he was carrying pepper spray for self-protection, and the service providers explained that they would have to take it while he was in the shelter. While this initially made him feel anxious, after he was given a tour of the residence and a description of the services, he was able to feel calmer and "pretty cool." Once he settled into his room, he was bothered by the policy allowing service providers to conduct room checks at night when deemed necessary. Jake was very upset that someone may come to his room at night, and he always propped something against his door so that it would fall and alert him if someone entered his room. Jake's fear was linked to his history of sexual abuse while in the care of Children's Aid Society, which frequently occurred at night while he was in bed, and the resulting trauma response of chronic bed-wetting. After five days, he finally brought his concern to the attention of staff:

> About the fifth day of being there, I said, "This is crazy, you guys aren't going to come into my room anymore." They reassured me that only staff had the key … but it was other issues. It was issues from being in the group home. I was always wetting my bed. So how do I explain that to a kid if I'm always doing my laundry, and like … even the staff. I didn't want certain staff knowing that, and I knew it would get back to the kids. So at the end of the day, I had to sit down with the staff and say, "Look, this is what's going on. I need help." And I got help, you know? Then I started advocating for myself.

Jake found the service providers open and receptive to his concerns, and together they developed a plan that worked to put Jake at ease. This successful negotiation helped build his confidence to engage in further self-advocacy and to "not take no for an answer."

While the ability to negotiate with service providers was validated by many young people, Jean-Olivier (age twenty) suggested that it could be challenging for service providers to deal with all of the youth effectively, and sometimes they let their frustration get in the way of positive service delivery:

> You get a lot of angry kids that are just like, "Fuck all of you, I don't

*want to do chores." … Just a lot of attitude. But a lot of staff, they
take it in, and … they're angry. And that's the kind of staff that if
[they] come to me and ask me to do chores, and I'm not in a good
mood, and I say "No," [they're] going to give me attitude over it.
Whereas other staff, they don't let it get to them. So I think staff
need to work on that. I really do. It's a learning thing, you learn
from every situation.*

Since Jean-Olivier had experienced relatively long-term homelessness and
serious mental health complications, it was inevitable that his motivation
would be low some days, affecting his choices about participating in chores.
While a service provider's occasional frustration may be understandable, it
is important to remember that youth may be dealing with significant hard-
ships that could affect their motivation.

Christine (age twenty-one) experienced a strong internal reaction to the
stigma of homelessness when she was first on the street, and this appears to
have been reinforced through her interactions with service providers. Once
she became homeless, she felt out of place and like she did not belong in
public spaces. She linked her feeling of stigma with the vulnerable position
of needing to ask for things in the youth shelter where she had a brief stay:

*Because when I was homeless, I mean, the way that people looked
at me and talked to me was … horrible. And I was like, are you
serious? I'm just like you. I'm just here temporarily, and I guess you
don't know that. But I mean … this is crazy, the way they talk to
you. Like even the staff … you know, you feel like you're talking to
a prison guard or something. Like you have to ask them things. …
It's a very incarcerating feeling.*

Christine felt that having to negotiate with service providers to meet her
needs was disempowering. This feeling could be linked to her age, since she
was at the upper age threshold for accessing youth services and had had a
greater degree of autonomy prior to experiencing homelessness. Being in the
shelter environment made her feel that many of her freedoms were taken
away and her behaviour was monitored. When Bryce (age eighteen) received
notice that he would be evicted from the [transitional housing program], he
made an effort to extend his stay by obtaining an "intent to rent" form for
a property that he did not intend to rent. When we spoke, he was hopeful

that if he showed service providers that he was likely to move into a new property in a month, they would allow him to extend his stay at the shelter for at least the month of January, which would keep him off the streets in winter and give him more time to make a plan. Bryce and Christine both felt that it was difficult to connect with staff and advocate for their needs, with Bryce inventing a creative solution to extend his stay in housing.

From the youth perspective, negotiating on a case-by-case basis allows for flexibility and tailored programming that is beneficial to the changing needs of young people. However, this approach also relies on constant interaction, and, as highlighted by Chad (age seventeen) and Jean-Olivier (age twenty), it can be highly influenced by the relationship between young people and service providers. Overall, many young people felt that service providers in the shelters were approachable and adaptable in their delivery of services, with some young people raising concerns about how service providers responded to young people who resisted the shelter rules.

In Sue-Ann's study, youth frequently aired their discontent with services. Francis (age sixteen) believed that he was treated differently by frontline workers, in particular shelter workers and drop-in staff, because of his young age. He said these workers often treated him "as less than an adult" and that "sometimes they don't realize that maybe youth can think on the same level." In his words, "Sometimes they forget that youth may be just as able to make competent decisions as an adult." At least half of the group in Sue-Ann's research echoed these sentiments. They felt that they were not spoken to or treated as adults would be and were instead seen as vulnerable and requiring protection ("at-risk") or more drawn to deviant acts and requiring close monitoring. Lucchini (1996) found that as they aged, street children were seen less as victims and more as delinquents. This shift in perceptions over time was certainly true of youth perceptions in our research, as youth felt that the younger they were, the more likely they were to be perceived as vulnerable. This image was not always disadvantageous, however, as many youth described using this social representation of vulnerability to their benefit. Several youth admitted to playing up their young age and using their charm in order to obtain the services and materials they needed.

NAVIGATING ADDITIONAL SERVICES

Because the youth shelters are located within a larger multi-service agency that includes a drop-in centre as well as multiple mental health, drug treatment, and resource programs, the young people in Benjamin's study reported that the services they needed were accessible, and many had chosen to use these additional supports. Jake (age nineteen) accessed counselling and was very impressed with the broad range of services available. He said, "I think that the individual counselling that I've received has actually made me a stronger person. They offer food, you can do your laundry, they have a health clinic, the dentist, the services are never-ending." Similarly, Pete (age eighteen) became connected with a treatment group for young people with concurrent disorders, which he experienced as very positive. He felt that it was a positive space where he was celebrated for working towards his goals, and he contrasted this with some of the negative feedback he had been receiving from other sources in his life:

> I just feel a sense of accomplishment … 'cause most of the time I was told that I wasn't doing anything right in my life, and that I was starting to be a fuck-up. And as soon as I get there, it's more like … you get this kind of warm feeling. It's like, "Wow, I'm actually being recognized for doing this. This feels good." It's a positive space to share your stories and get feedback from everybody else. Those people are actually doing stuff with their lives and moving forward, and they want to share with people how they did it and how good they feel about it.

While many young people in Benjamin's study shared similar stories of becoming connected with additional services within the agency, one story highlighted the importance of accessible services for young people who may not be motivated to seek out supports on their own. Prior to his stay in a youth shelter, Dustin (age sixteen) had mugged people on the street and robbed pharmacies for money to purchase drugs and basic necessities. This changed when a representative from the provincial agency responsible for social assistance visited the youth shelter:

> It's weird. When I was at the shelter, I just woke up one day, and this girl from welfare comes in, and that day I was signed up. I

never even thought maybe I should apply for welfare ... nothing like that. She just came, and she's like, "Okay, you'll be getting your cheque next month. Just make sure you go to school." I was like, "Sweet." Now I get my welfare check, and I haven't done it.... I haven't robbed anybody in like a month. I've just been living off my welfare, and whatever money I get, I'm happy to get it, and that's about it. Because before, I was literally a kid with absolutely no income who wanted to use drugs. So now I have some legal way to pay for it. I'm not trying to get arrested and screw everything up for something that I can pay for legally.

Dustin indicated that he would not have considered seeking out social assistance on his own, but since the opportunity was presented to him at the youth shelter, he was glad to be enrolled. While he admitted that he used the money to purchase illegal drugs, he was happy to finally have a legal source of income. Even so, his hiatus from committing robbery was fragile. Dustin admitted,

If something were to happen.... That's what I know. That's how I know how to get money, so you never know. I don't want to, but some people are used to working in law firms, some people are used to working at Dollarama, I'm just used to [robbery]. That's how I know how to get money.

Dustin's rationale for committing robbery suggested that his abstinence from crime was not the result of a cognitive shift but rather because his needs were met through services provided by the shelter.

Navigating Structural Obstacles

One of the most important findings drawn from the young people's narratives are that structural barriers pose enormous obstacles to getting off the streets, and that these are particularly acute for young people under eighteen who cannot access adult services. These constraints often push youth to make "dangerous" choices (e.g., renting a room in a rooming house, working under the table) that may lead to exploitation or poor health. While there is a tendency to view this younger cohort as vulnerable and requiring protection, there is also a lack of resources serving this population, especially since they are denied access to adult services such as social assistance, shelters, housing and labour markets, and addictions services. Several participants revealed that the social assistance system for sixteen- and seventeen-year-olds was too onerous and impossible to obtain, so they did not even apply, though this stands in contrast to Dustin's experience.

Housing systems represent another hurdle for this age group. While there are some affordable social housing units, there are not enough to meet the demand, nor is there enough choice. The private housing market poses many barriers for youth because of landlords' lack of knowledge of tenant rights and age criteria, or discrimination against youth based on their age and association with the streets. These factors push youth into arguably dangerous places to rent (e.g., rooming houses) and precarious rental arrangements. Youth were often unaware of their tenancy rights and were frequently exploited or evicted without just cause.

Young people's ability to subsist on the streets was greatly affected by structural constraints and symbolic barriers, and was further reinforced by discrimination they encountered because of their association with street life. The limitations imposed by the welfare system, supportive housing, and shelters forced many youth to find creative strategies to survive, and generally pushed them into more dangerous high-risk contexts. This creation of risk by the very institutions that exist to help marginalized homeless youth is a phenomenon that adds complexity to how they navigate through homelessness (see Nichols 2014). The gaps and structural constraints created by the service sector itself, particularly for sixteen- and seventeen-year-old youth, who do not have access to the same resources as adults and are not allowed the same autonomy as adults to make decisions about their well-being, need to be considered as potential risk factors for the "at-risk" youth they serve.

Acknowledging the potential for service agencies to cause harm to their clients, and despite the negative comments made about experiences with specific policies and service providers, the majority of youth in Benjamin's study expressed some degree of gratitude for the services provided through youth agencies. It is clear that a large number of youth value these services, and many young people expressed an interest in working in service provider roles in the future because of the help they had received. And while the one-stop shop or continuum of services models can be extremely useful to connect youth with necessary resources, this can also pose an obstacle to youth who have had a poor experience within the agency or have been barred from services. But young people are not merely passive recipients of these services, instead demonstrating their agency in active negotiation with service providers to get what they believe they need to be healthy.

Youth spoke of many failures of the system: ineligibility for income assistance; inability to rent an apartment due to poor, non-existent, or irregular incomes; the lack of safe and affordable housing; discrimination by landlords based on appearances or the mistaken belief that renters have to be eighteen years of age; and the lack of choice in the shelter system. All of these factors combine to place homeless youth at increased risk for victimization by pushing them into precarious rental agreements (if they can access them), often in dangerous areas (e.g, rooming houses because that is all they can afford). Youth are forced to manipulate systems to their advantage, as when Chris lied about his age in order to access the adult shelter system. It pushes these younger and arguably more vulnerable individuals into adult systems, in which there might be greater opportunities for exploitation and victimization. Homeless youth described the creative strategies they employed and the risks they took in order to manage life on the streets, precisely because social safety nets did not respond to their needs.

These findings are but a starting point for an examination of the structural and symbolic constraints that exacerbate a climate of risk-taking and inadvertently encourage youth creativity, adaptability, and resilience in their efforts to survive or get off the streets.

8. POSITIVE ADAPTATION IN ADVERSITY

It changes you. You become a lot smarter. You're not an idiot. If you left home an idiot, you're going to go back home a smart mother-fucker....You're gonna know what you did to end up homeless was fucking stupid. You're young, you shouldn't be homeless at this age, you should be doing the right stuff to get your life done. I used to be an off-the-wall little fuckin' maniac. Now ... now I'm calm, I've got actual friends, I've got people that care about me, and I know that. I didn't know that when I was younger, and now I do. So I.... It might not even be actually being homeless, it could just be aging.... You're not a fuckin' stupid little child anymore, but it could be.... I'm pretty sure it is being homeless, man, 'cause I know that I wouldn't be like this right now if I wasn't homeless at some point.

A central theme that emerged in our work with young people was that experiencing homelessness can bring about a large number of personal changes. When this simple question was asked, "I've been hearing from other young people that experiencing homelessness can change you. Is this true for you?" a resounding and almost knowing "Yes" echoed back, as if there was some sense of shared experience that young people gathered through homelessness. The responses to this question were surprising because young

Note: Parts of this chapter originally appeared in B. Roebuck and M. Roebuck (2016), "The strengths of young people who are homeless," *Canadian Journal of Community Mental Health*, 35, 2: 43–54.

people frequently described these changes as positive. Some young people did mention changes that they perceived to be negative, such as becoming more "pissy" (Dustin, age sixteen) or further involved in drugs and criminal behaviour, which was a relatively common experience, as described previously. However, and somewhat surprisingly, almost all of the young people in Benjamin's study volunteered the perspective that homelessness had triggered some degree of personal growth.

Literature on youth homelessness frequently highlights the risk factors and high social costs of homelessness; however, like any crisis, homelessness has the potential to bring out the worst and the best in people. Young people living on the street may begin to develop new strengths that relate to management of their environment or overall life maturing, and these valuable resources help them navigate and negotiate their surroundings, often becoming the building blocks to exiting the streets. These positive developments have begun to be captured by researchers, but there is room for the development of a more strength-based research agenda (see Bender et al. 2007; Kidd and Davidson 2007; Lankenau, Clatts, Welle, Goldsamt, and Gwadz 2005).

Understanding how young people develop strengths through their experiences of homelessness is central to understanding the process of resilience: what are the strengths that young people develop on the streets, and how do they manage to grow despite facing adversity? Service providers and young people in this study seemed to believe that young people with more internal and external resources navigate out of homelessness faster than those without these resources, but they also acknowledged that homelessness provides a steep learning curve, during which young people are constantly trying new things, facing new challenges, and learning from the outcomes. In the words of Max (age twenty) and Aaron (age twenty-three), "What doesn't kill you makes you stronger."

VISIBLE STRENGTHS

Based on Rawana and Brownlee's (2009) notion that strengths are competencies and characteristics that people develop throughout their lives, it is possible that adversity may provide a training environment for existing strengths to be practised and further developed. A number of distinct visible strengths were identified in this research by young people and service providers, which we have grouped into the following categories: street smarts, life skills, and attitudes.

Street Smarts

It was common for young people and service providers to refer to street smarts as one of the things that young people developed because of homelessness. This term seems to be common in the homelessness sector, since it is used frequently by people with lived experience, service providers, and academics (see Bender et al. 2007; Kidd and Davidson 2007; Lanekau et al. 2005). It is not easily defined; the common attributes that were described as street smarts were "smartening up" and "avoiding drama."

"Smartening Up"

Jay (age seventeen) first experienced homelessness at the age of fourteen after a series of family conflicts and out-of-home group home placements. He described himself as a naïve kid out on the streets at the beginning; he was scared and did not know where to go. However, the time spent on the streets over the past several years helped him to develop street smarts and to be motivated to take steps to sort out his life, such as working towards completing high school.

In this personal reflection, Jay considered whether the changes that he experienced in his life were related to aging or homelessness, and chose to believe that he had matured because of homelessness rather than the simple maturing that comes from age. He reflected on what he had learned, indicating that he was not alone and that people cared for him. This was further expanded in his discussion of getting to know people because of homelessness. Jake (age nineteen) and Aaron (age twenty-three) also shared the perspective that homelessness had helped them to "smarten up," with Jake sharing that he had learned to consider his choices more carefully, and Aaron explaining that he had calmed down and could now make plans to proactively create the type of future that he wanted.

"Avoiding Drama"

As has been illustrated in earlier chapters, street life drama can be volatile, and there are frequent conflicts between different groups of young people on the streets. Several of the young people we interviewed and interacted with explained that it is important not to anger other youth on the streets, because if they come after you, they may have a whole group with them. Before becoming homeless, Chad (age seventeen) had been caught in a cycle of gang violence, but now that he was homeless in a different city and no longer aligned with a gang, he chose to avoid drama and tried to calm down when he was insulted. He explained that when he was younger, he was also very emotional and highly reactive. He said, "I find since I've been on the street, I'm not as violent." Chad also tried to "lay low" by choosing friends "who do their own thing and avoid all the drama." He explained, "Basically, just try and avoid confrontation at all costs, like … don't piss anybody off, just keep your mouth shut real good. Avoid … certain people who you know don't like you, and make sure you stay friends with the right people."

Avoidance of drama often encouraged the development of a skill, that of hypervigilance, commonplace among trauma survivors who have had to survive within contexts of adversity and active threats (Herman 1992).

Life Skills

Young people living on the streets become fully responsible for managing their own lives, without the support and assistance of parents. At times, this can be challenging. One young person reported that once she became homeless, she lost the will to care for her hygiene and did not bother with brushing her teeth. However, many of the young people that we met were very active in caring for their health, making doctor appointments, visiting drop-in health care services, and using the laundry services at the drop-in or in the shelters to clean their clothes.

Young people who are homeless become responsible for managing their health and their budgets, paying cell phone bills, doing laundry, and searching for employment and housing — and many are struggling to succeed in school at the same time. Service providers and young people shared the view that young people on the streets are developing much more advanced skills in this area than young people who are living at home, where parents may still take care of most of the responsibilities. "Kids at home are learning different things. Kids on their own, or on the streets, or in shelters are learning a lot of things on their own, problem-solving … that sort of thing. But kids at home are getting other sorts of skills and supports," said Lisette, a service provider.

This perspective highlights that young people who are homeless are learning independently and are constantly engaged in problem-solving. As stated previously, homelessness provides a steep learning curve, and to survive, young people need to quickly develop a wide range of skills. While many of the young people we interviewed appeared to have developed independence and self-reliance, many felt torn about the level of responsibility they had to manage, arguing that it came with a heavy cost. Paul (age nineteen) said, "So I learned to become independent. I never really had a childhood. I had to be grown up all the time." And Kristin (age eighteen) grieved, "The fact that we as eighteen-year-olds, sixteen-year-olds, fifteen-year-olds, fourteen-year-olds, have to pick ourselves up and carry ourselves as thirty-year-olds to be able to get anywhere in life does not help, because that's our whole childhood gone. You don't get to be a kid again. And when you do, if you do ... you get judged obviously, because it's not right." Aaron (age twenty-three) felt quite differently about the skills he had developed while homeless:

> *Homelessness is actually ... not a gift, but it'll make you learn more about yourself than anything, because ... if you're homeless and you're trying to do it all for yourself, you're actually building character, you're building your motivation ... I see it in myself.... Being on the streets, it actually built up skills I wouldn't have learned in a home, having my brother help me out with everything.*

Young people who are homeless experience the weight of responsibilities that are typically reserved for adults in Western society, and while they often learn to manage these roles, it can be a bittersweet experience. Hagan and McCarthy (2005) validate the tension in the lives of young people transitioning to adulthood in the context of homelessness, pointing out that young people who are homeless generally have challenges meeting the goals that typically signify the end of adolescence, such as completing high school, enrolling in college or university, and entering full-time employment. At the same time, young people who are homeless may become responsible for other roles typically reserved for adults "before they acquire the skills, credentials, experiences, psychological resources, connections, social support, and other assets that increase the likelihood of success" (Hagan and McCarthy 2005: 178). In our research, young people appeared to feel torn between feelings of pride that they were able to take responsibility for their own lives, and a sense of grief over the perceived need to grow up too quickly.

The fast-track to self-reliance that young people experience because of homelessness appears to spark some forms of personal growth, but it also increases vulnerability and exposure to harm. For this reason, Karabanow (2004) cautions about glorifying the positive traits that young people may develop through homelessness at the expense of recognizing the harms. Here, we attempt to provide a balanced discussion that recognizes the adversity that young people experience connected to homelessness and also explores the strengths and resilience that can emerge in parallel.

Attitudes

Other strengths young people reported related to their attitude towards circumstances and how their attitude may have shifted throughout their experiences of homelessness. These attitudes appeared to help young people stay motivated and tackle obstacles in their lives.

Gratitude

Several young people explained that their experience of homelessness had caused them to feel more gratitude for the good things in their lives, and that experiencing gratitude was a personal strength that helped them to deal with their challenging circumstances. For Jake (age nineteen), gratitude was sparked as a reflection on what he had taken away from the challenges of homelessness. "I think that my experience has made me a lot stronger in areas that normally I wouldn't be if I didn't experience some of the stuff that I have. So I'm very grateful, l guess, for some of the situations that I've been in.... I've learned." Pete (age eighteen) found that his nights sleeping outside made him feel grateful:

> We'd be out at Britannia Beach, and we'd sleep out on the rocks at the beach there. You kind of get those moments ... like when you're camping, and it's quiet out and you see the stars in the sky.... You're just appreciative for waking up the next morning and actually having something in your stomach, or just ... cigarettes, or different people beside you. It's another wide eye-opening experience to have to live with that and deal with that for six months.

For Thomas (age nineteen), cultivating an attitude of thankfulness was a deliberate strategy for countering feelings of anger and frustration:

When something wrong happens and I get mad, I think positive … because I wake up and I can do everything: I can speak, I can see, I can feel, I can touch, I can move, I can walk. So those little things that happen in the day will be little compared with the huge things that I have. I am grateful for everything that I have, and I don't think about what I don't have.

During the focus groups, service providers eagerly validated that young people who are homeless often express gratitude. This was seen in expressions of thankfulness for the resources provided in youth shelters and drop-in centres, and in thank-you notes and personal expressions of thanks when young people received help or transitioned out of homelessness. Daryl, a service provider, also offered the perspective that experiencing homelessness seems to counter a culture of entitlement: "Youth struggling, going through homelessness, going through systems, trying to make it on their own…. I think it really breaks that down and gives them more respect for the things they do get, and they don't take things for granted as much."

Openness and Empathy for Others

In a similar way, several youth indicated they felt that experiencing homelessness helped them to better understand other people on the street and to express more openness and empathy. This phenomenon was typically described as a change resulting specifically from having lived the experience of homelessness. June (age eighteen) explained, "I think it's made me a little more open-minded. Like … I always think to myself … the thing I live by is be kind because everyone is fighting their own war." Similarly, Vince (age twenty) felt like living through homelessness softened his approach with people he did not know. He explained that prior to being homeless, he did not like talking to anyone apart from his closest friends, but homelessness had changed that: "After that I became more open talking to people … and I was giving them a chance. 'Cause I used to not like talking to anyone … not even a person on the street that would open the door for me, I wouldn't say thank you. So now it's funny that I'm a lot more polite and everything … more caring … 'cause I've lived it. Treat people the way you want to be treated." Chad (age seventeen) discussed how his experience has caused him to wonder about how other people ended up on the street:

> *But now, I see someone on the street, I'll actually think, "Why are you on the street? What did you go through? Like, why are you smoking crack? What are you trying to forget about?" I feel like I can relate more to people than before. 'Cause before when you're not living on the street ... like when you have a place to live and it's not that bad, you can turn a blind eye to everything else, but when you're on the street, you can't turn a blind eye to anything ... 'cause you're a part of it.*

Although judgment of peers continues in street life, service providers affirmed in the focus groups that young people on the streets and in drop-in centres develop a degree of respect and tolerance for people who are different from them. People from visibly different groups that would likely not associate in high school easily mix at the drop-in, connected by their common experience of homelessness and marginalization, although it should be also be noted that this is a supervised space, which can create a safer environment.

Minimizing Harm with Humour

In a focus group with service providers, Cassandra mentioned that she was amazed at how young people living with such difficult circumstances were able to minimize their challenges and find humour. She provided the following example:

> *One of them yesterday was putting on make-up before the evening, and says, "I'm brushing my hair. It's kind of hard to look good when you've been sleeping out on the street. Ha ha ha." And to me, it's like, wow, some other people would probably crumble, but these people kind of just see it as that's what they're facing right now, and then let's move on. I find that incredible.*

While humour can be a source of strength for some, other young people also acknowledged that they had lost their sense of humour when they became homeless, making fewer jokes and spending more time in a serious frame of mind.

Dreaming about a Better Future

The majority of young people talked at length about finding housing and finishing school. We were very interested to hear more about how young people thought about the future and what role these thoughts played in their lives. Thinking ahead seemed to be an important coping mechanism for many young people in difficult circumstances, and to some extent, this seemed to be linked with resilience. Jay (age seventeen) tried to think about where he was going, rather than dwelling on the past. "I try not to look back," he said. "I try to look towards the future and what I can do, and not what I have done." In this way, Jay chose not to spend his mental energy dwelling on his past experiences of abuse, or his limited opportunities in school, or his involvement in drug dealing, instead spending time considering the things that he had the power to accomplish such as getting into an alternative school to finish his high school education.

Thomas (age eighteen) held a more cautious view of the future and made an important distinction between the future and dreams. "I have a theory. There's future and there's dreams. The future, you don't know about it; dreams you know because you want it and you try to do it every day. So, I prefer my dreams than my future." As a trans person of colour born abroad, with no remaining family members, without educational qualifications, and now homeless in a new country, Thomas was very aware of the obstacles and potential discrimination that lay in his future. He found motivation by focusing on more holistic dreams. His primary dream, apart from a career, was to find companionship. "I just dream of a love for my life that I could trust, and it could be for all my life. That's it." Thomas did not need to be important or to have a big house; he just wanted to be loved.

Other young people had a number of material objectives in mind. Chad (age seventeen) had some very specific ideas about what he would like to achieve later in life. "I just want a cottage … a cottage and a motorcycle, and I'm good to go," he laughed. "I guess … and a house where I'm not in a bad part of town … but you know, just … have my cottage and my motorcycle. I'll have my car, be a mechanic…. I'm a happy man." In their study with forty-five homeless and street-involved youth at a youth drop-in centre, Foster and Spencer (2011) conducted narrative interviews where they asked young people about their past, present, and future. They found that while some young people discussed futures that were linked to their past and present (a "connected narrative"), many youth presented elaborate ideas or big dreams that would be difficult for anyone to achieve. At the same time, they found that young people had clear ideas about the type of future they wanted to avoid, and that virtually all of the young people they interviewed wanted to transition out of homelessness at some point. Many youth in their study indicated that in the future, they wanted to be able to have the money to get what they needed and what they wanted. While Foster and Spencer's article provides an excellent discussion of how young people think about their futures, the authors do not return to analyze the role that big dreams play in the lives of young people who are homeless, even though these seem to be so common. We would like to further explore "big dreams" here.

When Benjamin asked Chad (age seventeen) if he thought about his dreams often, Chad presented a very connected narrative despite having dreams that may appear unattainable:

> *Every day. It's what gets you through the day. Dreams is what gets you through that, 'cause like ... when you're staring down the barrel of a gun, all you're thinking is, "Man, I'm gonna fucking die right now," and you get sad 'cause you're like, "Man, I haven't accomplished shit." So you think of your dreams and you're like, "Man ... if I get through this, that's what I want.... I want out. I just want this, and I'm done." You know?"*

For Chad, dreams help him to stay motivated and to centre himself following traumatic aspects of street life. Dreams play a role in his day-to-day survival. Chad's narrative suggests that for some young people, the specific nature of their big dreams may not be as important as the role that the dreams play in their lives. In a focus group, Yvette, a service provider, shared a similar perspective:

> *They keep on dreaming. There's always a dream.... I think a lot of them picture themselves in different places at some point. It may be crappy right now, but eventually they know or they dream that they will be better, in a better place. So the time right now is really difficult, but yet, they still, in their minds, fantasize about when it will be better.*

We interviewed many young people who presented narratives that seemed to connect their past, present, and future. These young people appeared to be strategic thinkers — some had entered homelessness already considering strategies for exiting, and others had used the loneliness, isolation, and unstructured time they encountered during homelessness to contemplate the life that they wanted to live in the future, and the future they wished to avoid. Ella (age sixteen) explained the importance of taking the time to think things through to avoid becoming a homeless adult:

> So basically, you have to think if you want to live this life forever and end up at [an adult shelter], or if you want to do something about it and have a better life. 'Cause I don't think anyone would want to be stuck down here forever. Even if you talk to people in the adult shelters, you'll realize how most of them don't want to be there. They're just stuck there because some of them didn't get a proper education. Some of them, they can't get out of the city because of probation, or some of them just have bad drug addictions and they don't want to be, but they're stuck here. So that's why you've got to make those decisions when you're younger, so you don't have to end up like that ... just stuck.

Ella's belief about the aspects that contribute to long-term homelessness were evident in her decision-making in the present. She chose not to use drugs to avoid addiction, she was continuing her education in an alternative school despite multiple setbacks, and she was re-evaluating her career plans based on her current assessment of her abilities, choosing not to become a paramedic since that would require more skills in math and science than she felt she possessed. She also made a choice not to receive a free apartment from a drug dealer, since she was concerned that "getting booked" or charged for a drug offence would limit her future possibilities. This type of strategic thinking was echoed by Pete (age nineteen), who regularly made a six-month plan for what his next steps would be, and Vince (age twenty), who used his time sitting in the "drunk tank" to develop a set of goals. Vince then evaluated his life choices through the lens of his goals, which impacted his decision-making. He had been sober for an extended period of time and even refused to allow friends to house him, since he feared that he would become too comfortable and stop working towards his future goals.

Many of the decisions that young people make about their futures also come with a cost, such as experiencing the unwanted symptoms of drug withdrawal, checking into residential drug treatment programs, enduring hospitalization as a result of disclosing mental health challenges, and losing the comfort and protection of friends and status on the street. Chad (age seventeen) was very honest about some of the difficult decisions that he would have to make to achieve his desired future. "As sad as it sounds, I'm probably going to have to drop a lot of my friends. Like … I know that, 'cause if I'm clean, I can't be around people who are using drugs, you know?" Weighing the pros and cons of life decisions and sifting through personal ambivalence is an important aspect of making decisions about exiting the streets.

The ability to imagine a positive future, despite immediate and pressing circumstances, is a strength that young people use to pass through difficulty, overcome daily challenges, and transition out of homelessness. Some of the dreams that young people entertain may not be grandiose, but the capacity to dream through adversity is a strength and indicator of resilience. Courage and determination shape a framework for all of the decision-making that young people have to do on the streets.

Courage and Determination

Perhaps the most obvious visible strengths of youth on the streets are courage and determination, qualities that have been demonstrated through the many case studies and narratives presented in the book. Service providers were more likely than the youth to highlight how courageous the young people were, while both service providers and young people highlighted the importance of determination and conviction in facing each new day with hope. For Donny, a service provider, courage was the dominant theme in how he described the young people:

> *A lot of times we get asked, "What's a success story?" Well, I think a success story is someone who's got the balls to walk through our doors right in front, to come in the building and say, "This is me, take me as I am." That's courage right there. You might not talk to anybody. It might take you two weeks to feel comfortable to talk to somebody, but you walked through the door. So that tells me something right off the get go. You have that.*

For all the service providers interviewed, the most common form of resilience described was how, despite incredible adversity, the young homeless people they work with keep waking up day after day, working through their issues, and trying for a better life.

HIDDEN STRENGTHS

While young people may develop clear strengths through homelessness, some of the strengths are less obvious and lie beneath the surface. Marshall (age seventeen) grew up in an abusive home where his father was violent and mocked him for his eating disorder. He explained that his mother left when he was young, and the experience triggered suicide attempts and other mental health challenges, resulting in hospitalization and mental health treatment. Eventually Marshall was placed in foster homes and group homes, where he experienced sexual abuse and began to run away to escape the ongoing victimization. Shortly before an interview with Marshall, he had a significant experience at the drop-in centre when a young woman attacked him because she wanted to use the computer he was on:

> Some chick came and punched me in the face because she wanted to see the computer. At first, I just stood there and let her punch me in the face a couple of times. And I got up and said, "I'm sick and tired of being a fucking twinkie." I got up and said like, "No, it's not happening!" And then I stopped her, I pushed her out of the way.

This action of standing up for himself was a pivotal moment for Marshall. As he had experienced high levels of victimization in his early years, he typically tended to run away or retreat into himself and engage in self-injury. In this instance, he took a stand for himself and said, "No, it's not happening." So while he did end up in a physical altercation in the drop-in, he also described this as one of the first times that he had actively confronted someone who tried to abuse him:

> You know what? Now I feel better about myself. And I [hadn't eaten] for six days, and now ... I started trying to eat again. I guess that doing what I did yesterday kind of made me realize what I have now, that I have the power to stand up for what's going on. Before, I never stood up for anything. And actually ... I would say I actually

enjoyed being homeless, 'cause I think it's changed me, changed what I've went through.

In this case, Marshall appeared to be learning that he had the capacity to resist abuse, and this realization improved his self-image and his personal sense of power. This would not be the most logical conclusion to draw for an onlooker who had witnessed the fight in the drop-in; the value of the incident and the strength that Marshall was developing lay beneath the surface. This example aligns with the work presented in Michael Ungar's (2004b) book *Nurturing Resilience in Troubled Youth,* which argues that certain behaviours that may be designated as "trouble" by external observers or social workers could carry a more meaningful interpretation for the person living the experience. For Marshall, through this experience he came to accept that he has value and does not deserve to be abused.

BIFURCATIONS AWAY FROM THE STREET

Many homeless youth described significant events that were catalysts that encouraged their exit from or altered their entrenchment in street life in some way. Bifurcation describes the process whereby participants pulled away from their identification as homeless youth and embarked on a new course. A term used by chaos theorists and mathematicians to connote a radical change process and a change of direction, bifurcation occurs when a "system's instabilities of some sort can have become so serious that for it to continue operating as it has been is not a practical option. It must make a radical change — take a fork in the road, travel into new territory" (Jacobs 2000: 87). This term seemed particularly apt to describe the radical decisions that youth made when their lives became too unstable or conditions too intolerable. These decisions birthed significant changes, altering their path. Olivia used the term "revolutionary" to describe how her life changed once she found out she was pregnant. As in Karabanow et al.'s (2005) study of homeless youth, significant and traumatic events often triggered disengagement from street life and prompted subsequent changes in behaviour. The next vignette highlights how a descent into drug addiction and homelessness served as a wake-up call for one young man to "straighten himself out."

Daniel's Story

Daniel (age seventeen) grew up in a small town outside of Ottawa. His parents divorced when he was six years old, and his father moved to the city. He lived with his mother, younger brother, and older sister until the age of fifteen. He described both of his parents as working professionals with secure, well-paid jobs. At age fifteen, he was sent to live with his father in the city because he was "partying, drinking and using ecstasy, and cutting class," and his mother was tired of dealing with his delinquent behaviour. Once in Ottawa, Daniel began using more substances, dropped out of school, and started stealing from his father to pay for his drugs. His father evicted him after finding out about the theft and drug use. The only place a landlord would rent to him was a room in a rooming house where most of the tenants were using crack. It was not long before he was addicted to crack; he revealed he was "spending all of my ow [Ontario Works social assistance] on crack." He recalled, "My parents told me they won't let me move back home 'til I clean up my act. I came from a normal family and everything, but I just screwed up." Eventually, he was evicted and ended up staying at a shelter. Leaving the rooming house life behind, Daniel made the decision to stop using crack and switched to softer substances.

Daniel was very preoccupied with finding employment. He worked several odd jobs in the formal economy, sold marijuana in the informal economy, and, by the end of the study, had secured a full-time job as a baker and stopped dealing drugs. He moved into a supportive housing complex, and subsequently moved in with his girlfriend, stopped using drugs, and disengaged from street life entirely. Daniel expressed remorse for his "screw-ups" and sadness about not being able to "go back to my life." At one point, when he had secured employment, his father agreed that he could move back in with him but reneged on the offer at the last moment. Daniel was very disappointed:

> Yeah, my dad had told me I could move back in with him once I clean up my act, you know, once I have a job and stop using drugs. But once I did these things he changed his mind. He decided that we just don't do well together.... My mom is splitting up with her boyfriend and has decided to take a job in the U.S.A., so I can't move in with her. I guess I have to grow up sometime, so it might as well be now.

In Daniel's case, there were two identifiable moments that affected his subsequent decisions and the direction his life took. The first was overcoming his crack addiction by removing himself (involuntarily) from the place he associated with using drugs. The second turning point came when his parents refused to allow him to return home. Daniel viewed both of these moments as catalysts for his development of agency, autonomy, and resilience.

Indeed, some youth credited significant events with changing the course of their street lives. Ingrid revealed that witnessing her previous boyfriend's murder had a huge impact on her street life, at least for a time. After the murder, she became romantically involved with her previous boyfriend's best friend, stating, "He's the only one I can be with after what happened." They moved into an apartment together, marking the first time Ingrid had had housing in five years. However, after a few months of overcrowded apartment living and heavy morphine use, their place had become a "crash pad" for all of their friends. Ingrid and her boyfriend decided to leave street life behind and move back to her parents' house in the country. During this time, Ingrid drastically cut down her morphine use and eventually quit using altogether, at least for several months. Eventually, the monotony of living with her parents, holding down a "boring job," and being disconnected from street life (especially substance use) triggered her return to the streets. In email correspondence, she wrote, "Homelessness sux. When u do good and fall back down it gets harder and harder to get back up." She emphasized the significant impact of her previous partner's murder on her decisions — it affected her choices regarding intimacy, her desire to disengage from street life, and her efforts to quit using drugs.

Similarly, several female youth cited pregnancy or abortion as significant life-changing events. Annie and Tanya both chose to terminate their pregnancies, a decision that significantly affected their future life decisions. Both decided to limit their drug use, be more discriminating about whom they were spending time with (intimately and otherwise), and become more invested in their future (e.g., return to school, find jobs and housing). They felt guilty for not taking precautions against pregnancy and agreed that they were going to be more responsible in the future. Marie and Olivia, on the other hand, decided to become mothers and accepted this responsibility even though it was unplanned, with obvious consequences for the future course of their lives.

Three years from when Sue-Ann first met her, Annie revealed that her life had changed drastically. After undergoing painful back surgery a year earlier and getting pregnant a second time, she decided to stop living on the streets and using drugs, though she continued to remain connected to other street youth and the services associated with homeless youth. She and her boyfriend obtained a subsidized apartment and raised their baby together. She decided to go back to school while her boyfriend worked full-time, and they both abstained from alcohol and drugs. Annie had also reconnected with her family. Her mother had stopped drinking, and to her surprise, her relationship with her stepfather had improved. She declared that "even he can see that I've changed my life around" and that now "my mom is like my best friend." When asked about how she made these changes, she replied, "I don't really know how it happened … but it just kinda did…. One thing led to another. Y'know I am almost twenty now, so I had to grow up. I couldn't keep living that life."

In another case, a couple was expecting a baby and had transitioned into housing since the young woman's mother was keen to support her coming granddaughter and decided to allow the couple to rent one of her properties. For the male partner, Aaron (age twenty-three), expecting the baby provided a high level of motivation to maintain employment and stable housing, and to clear up past charges from the criminal justice system. When June (age eighteen) found out that she was pregnant, she initially planned to have an abortion since raising a child while homeless or giving the baby away were not options she wanted to pursue. On the day of her appointment, she was surprised by her reaction:

> *I actually made an appointment for an abortion. But when it came down to it, I just … I was crying all day… It was so sad. I couldn't do it…. I couldn't do it. And I knew if I actually went through with it … I wouldn't be the same ever again. I wouldn't feel happy with myself. I'd rather carry the baby and give it to a family instead of kill it. I couldn't do that. Especially like … when you're pregnant, you can feel being pregnant; you can feel the baby inside you. I don't know how a woman could go through with it. Like before being pregnant, I always thought whatever … people can make their own decisions. But now … I have no idea how a woman could do that.*

For June, the decision-making process around her unplanned pregnancy while cycling through homelessness was difficult and constrained by many structural obstacles. Yet, after choosing not to terminate the pregnancy, she was able to work with her partner and her family to establish housing, an income, and plans to raise the child. June stressed that the decisions she had to make while homeless were very difficult, but she was grateful for the support of her partner, and their experiences drew them closer together.

For other young people on the streets facing pregnancy, partnerships can cause conflict. After breaking up with his girlfriend, Chad (age seventeen) learned that she was pregnant. Although he was excited and motivated to leave the streets when he learned that he would be a father, his excitement turned to frustration and anger when he learned that the mother-to-be was continuing to drink alcohol and use drugs while pregnant. Adam (age eighteen) felt guilty about the miscarriage of the baby that he was expecting with his fiancé when she blamed the pregnancy loss on the stress of him being homeless and broke off the relationship. However, Adam also described this experience as part of the "wake-up call" that he needed to transition off the street and find housing.

Other participants also revealed that they had made significant life changes because of new responsibilities, echoing Annie's rationale about having to "grow up." Olivia's and Marie's life changes mirror those of Annie. Once pregnant, they left street life, obtained housing, went back to school, and raised their children. Other youth shared that they became tired of street life, its hazards, the instability, the drama of downtown life, and the dependence on drugs, factors that gradually added up and led them to change course. To cite a few examples, Ingrid moved to her parent's home in the country at one point, Daniel and Michelle obtained their own apartments, and Laura went to a residential treatment centre to seek help for her drug addiction. All of these youth had been more active risk-takers at the beginning of the study. When they decided to leave the streets, they began to distance themselves from that context and developed a new appreciation for the risks associated with street life. As a result, they made significant lifestyle changes, from quitting drugs to finding housing and work in the formal economy.

Karabanow (2004: 176) describes this disenchantment with street life as an exit process that involves a multitude of factors; he found that former street youth emphasized "the importance of leaving the street lifestyle, particularly the physical location, in order to gain stability." Karabanow (2004: 175) states,

When a young person decided to get off the street, he or she [began] to imagine the processes of transitioning off the street and into a more stable environment. The most common aspect of this contemplation involved leaving the downtown core and severing ties to the street. At this point, participants conceptualized street culture as a very unhealthy (physically, emotionally, and psychologically) setting.

During encounters with Ingrid, she never blamed her family, friends, or the system for her homelessness or drug use. She never viewed herself as a victim, never blamed anyone but herself for her decisions, and vacillated between being exceptionally self-monitoring to admittedly reckless. She did, however, cite the significant event of her previous boyfriend's murder as having a huge impact on her life course, including current choice of boyfriend, disengagement from street life, and efforts to quit using drugs.

Some experiences were also imposed. Annie's back surgery was needed because of strain from excessive backpacking. She described spending a few months in the hospital and then "losing the taste for street life" and deciding to get an apartment. Other female youth described rape as the incentive for changing their practices to always carrying a weapon, never sleeping outside alone, using drugs in the company of people they trusted, using "softer drugs," or getting off the streets.

Death and Self-Reflection

In their research on exiting homelessness, Karabanow, Carson, and Clement (2010) found that many young people who are homeless witness the death of friends on the streets, and this may become a pivotal moment in their trajectories. This was also true for several of the young people interviewed for our study, where it was relatively common for young people to mention a peer or a partner who had died on the street. Several youth explicitly discussed witnessing the death of a friend or partner, and this was often a trigger for making a big change in their life course. For Chad (age seventeen), who grew up involved in gang violence before moving to Ottawa, where he became homeless, the loss of three of his closest friends to violence before he turned sixteen motivated him to make the most of his life. "I think it's another thing the streets taught me, like ... I have to live my life for my friends that died ... 'cause they didn't get the chance.... Like, their turn at life got ended before it even begun." Similarly, Kristin (age eighteen) found that witnessing the death of a close friend from an overdose had become a powerful motivator to leave the streets but explained that it was challenging to feel motivated to change when she remained surrounded by peers who used drugs and a lifestyle where drugs were constantly accessible:

> *I had a friend die in my arms. She overdosed. She tore her skin to pieces. Like … that's why I'm trying to be sober, but you know…. What else do you turn to when you have no other comforts? And what's the easiest accessible comfort when you're on the streets? Weed … alcohol … worse. You know?*

For young people who are homeless, traumatic experiences on the street provide opportunities for reflection, and sometimes motivation to consider exiting street life. However, there are many obstacles to exiting homelessness that can discourage or delay the process. Traumatic experiences are also integrated at different moments in time and in a nonlinear fashion, a tension that can produce feelings of powerfulness or the opposite, complete powerlessness. At times these experiences act as accelerators to make big life changes, and at other times they keep youth mired in a cycle of violence, cutting their wings.

Significant events represented turning points that impacted youth disengagement from homelessness and/or substance use, or altered their choices in some way, which consequently affected their risk perception and practices of self-regulation. For many youth, these included traumatic events that forever altered their understanding of street life; for others, the experience of homelessness and substance dependency provided the springboard for change. Within these turning points were varying degrees and dimensions of self-regulation and responsibility. While some youth internalized responsibility, underscoring the "privatization of risk" thesis (Foucault 1978), others projected blame onto others, including families, friends, systems, and the environment, for their circumstances, disproving linear and singular notions of an individual "culture of blame" phenomenon (Douglas 1985).

We have employed the strength-based perspective in our analysis, but we also wish to acknowledge Jeff Karabanow's (2004: 68) words of caution: "While there may exist some redeeming aspects to street life (such as independence, freedom, a sense of community and support), for the vast majority of children, this lifestyle offers a problematic and unhealthy existence." Our research has shown that young people can experience personal growth and build strengths through the experience of homelessness; however, these lessons come with a high cost. Not every young person successfully navigates through homelessness, nor does anyone ever come out unchanged, and some are deeply scarred by it. Despite the transformation that many young people experience on the streets, given the choice, most would prefer to grow up in the safety and security of a loving family (or community) and feel supported (materially and emotionally).

9. UNDERSTANDING THE EXPERIENCES OF HOMELESS YOUTH DIFFERENTLY

Our aim is not to prescribe specific interventions but to offer a jumping-off point for exploration into how homeless youth understand their experiences. Several assumptions and paradoxes were uncovered over the course of this work. The streets were seen by youth as not only places of danger but also generators of excitement and opportunities for self-discovery, a finding that parallels what other researchers have found (Bellot 2001; Parazelli 1997). Many youth felt they had more control over their lives and choices on the streets than in their previous lives, despite finding themselves in an arena of constrained options. Many described their experiences of homelessness as character building. Some described themselves as "warriors" (e.g., Ingrid), and many viewed themselves as resourceful and creative survivors who actively resisted those who tried to exert authority over them (e.g., police, other youth). Instead of the pervasive stereotype of youth as impulsive, rebellious, and cognitively stunted, this study found that many youth were thoughtful about their lives, their identities, and their relationships with others, and were very conscious of social stigma and structural obstacles.

The youth we met were survivors who were creative and adaptive in the face of present-day constraints, which were often added to ongoing struggles from childhood. Whether they identified as the family scapegoat, the target of group victimization, or the powerful street hustler, they told us stories about surviving difficult experiences and responding creatively to their constraints. Identities were constantly shifting, being experimented with, or reshaped in light of new experiences or responsibilities (e.g., becoming a parent). Their various roles and shifting identities all affected the kinds of decisions they made in the face of threats or opportunities.

It is important to highlight youth agency and dynamism and to outline an alternative conceptualization of homeless youth as resilient and adaptable. The images of youth that circulate in the collective imagination (academic and mainstream) are generally flattened and limited. The paucity of research on their lived experiences from their point of view means that the existing literature highlights the negative impact of early childhood experiences and/ or the negative sequelae of street involvement, which reinforces stereotypes of street youth as victims or deviants (Bellot 2001; MacDonald 2010). Methodologically, research with this population has been limited because they are marginalized and much of their behaviour is highly stigmatized (Benoit, Jansson, and Anderson 2007; LaBoy 2018; MacDonald 2016), leaving a dearth of knowledge about how youth conceptualize their own experiences and promoting an essentialized expert discourse in its place. Researchers have noted that while homeless youth have been deemed an "at-risk" group, they are the least likely to reach out for help. Relatively little is known about how they get by on the streets. At the same time, there is a moral imperative to intervene due to their fragile social status and "at-risk" label.

Youth described the risks they would take, such as joining the carnival or hitchhiking across the country, and they were thoughtful about the consequences of these gambles. These experiences and other significant life events affected their understanding of themselves and who they wanted to be. Conceptualizations of life on the streets thus changed over time as experiences both negative and positive accumulated. Most importantly, youth tended to view risk-taking not simply as deviant or victimizing but as experimental and character forming. While youth described certain risks as necessary for their survival, they responded to these situations in ways that demonstrated their creativity and resilience. This process allowed them to discover new things about themselves and who they wanted to become, consequently altering their practices and perceptions of risk.

Young people's shifting understandings of street life served to shape and reshape the construction of their identities, contrasting sharply with point-in-time data that keeps youth frozen in a passive otherness. Significant events in their lives greatly transformed their notions of responsibility and dramatically altered their life paths. For some, pregnancy forced them to radically alter their behaviours and environments (e.g., quit drugs, find housing). The violence of street life and health consequences of drug use were also catalysts for change. These experiences pushed youth to consider the risks (good and bad) inherent to street life, and for some this led to an epiphany about the instability of their current lives. The changes they subsequently made greatly affected their ideas about responsibility, agency, and identity.

A major paradox of youth experiences is that drug use was seen as both constraining and liberating. It is important to highlight the ambivalence youth felt towards drug use and how they got their drugs. They described their complex relationships with addiction — with the substances themselves and the tiring pursuit of them, as well as the inherent dangers of obtaining them — and how this affected their identities on the street. Several youth described the stigma associated with substance use and the need to lead a double life, hiding their consumption to maintain relationships. The risks involved in drug acquisition for young women, especially the risk of sexual exploitation, were particularly salient. It is important to take a broad view of risk when assessing drug use, integrating a harm reduction approach that goes beyond simple consumption to include the context of acquisition and a recognition of asymmetrical and gendered power dynamics. Moreover, exploring the benefits and drawbacks of drug use is a better starting point for intervention because it recognizes the ambivalence many youth feel about their use, which manifests itself as a push-pull paradox of freedom and captivity (MacDonald 2014).

TOWARDS A STRENGTH-BASED, CONSTRUCTIVIST VIEW OF RESILIENCE

> *I think it's part of resilience, to be able to change goals and adapt to life situations, and not to cling on to what someone has done to you, or cling on to what someone said to you, or how someone treated you, because by putting it in the past and growing from it, I'm able to interact with new people and not resent them for reminding me of someone. (Syrus, age twenty-one)*

This description provided by Syrus closely matches the common notion that resilience is a process of positive adaptation despite experiences of significant adversity (Masten and Powell 2003). All young people who are homeless experience adversity, and yet many of the risk factors they encounter may trigger a degree of personal growth and transformation. Based on the interviews we conducted and the interactions we had with youth, we learned that a risk factor like family breakdown has the potential to strengthen autonomy, independence, and problem-solving; disconnection from peers can trigger experimentation and self-discovery; having few possessions can increase feelings of gratitude; and accessing multiple community services can enhance organizational skills, initiative, and the capacity for negotiation and self-advocacy. The development of these strengths validates the notion that young people who are homeless may experience many forms of positive adaptation in light of the adversity they face; however, because of the way that resilience is generally defined in an objective way, where youth are expected to achieve a number of normative benchmarks of the typical transition to adulthood, these same young people are unlikely to be seen as resilient. They may not be in school; they may be unemployed, selling, or using drugs, and committing criminalized acts to meet their basic needs. However, most of the youth we met engaged in self-reflection and recognized that some of their problem-solving behaviours that might be considered undesirable were temporary and necessary to survive homelessness but did not define who they were as people. A constructivist model of resilience (Ungar 2004a, 2004b, 2005, 2008) addresses this disconnect by acknowledging the skills used by marginalized young people to navigate and negotiate the tensions of life on the streets, and understanding them as indicators of resilience.

A constructivist model of resilience (Ungar 2004a, 2004b, 2005, 2008) has been used throughout our work to frame the way that young people navigate through homelessness. This perspective draws on the interactionist theory of structuration, which suggests that human agency and social structures exist in a continual feedback loop, where individual decisions are shaped by social structures, and social structures are reinforced or transformed as many individuals make decisions (see Giddens 1976, 1979, 1983, 1984). In this way, Giddens bridges macro structures with micro decision-making. Many researchers studying youth homelessness have focused on the macro structures that impact the lives of young people without much focus on individual decision-making and how this decision-making is shaped by negotiation with other human agents and the subjective and symbolic interpretations of these interactions. In this research we have used tools from a symbolic interactionist perspective to further develop the dialogue around the decision-making of young people who are homeless and how young people present themselves in everyday life to aid in their negotiations with peers and service providers. This builds on Ungar's (2004a, 2004b, 2005, 2008) constructivist model of resilience, adding concepts from symbolic interactionism such as the presentation of self in everyday life as tools to explore how young people negotiate with themselves and with others.

The process of resilience is not solely individual and occurs in the context of available external resources and social networks that support people in their process of personal growth (Bender et al. 2007; Lankenau et al. 2005; Masten and Powell 2003; Ungar 2005). It is ongoing, shaped and constrained by personal agency and structure. Young people in this research identified community resources as an essential source of support for meeting their physical and emotional needs. There was also a strong alignment between how service providers described their work with young people and how the young people described their interactions with service providers, who were generally nonjudgmental and created safe spaces. However, not all the youth we encountered supported this analysis. Most of the youth indicated that the accessibility, relevance, and flexibility of the services available in the community were linked to many of the positive outcomes they experienced. However, other youth mentioned that they felt there was ample room for improvement in services, particularly related to accessibility but also lack of options and diversity in available resources. Some of the younger youth also mentioned feeling discriminated against or being the targets of paternalistic and sometimes overprotective interventions, however well intentioned, causing them to withhold certain requests or personal information.

Finally, this research has framed the "positive adaptation" component of resilience around the concept of strengths, both visible and hidden. Critics of resilience discourse object to the practice of describing young people as "at-risk youth" and the expectation that young people described as resilient are achieving a normative set of expectations related to housing, school, and employment (Foster and Spencer 2011; France 2007; Kelly 2000, 2006; Mallett et al. 2010; Martineau 1999; te Riele 2006). As an alternative, this research has explored the strengths young people possess and the strengths they are developing through their experiences of homelessness. This development of strengths has been used as an indicator of positive adaptation.

Strengths were described by young people directly and by service providers, and also identified through our own interactions with youth and analysis of the narratives they presented. This strength-based approach is importantly linked to a constructivist perspective of resilience since many of the strengths required to survive homelessness may counter normative values and contradict traditional understandings of risk and protective factors. The young people we interviewed are strong and overcome many obstacles daily, even if the way they navigate and negotiate looks different than the negotiations of young people with more economic resources. This research has found that a constructivist, strength-based model of resilience is well suited to understanding the process of resilience in the lives of young people who are marginalized and economically disadvantaged.

THE PARADOX OF RESILIENCE

Young people who are homeless may have courage and strength, but they also experience unimaginable exposure to trauma. Youth report experiencing physical and sexual violence (which often starts in childhood and continues on the streets); witnessing the deaths of friends through murder, suicide, or overdose; having their belongings stolen; being judged by strangers; sleeping in stairwells and parking garages; having to steal to eat or engage in sex work or sexual exploitation for money, shelter, or drugs; being mistreated by police officers; enduring countless sleepless nights; struggling with addiction and substance abuse; and facing humiliation when seeking help to access social welfare, housing, or education. All of these challenges occur within the context of the developmental process of transitioning to adulthood and reflecting on the type of people they want to become. With such exceptional obstacles, youth often engage in behaviours that run counter to their values as a means of survival, and it is precisely these behaviours, often considered "deviant" or "high risk," that may be indicators of resilience. We have highlighted the many paradoxes of life on the streets, but perhaps one of the greatest is that survival behaviours themselves are evidence of the will to live, to move forward, to achieve a sense of belonging and well-being. Normative models of resilience would not likely point to a homeless sixteen-year-old selling drugs in local high schools to set aside enough money for first and last months' rent as an example of resilience, but the strength-based constructivist model tells a different story. Many of the choices that young people make as they navigate homelessness, though controversial to external observers, are rational given the complexities of their daily lives and the constraints imposed on their choices. What lies beneath the surface may be most important, a process of positive adaptation in its early stages, not yet fully developed. As Cronley and Evans's (2017: 1) systematic review exploring resilience among youth experiencing homelessness aptly points out, "researchers need to exercise more self-awareness about how stereotypical pejorative paradigms may constrain innovative, strengths-based scholarship." Indeed, young people on the streets often develop significant and culturally valued strengths through their experiences of adversity and problem-solving. And while it is important to celebrate these strengths and the truth in the expression "what doesn't kill you makes you stronger," which we heard from so many young people, it is also true that not all young people live to become stronger.

All young people deserve housing. All children are deserving of love, of having their basic needs met, of safety and security. And yet, for many young people in our communities, this is not the reality. While researchers will continue to study how homeless youth manage to survive, navigating and negotiating their way through the complexities of street life and demonstrating resiliency, this onus on youth to be resilient is a paradox. One young person from a stable home goes to school and stresses about an upcoming test, while another sleeps under the bleachers at her high school so she can make it to class in the morning. We need to recognize that some youth face much more hardship and disadvantage than others, and it is unfair to judge their choices, progress, and success from normative standpoints. They are making decisions within very limited and constrained options that deviate from mainstream expectations of this age group. We can and must do better to address these inequalities and support the innate potential in all youth.

It is our hope that the voices heard in these pages will have a positive impact in terms of lobbying for better housing, employment, and resources for homeless youth, including peer supports and peer-led initiatives. We also hope that our research demonstrates the heterogeneity of this population and their experiences. This diversity among homeless youth underlines the importance of engaging youth in service planning and provision to better meet their needs and combat one-size-fits-all approaches, especially since their creativity has been amply shown throughout their stories. Active youth engagement and collaboration at all levels, including governance structures (power-sharing arrangements), is key for developing practice rooted in respect, choice, and flexibility. The insights and knowledge of homeless youth should be woven into the core of practice, interventions, and policy-making. One of the impacts that we hope for is a move away from a two-dimensional view of young people's experiences as ones of victimization or deviance, and a move towards recognizing the strengths of youth: their creativity, adaptability, reflexivity, and power. Indeed, what may be considered acts of resistance by some (or noncompliance by others) are demonstrations of their ability to act in their own best interest, to hold onto and exert their power in a context of limited and constrained options.

We have offered an intimate portrayal of the lives of homeless youth from their point of view. This meant prioritizing methods that facilitated long-term partnership and engagement with youth, where they could lead discussions, express themselves at will, and create meaning out of their experiences. Learning from youth in this manner is essential since they often have solutions to the barriers they encounter (Gomez and Ryan 2016). In this way, their knowledge is valued and they are perceived as thoughtful, active agents finding creative ways to eke out a living, and not simply as marginalized passive victims or offending delinquents requiring protection or punishment. Young people's own voices and perceptions are often excluded from decisions impacting their well-being, which are often made instead by adults with power. Learning from youth experiences confronting oppression and navigating and negotiating life on the streets is an essential step in working together to end youth homelessness.

The complexities we have presented should also make it obvious that housing alone is not the solution to youth homelessness, and that multi-sector planning and policy fusion are required to address the broad range of structural obstacles that young people encounter when they are homeless and continue to encounter as they make efforts to transition out of homelessness (Karabanow, Kidd, Frederick, and Hughes 2018). Young people's own voices on their individual efforts to confront, engage with, and negotiate the various risks associated with street life are starting to receive more attention in research, and it is clear that much of their energy, strength, creativity, and problem-solving are invested in trying to find adequate shelter, food, and resources rather than focusing on education, career paths, health, or relationship goals typical of peers with access to housing. Given the poor outcomes associated with youth homelessness in the areas of mortality, mental health, substance abuse, victimization, and criminal offending, as well as the disproportionate impacts on youth leaving care, girls, LGBTQ2S youth, and Indigenous youth, there is a critical need for multi-sectoral engagement in the prevention and elimination of youth homelessness. The normalization of youth homelessness — its generalized acceptance combined with assumptions about who these youth are and what they are capable of — acts as a barrier to finding solutions. Gaps in service delivery and the ways that social services, housing, and health agencies compete for funding within their siloed mandates create a climate where young people fall through the cracks (Nichols, 2014). Coordinated prevention has the capacity to interrupt a downward spiral of negative outcomes associated with life on the street and to generate significant social, political, and economic benefits. Young people who are homeless have wisdom from their lived experience and need to be included in planning solutions. The youth we spoke with had tremendous strengths and talents they were drawing on to survive life on the streets. How would their lives look if they were able to use these same strengths and talents in a context of safe and stable housing, supportive environments, and respectful relationships that affirm their dignity?

NOTES

1. May 16, 2018 <https://twitter.com/homelesshub/status/996782839160098821/photo/1>.
2. International Covenant on Civil and Political Rights (ICCPR), the International Covenant on Economic, Social and Cultural Rights (ICESCR), the Convention on the Rights of the Child (CRC) and the International Convention on the Elimination of All Forms of Racial Discrimination (ICERD).
3. This has changed a bit in recent years, particularly in youth shelters that are adapting their practices to allow for gender fluidity. Furthermore, a new shelter and transitional housing facility specifically for transgender youth has recently opened in Toronto (Sprott House).
4. The Child, Youth, and Family Services Act is now fully implemented in Ontario, raising the age of child protection to eighteen, though with the requirement that sixteen- and seventeen-year-old youth need to consent to child welfare involvement.

REFERENCES

Abramovich, A. 2013. *Questions of Homeless LGBTQ Youth Study*. <homelesshub.ca/gallery/questions-homeless-lgbtq-youth-study>.

Abramovich, A., and J. Shelton (eds.). 2017. *Where Am I Going to Go? Intersectional Approaches to Ending LGBTQ2S Youth Homelessness in Canada & the U.S.* Toronto: Canadian Observatory on Homelessness Press.

Ahern, N. 2006. "Adolescent resilience: An evolutionary concept analysis." *Journal of Pediatric Nursing*, 21, 3: 175–185.

Archer, M. 1982. "Morphogenesis versus structuration: On combining structure and action." *British Journal of Sociology*, 33, 4: 455–483.

Armaline, W.T. 2005. "'Kids need structure': Negotiating rules, power, and social control in an emergency youth shelter." *American Behavioral Scientist*, 48, 8: 1124–1148.

Aubry, T., F. Klodawsky, E. Hay, and S. Birnie. 2003. *Panel Study on Persons Who Are Homeless in Ottawa: Phase 1 Results*. Ottawa, ON: University of Ottawa, Centre for Research on Educational and Community Services.

Aubry, T., F. Klodawsky, R. Nemiroff, S. Birnie, and C. Bonetta. 2007. *Panel Study on Persons Who Are Homeless in Ottawa: Phase 2 Results*. Ottawa, ON: University of Ottawa, Centre for Research on Educational and Community Services.

Avila, R., C. Campbell, and P. Eid. 2009. *La Judiciarisation des Personnes Itinérantes à Montréal: Un Profilage Social*. Québec: La commission des droits de la personne et des droits de la jeunesse.

Bajoit, G. 1999. "Notes sur la construction de l'identité personnelle." *Recherches Sociologiques*, 30, 2: 69–84.

___. 2000. "Qu'est-ce que la socialisation?" In G. Bajoit, F. Digneffe, J.-M. Jaspard, and Q. Nollet de Brauwere (eds.), *Jeunesse et Société: La Socialisation des Jeunes dans un Monde en Mutation*. Belgium: De Boeck Université.

Baker Collins, S.D. 2013. "From homeless teen to chronically homeless adult: A qualitative study of the impact of childhood events on adult homelessness." *Critical Social Work*, 14, 2: 61–81.

Barker, C. 2005. *Cultural Studies: Theory and Practice*. London: Sage.

Barnaby, L., R. Penn, and P.G. Erickson. 2010. *Drugs, Homelessness & Health: Homeless Youth Speak Out About Harm Reduction. The Shout Clinic Harm Reduction Report, 2010.* Toronto: Wellesley Institute.

Baron, S.W. 2003. "Street youth violence and victimization." *Trauma, Violence, & Abuse,* 4, 1: 22–44.

Baron, S.W., D.R. Forde, and L.W. Kennedy. 2007. "Disputatiousness, aggressiveness, and victimization among street youths." *Youth Violence and Juvenile Justice,* 5, 4: 411–425.

Bassuk, E.L., J.N. Perloff, and R. Dawson. 2001. "Multiply homeless families: The insidious impact of violence." *Housing Policy Debate,* 12: 299–320.

Bearsley-Smith, C.A., L.M. Bond, L. Littlefield, and L.R. Thomas. 2008. "The psychosocial profile of adolescent risk of homelessness." *European Child & Adolescent Psychiatry,* 17, 4: 226–234.

Becker, H.S. 1963. *Outsiders: Studies in the Sociology of Deviance.* New York: The Free Press.

Begun, S.J. 2017. "A mixed methods examination of pregnancy attitudes and HIV risk behaviors among homeless youth: The role of social network norms and social support." *Electronic Theses and Dissertations,* 1293. <https://digitalcommons.du.edu/etd/1293>.

Bellot, C. 2001. *Le Monde Social de la Rue: Expériences des Jeunes et Pratiques d'Intervention à Montréal.* Dissertation, École de criminologie, Université de Montréal, Québec.

Bellot, C., C. Chesnay, and M. Royer. 2007. *Judiciarisation des Populations Itinérantes de 2004 à 2006 : Extrait du Rapport Préliminaire.* Montreal: Centre international de criminologie comparée (CICC).

Bellot, C., I. Raffestin, M. Royer, and V. Nöel. 2005. *La Judiciarisation et Criminalisation des Populations Itinérantes à Montréal.* Montreal: Le Réseau d'aide aux personnes seules et itinérantes de Montréal (RAPSIM).

Bender, K., S.J. Thompson, H. McManus, J. Lantry, and P.M. Flynn. 2007. "Capacity for survival: Exploring strengths of homeless street youth." *Child Youth Care Forum,* 36: 25–42.

Bender, K., J. Yang, K. Ferguson, and S. Thompson. 2015. "Experiences and needs of homeless youth with a history of foster care." *Children and Youth Services Review,* 55: 222–231.

Benoit, C., M. Jansson, and M. Anderson. 2007. "Understanding health disparities among female street youth." In B.J.R. Leadbeater and N. Way (eds.), *Urban Girls Revisited: Building Strengths.* New York: New York University Press.

Bessant, J. 2001. "From sociology of deviance to sociology of risk: Youth homelessness and the problem of empiricism." *Journal of Criminal Justice,* 29: 31–43.

Best, A. 2007. "Introduction." In A. Best (ed.), *Representing Youth: Methodological Issues in Critical Youth Studies.* New York: New York University Press.

Bjarnason, T., T.J. Sigurdardottir, and T. Thorlindsson. 1999. "Human agency, capable guardians, and structural contraints: A lifestyle approach to the study of violent victimization." *Journal of Youth and Adolescence,* 28, 1: 105–119.

Boivin, J.-F., E. Roy, N. Haley, and G. Galbaud du Fort. 2005. "The health of street youth: A Canadian perspective." *Canadian Journal of Public Health,* 96, 6: 432–437.

Bourdieu, P. 1999. *Language and Symbolic Power*. Cambridge, MA: Harvard University Press.

Bournes, B., and T. Meredith. 2008. "Business plan for a youth health clinic." Prepared for the Youth Services Bureau. October 23. KPMG LLP. Ottawa, ON.

Bradley, J. 1997. *Stress, Social Support, and Adjustment*. New York: Garland.

Brown, S.M., S. Begun, K. Bender, K.M. Ferguson, and S.J. Thompson. 2015. "An exploratory factor analysis of coping styles and relationship to depression among a sample of homeless youth." *Community Mental Health Journal*, 51, 7: 818–827.

Bungay, V., J. Johnson, C. Varcoe, and S. Boyd. 2010. "Women's health and use of crack cocaine in context: Structural and 'everyday' violence." *International Journal of Drug Policy*, 21: 321–329.

Castel, R. 1998. *Les Sorties de la Toxicomanie*. Suisse: Editions Universitaires Fribourg Suisse.

Cauce, A.M., M. Paradise, J.A. Ginzler, L. Embry, C.J. Morgan, Y. Lohr, and J. Theofelis. 2000. "The characteristics and mental health of homeless adolescents: Age and gender differences." *Journal of Emotional and Behavioural Disorders*, 8, 4: 230–239.

Ceglowski, D. 2002. "Research as relationship." In N. Denzin and Y. Lincon (eds.), *The Qualitative Reader*. Thousand Oaks, CA: Sage.

Chesnay, C., C. Bellot, and M.-E. Sylvestre. 2013. "Taming disorderly people one ticket at a time: The penalization of homelessness in Ontario and British Columbia." *Canadian Journal of Criminology and Criminal Justice*, 55, 2: 161–185.

Cicchetti, D. 2003. "Foreword." In S.S. Luthar (ed.), *Resilience and Vulnerability: Adaptation in the Context of Childhood Adversities*. New York: Cambridge University Press.

Cochran, B., A. Stewart, J. Ginzler, and A. Cauce. 2002. "Challenges faced by homeless sexual minorities: Comparison of gay, lesbian, bisexual and transgender homeless adolescents with their heterosexual counterparts." *American Journal of Public Health*, 92, 5: 773–777.

Colombo, A. 2008. "La Reconnaissance: un Enjeu pour la Sortie de la Rue des Jeunes à Montréal." Dissertation, Études urbaines, Université du Québec à Montréal, Québec.

___. 2015. *S'en Sortir Quand on Vit Dans la Rue*. Montréal: Presses de l'Université du Québec.

Conrad, P. 1992. "Medicalization and social control." *Annual Review of Sociology*, 18: 209–232.

Coolhart, D., and M.T. Brown. 2017. "The need for safe spaces: Exploring the experiences of homeless LGBTQ youth in shelters." *Children and Youth Services Review*, 82: 230–238.

Cronley, C., and R. Evans. 2017. "Studies of resilience among youth experiencing homelessness: A systematic review." *Journal of Human Behavior in the Social Environment*, 4: 291–310.

d'Allondans, T.G. 2005. "Des rites de passage aux passages sans rite: Anthropologie de l'adolescence." In D. Jeffrey, D. LeBreton, and J. Lévy (eds.), *Jeunesse à Risque, Rite et Passage*. Québec: Les Presses de l'Université Laval.

D'Ercole, A., and E. Struening. 1990. "Victimization among homeless women: Implications for service delivery." *Journal of Community Psychology*, 18: 141–151.

Denov, M. 2010. *Child Soldiers: Sierra Leone's Revolutionary United Front.* New York: Cambridge University Press.

DiPaolo, M. 1999. *The Impact of Multiple Childhood Trauma on Homeless Runaway Adolescents.* New York: Garland.

Douglas, M. 1985. *Risk Acceptability According to the Social Sciences.* New York: Russell Sage Foundation.

Egeland, B., E. Carlson, and L.A. Stroufe. 1993. "Resilience as process." *Development and* Psychopathology, 5: 517–528.

Elder, G.H., M. Kirkpatrick Johnson, and R. Crosnoe. 2003. "Chapter 1: The emergence and development of life course theory." In Jeylan T. Mortimer and Michael J. Shanahan (eds.), *Handbook of the Life Course.* New York: Kluwer Academic/Plenum Publishers.

Ensign, J. 1998. "Health issues of homeless youth." *Journal of Social Distress and the Homeless,* 7: 159–174.

Erikson, E.H. 1968. *Identity: Youth and Crisis.* New York: Norton.

Falvo, N. 2016. "Homelessness in Canada: Its Growth, Policy Responses, and Advocacy." <http://homelesshub.ca/blog/homelessness-canada-its-growth-policy-responses-and-advocacy>.

Farrell, S., T. Aubry, F. Klodawsky, and D. Pettey. 2000. *Describing the Homeless in Ottawa-Carleton.* Ottawa, ON: University of Ottawa, Centre for Research on Community Services.

Farrugia, D., and J. Gerrard. 2016. "Academic knowledge and contemporary poverty: The politics of homelessness research." *Sociology,* 50, 2: 267–284.

Finlay, J. 2007. *We Are Your Sons and Daughters: The Child Advocate's Report on the Quality of Care of 3 Children's Aid Societies.* Ontario: Office of Child and Family Service Advocacy.

Foster, K.R., and D. Spencer. 2011. "At risk of what? Possibilities over probabilities in the study of young lives." *Journal of Youth Studies,* 14, 1: 125–143.

Foucault, M. 1978. *The History of Sexuality.* New York: Pantheon Books.

Fournier, M., S. Austin, C. Samples, C. Goodenow, S. Wylie, and H. Corliss. 2009. "A comparison of weight-related behaviours among high school students who are homeless and non-homeless." *Journal of School Health,* 79, 10: 466–473.

France, A. 2007. *Understanding Youth in Late Modernity.* Maidenhead, UK: Open University Press.

Fraser, M. (ed.). 1997. *Risk and Resilience in Childhood: An Ecological Perspective.* Washington, DC: NASW Press.

Furedi, F. 2006. *Culture of Fear Revisited: Risk-Taking and the Morality of Low Expectation.* London: Continuum.

Gaetz, S. 2002. *Street Justice: Homeless Youth and Access to Justice.* Toronto: Justice for Children and Youth.

___. 2004. "Safe streets for whom? Homeless youth, social exclusion, and criminal victimization." *Canadian Journal of Criminology and Criminal Justice,* 46, 4: 423–455.

___. 2009. "Whose safety counts? Street youth, social exclusion, and criminal victimization." *Finding Home: Policy Options for Addressing Homelessness in Canada.* Toronto: Cities Centre, University of Toronto.

____. 2014. *Coming of Age: Reimagining the Response to Youth Homelessness in Canada.* Toronto: Canadian Observatory on Homelessness Press.

Gaetz, S., C. Barr, A. Friesen, B. Harris, C. Hill, K. Kovacs-Burns, B. Pauly, B. Pearce, A. Turner, and A. Marsolais. 2017. *Canadian Definition of Homelessness.* Toronto: Canadian Observatory on Homelessness Press. <http://homelesshub.ca/sites/default/files/COHhomelessdefinition.pdf>.

Gaetz, S., and B. O'Grady. 2002. "Making money: Exploring the economy of young homeless workers." *Work, Employment and Society,* 16, 3: 433–456.

Gaetz, S., B. O'Grady, and K. Buccieri. 2010. *Surviving Crime and Violence: Street Youth and Victimization in Toronto.* Toronto: JFCY & Homeless Hub.

Gaetz, S., B. O'Grady, S. Kidd, and K. Schwan. 2016. *Without a Home: The National Youth Homelessness Survey.* Toronto: Canadian Observatory on Homelessness Press.

Gaetz, S., B. O'Grady, and B. Vaillancourt. 1999. *Making Money: The Shout Clinic Report on Homeless Youth and Employment.* Toronto: Central Toronto Community Health Centres.

Gattis, M. 2009. "Psychosocial problems associated with homelessness in sexual minority youths." *Journal of Human Behaviour in the Social Environment,* 19, 8: 1066–1094.

Giddens, A. 1976. *New Rules of Sociological Method: A Positive Critique of Interpretative Sociologies.* London: Hutchinson.

____. 1979. *Central Problems in Social Theory: Action, Structure and Contradiction in Social Analysis.* London: Macmillan.

____. 1983. "Comments on the theory of structuration." *Journal for the Theory of Social Behaviour,* 13: 75–80.

____. 1984. *The Constitution of Society. Outline of the Theory of Structuration.* Cambridge: Polity.

Gilbert, S. 2004. "L'Idéal du Moi comme Point de Mire et le Social en Toile de Fond: Une Compréhension de la Dynamique Sociopsychique de l'Itinérance des Jeunes Adultes." Dissertation, Département de psychologie. Montréal: Université du Québec à Montréal.

Goffman, E. 1959. *The Presentation of Self in Everyday Life.* New York: Doubleday and Co.

____. *1961. Asylums: Essays on the Social Situation of Mental Patients and Other Inmates.* New York: Doubleday and Co.

____. 1963. Stigma*: Notes on the Management of Spoiled Identity.* New Jersey: Prentice-Hall.

Gomez, R.J., and T.N. Ryan. 2016. "Speaking out: Youth led research as a methodology used with homeless youth." *Child and Adolescent Social Work Journal,* 33: 185–193.

Goodman, L., L. Saxe, and M. Harvey. 1991. "Homelessness as psychological trauma." *American Psychologist,* 46, 11: 1219–1225.

Greene, J.M., S.T. Ennett, and C.L. Ringwalt. 1997. "Prevalence and correlates of survival sex among runaway and homeless youth." *American Journal of Public Health,* 89, 9: 1406–1409.

Greene, J.M., and C.L. Ringwalt. 1998. "Pregnancy among three national samples of runaway and homeless youth." *Journal of Adolescent Health,* 23, 6: 370–377.

Greene, R.R. (ed.). 2002. *Resiliency: An Integrated Approach to Practice, Policy, and Research.* Washington, DC: NASW Press.

Hagan, J., and B. McCarthy. 1997. *Mean Streets: Youth Crime and Homelessness.* Cambridge, UK: Cambridge University Press.

___. 2005. "Homeless youth and the perilous passage to adulthood." In W. Osgood, E.M. Foster, C. Flanagan, and G.R. Ruth (eds.), *On Your Own Without a Net: The Transition to Adulthood for Vulnerable Populations.* Chicago: University of Chicago Press.

Haldenby, A.M., H. Berman, and C. Forchuk. 2007. "Homelessness and health in adolescents." *Qualitative Health Research*, 17, 9: 1232–1244.

Haley, N. 2007. "Health Problems of Street Youth… from Research to Action." Presentation given to ATEH Community Forum on Homelessness, November 22. Montreal Public Health Department.

Haley, N., É. Roy, P. Leclerc, J.-F. Boudreau, and J.-F. Boivin. 2003. "Characteristics of adolescent street youth with a history of pregnancy." *Journal of Pediatric Adolescent Gynecology* 17: 313–320.

Hall, G.S. 1904. *Adolescence: Its Psychology and its Relations to Physiology, Anthropology, Sociology, Sex, Crime, Religion, and Education (Vols. I & II).* New York: D. Appleton & Co.

Hamilton, A.B., I. Poza, and D.L. Washington. 2011. "Homelessness and trauma go hand-in-hand: Pathways to homelessness among women veterans." *Women's Health Issues*, 21(Suppl.): S203–S209. <http://dx.doi.org/10.1016/j.whi.2011.04.005>.

Heerde, J.A., and S.A. Hemphill. 2015. "Sexual risk behaviors, sexual offenses, and sexual victimization among homeless youth: A systematic review of associations with substance use." *Trauma, Violence, & Abuse*, 1–22.

___. 2017. "The role of risk and protective factors in the modification of risk for sexual victimization, sexual risk behaviors and survival sex among homeless youth: A meta-analysis." *Journal of Investigative Psychology and Offender Profiling*, 14: 150–174. <http://dx.doi.org/10.1002/jip.1473>.

___. 2018. "Exploration of associations between family and peer risk and protective factors and exposure to physically violent behavior among homeless youth: A meta-analysis." *Psychology of Violence.* Advance online publication. <http://dx.doi.org/10.1037/vio0000181>.

Herman, D.B., E.S. Susser, E.L. Struening, and B.L. Link. 1997. "Adverse childhood experiences: Are they risk factors for adult homelessness?" *American Journal of Public Health*, 87: 249–255.

Herman, J.D. 1992. *Trauma and Recovery.* New York: Basic Books.

Hoyt, D.R., K. Ryan, and A.M. Cauce. 1999. "Personal victimization in a high-risk environment: Homeless and runaway adolescents." *Journal of Research in Crime and Delinquency*, 36, 4: 371–392.

Jacobs, J. 2000. *The Nature of Economies.* Toronto: Random House.

Janus, M.D., F.X. Archambault, S.W. Brown, and L.A. Welsh. 1995. "Physical abuse in Canadian runaway adolescents." *Child Abuse & Neglect*, 19, 4: 433–447.

Jasinski, J.L., J.K. Wesely, J.D. Wright, and E.E. Mustaine. 2010. *Hard Lives, Mean Streets: Violence in the Lives of Homeless Women.* Boston: Northeastern University Press.

Jeffrey, D. 2005. "Conduites à risque et rites de passage à l'adolescence." In D. Jeffrey,

D. LeBreton, and J. Lévy (eds.), *Jeunesse à Risque, Rite et Passage*. Québec: Les Presses de l'Université Laval.

Jones, G. 1997. "Youth homelessness and the 'underclass'." In R. MacDonald (ed.), *Youth, the "Underclass" and Social Exclusion*. London, UK: Routledge.

____. 2009. *Youth*. Cambridge: Polity Press.

Kalke, T., A. Glanton, and M. Cristalli. 2007. "Positive behavioral interventions and supports: Using strength-based approaches to enhance the culture of care in residential and day treatment education environments." *Child Welfare*, 86, 5: 151–174.

Karabanow, J. 2004. *Being Young and Homeless: Understanding How Youth Enter and Exit Street Life*. New York: Peter Lang.

____. 2008. "Getting off the street: Exploring young people's street exits." *American Behavourial Scientist*, 51, 6: 772–788.

Karabanow, J., A. Carson, and P. Clement. 2010. *Leaving the Streets: Stories of Canadian Youth*. Halifax: Fernwood Publishing.

Karabanow, J., P. Clement, A. Carson, and K. Crane, and Community Action on Homelessness Research Committee Advisory Group. 2005. *Getting Off the Street: Exploring Strategies Used by Canadian Youth to Exit Street Life*. <halifax.ca/qol/documents/GettingofftheStreet.pdf>.

Karabanow, J., and S. Kidd. 2014. "Being young and homeless: Addressing youth homelessness from drop-in to drafting policy." In M. Guirguis-Younger, R. McNeil and S.W. Hwang (eds.), *Homelessness and Health in Canada*. Ottawa: University of Ottawa Press.

Karabanow, J., S. Kidd, T. Frederick, and J. Hughes. 2018. *Homeless Youth and the Search for Stability*. Waterloo: Wilfrid Laurier University Press.

Kelly, P. 2000. "The dangerousness of youth-at-risk: The possibilities of surveillance and intervention in uncertain times." *Journal of Adolescence*, 23: 463–476.

____. 2001. "Youth at risk: Processes of individualisation and responsibilisation in the risk society." *Discourse: Studies in the Cultural Politics of Education*, 22, 1: 23–33.

____. 2006. "The entrepreneurial self and 'youth at-risk': Exploring the horizons of identity in the twenty-first century." *Journal of Youth Studies*, 9, 1: 17.

Kemshall, H. 2010. "Risk rationalities in contemporary social work policy and practice." *British Journal of Social Work*, 40, 4: 1247–1262.

Kidd, S. 2004. "The walls were closing in, and we were trapped: A qualitative analysis of street youth suicide." *Youth & Society*, 36, 1: 30–55.

____. 2006. "Factors precipitating suicidality among homeless youth: A quantitative follow-up." *Youth & Society*, 37, 4: 393–422.

____. 2008. "Resilience in homeless youth: The key role of self-esteem." *American Journal of Orthopsychiatry*, 78, 2: 163–172.

____. 2009. "Social stigma and homeless youth." *Finding Home: Policy Options for Addressing Homelessness in Canada*. Toronto: Cities Centre, University of Toronto.

____. 2013. "Mental health and youth homelessness: A critical review." In S. Gaetz, B. O'Grady, K. Buccieri, J. Karabanow, and A. Marsolais (eds.), *Youth Homelessness in Canada: Implications for Policy and Practice*. Toronto: Canadian Homelessness Research Network Press. <homelesshub.ca/resource/

mental-health-and-youth-homelessness-critical-review-homeless-hub-research-summary-series#sthash.JCR4pThp.dpuf>.

Kidd, S.A., and L. Davidson. 2006. "Youth homelessness: A call for partnerships between research and policy." *Canadian Journal of Public Health*, 97, 6: 445–447.

___. 2007. "'You have to adapt because you have no other choice': The stories of strength and resilience of 208 homeless youth in New York City and Toronto." *Journal of Community Psychology*, 35, 2: 219–238.

Kidd, S.A., S. Miner, D. Walker, and L. Davidson. 2007. "Stories of working with homeless youth: On being 'mind-boggling'." *Children and Youth Services Review,* 29: 16–34.

Kidd, S., N. Slesnick, T. Frederick, J. Karabanow, and S. Gaetz. 2018. *Mental Health and Addiction Interventions for Youth Experiencing Homelessness: Practical Strategies for Front-line Providers.* Toronto: Canadian Observatory on Homelessness Press.

Kipke, M.D., T.R. Simon, S.B. Montgomery, J.B. Unger, and E.F. Iversen. 1997. "Homeless youth and their exposure to and involvement in violence while living on the streets." *Journal of Adolescent Health,* 20: 360–367.

Kirby, S., and K. McKenna. 1989. *Experience, Research, Social Change: Methods from the Margins.* Toronto: Garamond.

Kraus, D., M. Eberle, and L. Serge. 2001. *Environmental Scan on Youth Homelessness: Final Report.* Ottawa: Canada Mortgage and Housing Corporation.

Kruks, G. 2001. "Gay and lesbian homeless/street youths: Special issues and concerns." *Journal of Adolescent Health,* 12, 7: 515–518.

Krüsi, A., D. Fast, W. Small, E. Wood, and T. Kerr. 2010. "Social and structural barriers to housing among street-involved youth who use illicit drugs." *Health and Social Care,* 18: 282–288.

LaBoy, A. 2018. "'(I Want to) Change the World': An Analysis of Future Orientation of Homeless Youth in Atlanta." Thesis, Georgia State University. <https://scholarworks.gsu.edu/sociology_theses/72>.

Laird, G. 2007. *Homelessness in a Growth economy: Canada's 21st Century Paradox* (Report for the Sheldon Chumir Foundation for Ethics in Leadership). Calgary: Sheldon Chumir Foundations for Ethics in Leadership.

Lankenau, L., M. Clatts, D. Welle, L. Goldsamt, and M. Gwadz. 2005. "Street careers: Homelessness, drug use use, and hustling among young men who have sex with men." *International Journal of Drug Policy,* 16: 10–18.

Larouche, A. 2010. "Jeunes de la rue et prison: Constructions subjectives de l'identité." *Criminologie,* 43, 1: 31–56.

Larson, R. 2006. "Positive youth development, willful adolescents, and mentoring." *Journal of Community Psychology,* 34, 6: 677–689.

LeBreton, D. 1991. *Passions du Risque.* Paris: Éditions Métailié.

___. 2003. *L'Adolescence à Risque.* Paris: Hachette Littératures.

Levac, C. 2005. *La Rue, un Chemin Tracé d'avance? Une Recherche Anthropologique sur le Parcours de 21 jeunes Hommes de la Rue.* Refuge des jeunes de Montréal.

Lipsky, M. 1980. *Street-Level Bureaucracy: Dilemmas of the Individual in Public Services.* New York: Russel Sage Foundation.

Lucchini, R. 1996. *Sociologie de la Survie: l'Enfant Dans la Rue.* Paris: Presses

Universitaires de France.

____. 2001. "Carrière, identité et sortie de la rue: le cas de l'enfant de la rue." *Déviance et Société*, 25, 1: 75–97.

Luthar, S.S., D. Cicchetti, and B. Becker. 2000. "The construct of resilience: A critical evaluation and guidelines for future work." *Child Development*, 71: 543–562.

MacDonald, S.-A. 2010. "Staying alive while living the life: Conceptualizations of risk among homeless youth." Dissertation, École de Service Social. Université de Montréal: Montréal.

____. 2013. "The paradox of being young and homeless: Resiliency in the face of constraints." *International Journal of Child, Youth and Family Studies*, 4, 4: 425–446.

____. 2014. "Managing risk: Self-regulation among homeless youth." *Child & Adolescent Social Work Journal*, 31, 6: 497–520.

____. 2016. "Attempting to engage in 'ethical' research with homeless youth." *Intersectionalities: A Global Journal of Social Work Analysis, Research, Polity and Practice*, 5, 1: 126–150.

Macmillan, R., and J. Hagan. 2004. "Violence in the transition to adulthood: Adolescent victimization, education, and socioeconomic attainment in later life." *Journal of Research on Adolescence*, 14, 2: 127–158.

Mallett, S., J. Edwards, D. Keys, P. Myers, and D. Rosenthal. 2003. *Disrupting Stereotypes: Young People, Drug Use and Homelessness*. Melbourne: University of Melbourne.

Mallett, S., and D. Rosenthal. 2009. "Physically violent mothers are a reason for young people's leaving home." *Journal of Interpersonal Violence*, 24, 7: 1165–1174.

Mallett, S., D. Rosenthal, D. Keys, and R. Averill. 2010. *Moving Out, Moving On: Young People's Pathways in and Through Homelessness*. New York: Routledge.

Marshall, B.D.L., T. Kerr, C. Livingstone, K. Li, J.S.G. Montaner, and E. Wood. 2008. "High prevalence of HIV infection among homeless and street-involved aboriginal youth in a Canadian setting." *Harm Reduction Journal*, 5, 35.

Martineau, S. 1999. "Rewriting resilience: A critical discourse analysis of childhood resilience and the politics of teaching resilience to 'kids at risk'." Unpublished doctoral dissertation, University of British Columbia, Vancouver.

Masten, A.S. 2001. "Ordinary magic: Resilience processes in development." *American Psychologist*, 56: 227–238.

Masten, A.S., and J.P. Powell. 2003. "A resilience framework for research, policy and practice." In S.S. Luthar (ed.), *Resilience and Vulnerability: Adaptation in the Context of Childhood Adversities*. New York: Cambridge University Press.

McCarthy, B., and J. Hagan. 1992. "Surviving on the street: The experiences of homeless youth." *Journal of Adolescent Research*, 7, 4: 412–430.

____. 2005. "Danger and the decision to offend." *Social Forces*, 83, 3: 1065–1096.

McCarthy, B., J. Hagan, and M.J. Martin. 2002. "In and out of harm's way: Violent victimization and the social capital of fictive street families." *Criminology*, 40, 4: 831–865.

McMorris, B.J., K.A. Tyler, L.B. Whitbeck, and D.R. Hoyt. 2002. "Familial and 'on-the-street' risk factors associated with alcohol use among homeless and runaway adolescents." *Journal of Studies on Alcohol*, 63, 1: 34–43.

Mounier, C., and E. Andujo. 2003. "Defensive functioning of homeless youth in relation to experiences of child maltreatment and cumulative victimization." *Child Abuse & Neglect,* 27, 10: 1187–1204.

Narendorf, S.C., M.B. Cross, D. Santa Maria, P.R. Swank, and P.S. Bordnick. 2017. "Relations between mental health diagnoses, mental health treatment, and substance use in homeless youth." *Drug and Alcohol Dependence,* 175: 1–8.

Nichols, N. 2014. *Youth Work: An Institutional Ethnography of Youth Homelessness.* Toronto: University of Toronto Press.

Noell, J., P. Rohde, J. Seeley, and L. Ochs. 2001. "Childhood sexual abuse, adolescent sexual coercion and sexually transmitted infection acquisition among homeless female adolescents." *Child Abuse & Neglect,* 25: 137–148.

Novac, S., J. Brown, and C. Bourbonnais. 1996. *No Room of Her Own: A Literature Review on Women and Homelessness.* Ottawa: Canada Mortgage and Housing Corporation.

Novac, S., J. Hermer, E. Paradis, and A. Kellen. 2006. *Justice and Injustice: Homelessness, Crime, Victimization, and the Criminal Justice System.* Toronto: Centre for Urban and Community Studies, University of Toronto, and the John Howard Society of Toronto.

_____. 2009. "More sinned against than sinning? Homeless people as victims of crime and harassment." *Finding Home: Policy Options for Addressing Homelessness in Canada.* Toronto: Cities Centre, University of Toronto.

Novac, S., E. Paradis, J. Brown, and H. Morton. 2006. "A visceral grief: Young homeless mothers and loss of child custody." *Centre for Urban and Community Studies,* 34: 1–7. <http://www.urbancentre.utoronto.ca/pdfs/elibrary/Novacet-al-206-VisceralGriefHLMothers.pdf>.

_____. 2009. "Supporting young homeless mothers who have lost child custody." *Finding Home: Policy Options for Addressing Homelessness in Canada.* Toronto: Cities Centre, University of Toronto.

O'Grady, B., and S. Gaetz. 2009. "Street survival: A gendered analysis of youth homelessness in Toronto." In J.D. Hulchanski, P. Campsie, S.B.Y. Chau, S.H. Hwang, and E. Paradis (eds.), *Finding Home: Policy Options for Addressing Homelessness in Canada.* Toronto, ON: Cities Centre Press, University of Toronto.

O'Grady, B., S. Gaetz, and K. Buccieri. 2011. *Can I See Your ID? The Policing of Youth Homelessness in Toronto.* Toronto: JFCY & Homeless Hub.

O'Mahony, P. 2009. "The risk factors prevention paradigm and the causes of youth crime: A deceptively useful analysis?" *Youth Justice,* 9: 99–114.

Parazelli, M. 1997. "Pratiques de «socialisation marginalisée» et espace urbain: le cas des jeunes de la rue à Montréal 1985–1995." Dissertation, Études Urbaines, Montréal: Université du Québec à Montréal.

_____. 1999. "Prévenir l'adolescence?" In M. Gauthier, and J.F. Guillaume (eds.), *Définir la Jeunesse? D'un Bout à L'Autre du Monde.* Ste-Foy: Presses de l'Université Laval.

_____. 2000. "L'appropriation de l'espace et les jeunes de la rue: un enjeu identitaire." *L'Errance Urbaine.* Ste Foy: Les Éditions MultiMondes inc.

_____. 2002. *La Rue Attractive: Parcours et Pratiques Identitaires des Jeunes de la Rue.* Ste Foy: Presses de l'Université du Québec.

Public Health Agency of Canada. 2006. *Street Youth in Canada: Findings from Enhanced*

Surveillance of Canadian Street Youth, 1999–2003. <phac-aspc.gc.ca/std-mts/reports_06/pdf/street_youth_e.pdf>.

Rawana, E., and K. Brownlee. 2009. "Making the possible probable: A strength-based assessment and intervention framework for clinical work with parents, children, and adolescents." *Families in Society: The Journal of Contemporary Social Services,* 90, 3: 255–260.

Reid, S. 2011. "The untapped potential in our communities to assist youth engaged in risky behaviours." *International Journal of Child, Youth and Family Studies,* 1, 2: 170–203.

Riley, J., and A. Masten. 2005. "Resilience in context." In R. Peters, D. Leadbeater and R. McMahon (eds.), *Resilience in Children, Families and Communities: Linking Context to Policy and Practice.* New York: Kluwer Academic/Plenum Publishers.

Roebuck, B. 2008. *Homelessness, Victimization and Offending: Knowledge and Actionable Recommendations.* Ottawa: Institute for the Prevention of Crime.

Roebuck, B., and M. Roebuck. 2016. "The strengths of young people who are homeless." *Canadian Journal of Community Mental Health,* 35, 2: 43–54.

Roebuck, B., M. Roebuck, and J. Roebuck. 2011. *From Strength to Strength: A Manual to Guide Strength-Based Interventions with Young People.* Ottawa: Youth Now Intervention Services (YNIS).

Roebuck, M., and B. Roebuck. 2013. *Group Care in the Child Welfare system: Transforming practices.* Ottawa: Youth Now Intervention Services.

Roy, E., N. Haley, P. Leclerc, L. Cédras, L. Blais, and J.-F. Boivin. 2003. "Drug injection among street youths in Montreal: Predictors of initiation." *Journal of Urban Health,* 80, 1: 92–105.

Roy, E., N. Haley, P. Leclerc, B. Sochanski, J.-F. Boudreau, and J.-F. Boivin. 2004. "Mortality in a cohort of street youth in Montreal." *Journal of the American Medical Association,* 292, 5: 569–574.

Saleebey, D. 2013. "Introduction: Power in the people." In D. Saleebey (ed.), *The Strengths Perspective in Social Work, 6th Edition.* Upper Saddle River, NJ: Pearson.

Schwan, K., S. Kidd, S. Gaetz, B. O'Grady, and M. Redman. 2017. *Mental Health Care for Homeless Youth: A Proposal for Federal, Provincial, and Territorial Leadership, Coordination, and Targeted Investment.* Toronto: Canadian Observatory on Homelessness Press.

Schwartz, D.R., C.A. James, A.C. Wagner, and T.A. Hart. 2014. "Sexual risk behaviours and sexual health outcomes among homeless youth in Canada." In M. Guirguis-Younger, R. McNeil and S.W. Hwang (eds.), *Homelessness and Health in Canada.* Ottawa: University of Ottawa Press.

Scott, S. 2016. *Negotiating Identity: Symbolic Interactionist Approaches to Social Identity.* Great Britain: Polity.

Sharland, E. 2006. "Young people, risk taking and risk making: Some thoughts for social work." *British Journal of Social Work,* 36: 247–265.

Shaw, I.F. 2003. "Ethics in qualitative research and evaluation." *Journal of Social Work,* 3, 1: 9–29.

Simons, R.L., L.B. Whitbeck, and A. Bales. 1989. "Life on the streets: Victimization and psychological distress among the adult homeless." *Journal of Interpersonal*

Violence, 4: 482–501.

Sleegers, J., J. Spijker, J. van Limbeck, and H. van Engeland. 1998. "Mental health problems among homeless adolescents." *Acta Psychiatrica Scandinavica*, 97: 253–259.

Slesnick, N., S. Bartle-Haring, P. Dashora, M.J. Kan, and E. Aukward. 2008. "Predictors of homelessness among street living youth." *Journal of Youth Adolescence*, 37, 4: 465–474.

Stefanidis, N., J. Pennbridge, R.G. MacKenzie, and K. Pottharst. 1992. "Runaway and homeless youth: The effects of attachment history on stabilization." *American Journal of Orthopsychiatry*, 62, 3: 442–446.

Stermac, L., and E.K. Paradis. 2001. "Homeless women and victimization: Abuse and mental health history among homeless rape survivors." *Resources for Feminist Research*, 28, 3/4: 65–80.

Tanner, J., and S. Wortley. 2002. *The Toronto Youth Crime and Victimization Study: Overview Report*. Centre for Criminology, University of Toronto.

te Riele, K. 2006. "Youth 'at risk': Further marginalizing the marginalized?" *Journal of Education Policy*, 21, 2: 129.

Tisseron, S. 2009. *La Résilience*. Paris: Presses Universitaires de France.

Tremblay, R. 2005. "Disruptive behaviour: Should we foster or prevent resilience?" In R. Peters, D. Leadbeater and R. McMahon (eds.), *Resilience in Children, Families and Communities: Linking Context to Policy and Practice*. New York: Kluwer Academic/ Plenum Publishers.

Tyler, K.A. 2008. "Social network characteristics and risky sexual and drug related behaviours among homeless young adults." *Social Science Research*, 37, 2: 673–685.

Tyler, K.A., and L.A. Melander. 2011. "A qualitative study of the formation and composition of social networks among homeless youth." *Journal of Research on Adolescence*, 21, 4: 802–817.

Ungar, M. 2004a. *Nurturing Hidden Resilience in Troubled Youth*. Toronto: University of Toronto Press.

___. 2004b. "A constructionist discourse on resilience: Multiple contexts, multiple realities among at-risk children and youth." *Youth & Society*, 35, 3: 341–365.

___. 2005. "Pathways to resilience among children in child welfare, corrections, mental health and educational settings: Navigation and negotiation." *Child and Youth Care Forum*, 34, 6: 423–444.

___. 2007. "Grow 'em strong: Conceptual challenges in researching childhood resilience." In A. Best (ed.), *Representing Youth: Methodological Issues in Critical Youth Studies*. New York: New York University Press.

___. 2008. "Resilience across cultures." *British Journal of Social Work*, 38: 218–235.

Vaughan, B. 2001. "Handle with care: On the use of structuration theory within criminology." *British Journal of Criminology*, 41, 1: 185–200.

Walsh, F. 1998. *Strengthening Family Resilience*. New York: Guilford.

Whitbeck, L. 2009. *Mental Health and Emerging Adulthood Among Homeless Young People*. New York: Taylor & Francis Group.

Whitbeck, L.B., D.R. Hoyt, and K.A. Ackley. 1997. "Abusive family backgrounds and later victimization among runaway and homeless adolescents." *Journal of Research on Adolescence*, 7, 4: 375–392.

Whitbeck, L.B., D.R. Hoyt, and K.A. Yoder. 1999. "A risk-amplification model of victimization and depressive symptoms among runaway and homeless adolescents." *American Journal of Community Psychology*, 27, 2: 273–296.

Whittaker, J.K. 2000. "The future of residential group care." *Child Welfare*, LXXIX, 1: 59–74.

Winnicott, D.W. 1971. *Playing and Reality*. London: Routledge.

Worthington, C., B. MacLaurin, N. Huffey, D. Dittmann, O. Kitt, S. Patten, and J. Leech. 2008. *Calgary Youth, Health and the Street – Final Report*. Calgary: University of Calgary.

INDEX